Around the World in 65 Days
with George Griffith

The Journal of the Real Phileas Fogg
From Jules Verne to Tranquility Base

An anthology edited and compiled by
Robert Godwin

With a Special Memoir by
John Griffith

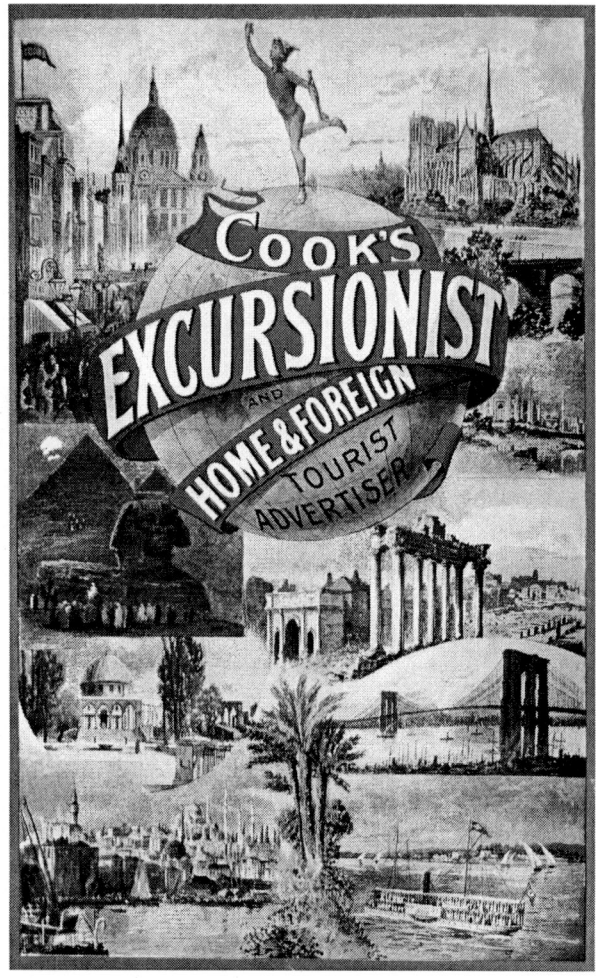

Around the World in 65 Days The Journal of the Real Phileas Fogg

Copyright © 2010 Robert Godwin ISBN 978-1897350-27-0

All rights reserved. No part of this book may be used or reproduced in any manner whatsoever without written permission except in the case of brief quotations embodied in critical articles and reviews. We acknowledge the financial support of the Government of Canada through the Book Publishing Industry Development Program for our publishing activities. Printed and bound in Canada. Apogee Books is an imprint of Collector's Guide Publishing Inc. Box 62034, Burlington, Ontario, Canada, L7R 4K2
www.apogeebooks.com

Contents

George Griffith - From Jules Verne to Tranquility Base	5
George Griffith's Legacy to Real Science - The Career of A A Griffith by John Griffith	29
How I Broke the Record Round the World	37
Across Europe in 45 Hours	39
Life on an Eastbound Liner	51
Eastward Ho!	59
Through the Desert Lands	69
From Aden to Eden	79
A Glimpse at the Pearl of the Sea	87
The City of the Lions	97
The Heathen at Sea	105
The Town of Three Names	113
The Skipper's Yarn	123
A Glimpse of Lilliput	131
Eastward to the Far West	141
A Week on Wheels	153
The End of the Run	163
A Railway Beyond the Clouds	177
A Ride to the City of the Sun	185
A Paradise of Tomorrow	197
The Most Majestic Mountain	205
Los Medanos	213
The Snake-dancers of Arizona	217
To France by Air	226
When Will the 20th Century Begin?	239

George Chetwynd Griffith-Jones* (c. 1899)

> A GALLOP ROUND THE GLOBE. London to London in 66 days. George Griffith is telling in PEARSON'S WEEKLY how he Broke the Record Round the World. With P.W. in hand, you can go with him in your armchair for a Penny a Week. First-class the Whole Way.
>
> COUNTRY RESIDENTS may have SATURDAY EVENING'S SPECIAL EDITION of the *Pall Mall Gazette* posted in time for delivery to the country on Sunday morning for 6s. 6d. per annum. Address THE PUBLISHER, *Pall Mall Gazette*, 18, Charing Cross-road, W.C.

He officially changed his name to just George Griffith by deed poll in 1894. The full family name was Griffith-Jones.

George Griffith

From Jules Verne to Tranquility Base

By Robert Godwin

In 1889 Hiram Stevens Maxim, an American living in England, had turned his considerable engineering skills to the problem of flight. Maxim was the inventor of the machine gun and had amassed a substantial fortune from sales of his revolutionary weapon. He was convinced that the secret of mechanical flight lay in the measure of power needed to drive a winged vehicle aloft. To that end, he spent several years building a high-powered aircraft at his estate in Kent. Two years before he would attempt to fly in his invention, Maxim had agreed to be interviewed for an article in one of Cyril Arthur Pearson's most successful London broadsheets, *Pearson's Weekly*. In amongst the prattle of everyday London life could be found the occasional item of merit; such as the August 13th 1892 interview with Maxim. This interview was a historic meeting between Maxim and Pearson's correspondent George Chetwynd Griffith-Jones.

Griffith-Jones was born in 1857 in Plymouth England. His father George Alfred Jones, an Anglican curate, had little money at his death, but had provided young George with access to his extensive library, which included the fantastic works of Jules Verne.

Griffith spent a good portion of his youth travelling around the world and at one point he described himself in *Who's Who* thus, "Sea apprentice; sundowner; sailor; stock-rider; butcher; globetrotter; schoolmaster; journalist and story-writer." His recreational pursuits included, "Loafing, travelling and sailing." By the time H.G. Wells was only five years old, George Griffith had sailed around the world three times, including three passes around Cape Horn (a particular accomplishment in those days). On retiring as a seaman, he returned to England and spent several years working as a teacher in the north of England, even though he had never successfully completed his own education. Later, while teaching in Brighton, he began writing for the local newspaper. It was at this time, down on his luck and short of money, that Griffith was hired by publisher Cyril Pearson. He was initially employed to just answer the mail and give trite answers to reader's questions about everything from wines to writing. By the time he settled down (somewhat) to his job as a mail-clerk and general gopher at

Pearson's, he had a well-rounded self taught background. Griffith was now set to become firmly ensconced in the world of popular magazines. You will see in the pages ahead that, as a correspondent, he crossed the Rockies as well as the Andes (three times).

This brings us to the summer of 1892 when he found himself face-to-face with the noted inventor Hiram Maxim. Probably as serendipitous a meeting as one might hope for.

During the course of their interview Maxim elaborated further on his solution for a winged, powered aircraft. He maintained that motive power was the key to successful flight and that the various methods of flapping, which were currently in vogue around the world, would never work. Maxim described his plans:

"The theory of my flying machine is briefly this:- It has been found that a thin flat plane will travel very easily through the air, and that if this plane be slightly tilted to the horizon, and sufficient velocity be imparted to it, the atmospheric pressure on the under side will exceed that on the upper, and thus very heavy weights can be raised from the ground.

"The first thing to be done was to find out how much power was required for flight, and my experiments showed that 250 pounds could be carried for every horse-power, and that the aeroplane worked well when the velocity was between 35 and 60 miles per hour.

"The next thing to be considered was the motive power, and this is the most important part of the machine. Gas and electricity are unavailable, as the motors required by their use would be too heavy. So I have had recourse to our old friend the steam engine; and here I have discovered a solution of this part of the problem.

"The boiler will consist of small copper tubes, which will be light enough yet sufficiently strong for the purpose. The condenser will be formed of a very large number of thin small tubes of aluminium, which will constitute part of the framework of the aeroplane. The atmosphere itself will thus be employed as a cooling agent.

"Petroleum will be the fuel used, and the motive power will be transmitted by two screw propellors attached to the sides of the aeroplane. The horizontal steering will be managed by varying the rates at which these two screws work. The vertical steering will be

more difficult. I propose to effect it by rudders attached before and behind."

As can be seen in this extract from Griffith's interview, Maxim was on the right track for powered flight. Most of the key principles are in evidence here. The sloped wing, a powerful engine using an appropriate liquid fuel (albeit in the wrong kind of engine), propellors (sic), rudders and even an extensive application of the newly refined light-weight metal of choice, aluminium. (Incidentally, using the aluminium airframe as a steam condenser to shed heat was seriously considered for America's first space shuttle design, the Bell Bomber-Missile, almost sixty years later.)

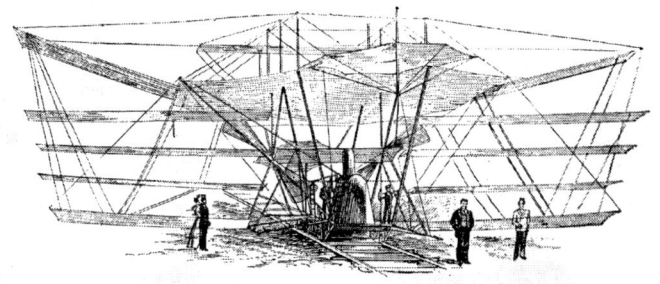

Hiram Maxim's 1894 aircraft from a period woodcut.

Almost exactly five months after Griffith's discussion with Maxim, a conversation took place between the staff and management of *Pearson's,* regarding a wildly successful serial that had just appeared in a competing weekly periodical. This story was the latest to appear in a popular trend of fictional future wars. The future war concept had reached new heights of popularity in 1879 in a short story called *The Battle of Dorking* by George T. Chesney, in which a complacent Britain is invaded by outside forces.

Pearson's editor, Peter Keary, wanted his own future-war serial and he was casting about for a volunteer author. Despite having no experience, but perhaps inspired by his recent encounter with Maxim, George Griffith stepped forward and produced a synopsis of just such a story—overnight! Even though he hadn't written the story yet, the synopsis appeared in its entirety in the January 14th 1893 issue of *Pearson's Weekly*, it took up one densely packed column. A week later Griffith submitted a 5000 word, two and a half page prologue, and so a remarkable writing career was born.

Griffith had remembered everything that Maxim had told him. Especially the inherent problems caused by the weight of a conventional steam condenser. He therefore decided to combine the principals of Verne's fiction with the reality advocated by Maxim and others. What resulted was a sort-of vertical lift-off hybrid that used streamlining to minimize drag, and sets of rotating propellers that could lift the Airship vertically and could then be retracted or tilted to provide forward propulsion. The resulting story was serialized anonymously over the course of the Spring and Summer of 1893, but it was so successful that the readers cried out for the identity of the neophyte author. Griffith's brilliant synergy of topical politics, vivid characters and cutting edge technology made his effort the unchallenged story of its kind. It was full of perceptive ideas and it struck a nerve with the paranoid British public. Griffith somehow managed to persuade Pearson to allow him to retain the book rights for his story. On July 3rd 1893 he accepted a 50/50 split with H.A. Moncrieff, owner of the Tower Publishing company of London, to take his remarkable serial and publish it in book form under the title *The Angel of the Revolution – A Tale of the Coming Terror*. The book was an instant success in England, it was also the first time Griffith's name was visibly attached to the story.

The basic premise of the story is that a group of disgruntled victims of the Russian monarchy have formed a globe-girdling network of "terrorists". Their ultimate objective is the peaceful subjugation of the entire planet, with the benevolent goal of bringing an end to war and the endless cycle of victors and victims. To accomplish this noble end the leader of the terrorists recruits a down-and-out scientist who has spent his last penny trying to solve the mystery of flight. The scientist succeeds and designs and builds a sort-of internal combustion engine that uses hypergolic fuels. One cannot help but see, in the first few pages, a parallel between Griffith's scientist, Richard Arnold, and the later work of Robert Goddard. Both devote themselves tirelessly to solving the problem, both are ridiculed, both never quit, and neither of them will divulge or share their secrets. (One is left wondering whether Goddard may have read Griffith' story since he was an aficionado of such things, but for some unfathomable reason, the story was never published in America until 1974.)

Even more extraordinary is the resonance with the true story of Nikolai Ivanovitch Kibal'chich who was executed for his involvement in the death of Czar Alexander II in 1881. Kibal'chich was part of *The People's Will,* a terrorist organisation bent on bringing about the downfall of the Czarist regime. On March 1st 1881 two bombs built by Kibal'chich exploded in a square in St Petersburg, the second one killing the Czar. Kibal'chich, along with five co-conspirators were captured, imprisoned and sentenced to death. Kibal'chich was described as a "calm and genial chemist" and during his final four weeks in prison he wrote down his ideas *for a reaction propelled aircraft.* The words in his short paper, written on March 23rd, make for agonizing reading.

"I am writing this project in imprisonment, a few days before my death. I believe in the realization of my idea, and this faith sustains me in my terrible predicament. Should my idea, after careful examination by scientific experts, be recognized as feasible, then I would be happy that I have rendered a service to my country and to mankind; I would then meet my death peacefully, knowing that my idea will not perish with me, but will exist among mankind for whom I was ready to sacrifice my life."

Kibal'chich theorised that explosives could allow a vehicle to rise off the ground in a controlled fashion, in such a way that it could accommodate a passenger. He knew that a military, or firework, rocket accelerated too fast to carry a passenger, but he came up with what seemed like a sensible way of controlling the expulsion of hot gas to allow for a more modest rate of acceleration. He then went on to say that by gimballing the rocket exhaust the vehicle could be steered in any chosen direction. He correctly dismissed other propulsion devices, such as steam and electric motors as being too heavy, and so he finally settled on explosive powders. He anticipated Robert Goddard's later design wherein the "candles" of powder would be reloaded automatically to maintain a consistent rate of acceleration. He made one small error, however, in that he thought the hot gas generated by the burning powder would provide additional lift, such as in a balloon.

When his lawyer first met him he was "struck by the fact that (Kibal'chich) was totally preoccupied with another matter". His plea, that his theory be confirmed, was ignored by the authorities and his writings would not be seen in public until after the 1917 revolution. Kibal'chich was hanged on April 3rd 1881, he was twenty-eight years old.

It is impossible for George Griffith to have known anything about Kibal'chich's theory, but his trial and execution would have made global news and certainly the undercurrent of revolution in Russia was still fermenting when Griffith began to write about his fictional characters, Richard Arnold and Alan Tremayne.

Once Arnold perfects a small working model of his airship he celebrates in solitude, the date is ostensibly September 3rd 1903, just three months before the date of the Wright Brothers actual first flight. The terrorists (who are essentially the 'good guys' in Griffith's world) are afraid that sooner or later a war will start which will be catastrophic. The words are eerily prophetic, *"Someone must soon fire the shot that will set the world in a blaze…"* Twenty one years later that exact phrase could have perfectly described the assassination of Archduke Francis Ferdinand of the Austro-Hungarian empire, a shot which precipitated the war-to-end-all-wars. Ironically, Griffith perceived that whomever would be able to master flight would have at their disposal the means to make war redundant, sadly this did not prove to be the case, at least not in World War I. By the end of World War II, however, the aeroplane would partly fulfill that destiny, predicted 52 years earlier by Griffith, when the *Enola Gay* dropped the world's first nuclear weapon in anger over the skies of Hiroshima, Japan, and hopefully brought an end to all-out global conflicts.

Meanwhile, Griffith' airship was described thus, *"You see that she is a combination of two principles – those of the Aeronef and the Aeroplane. The first reached its highest development in Jules Verne's imaginary "Clipper of the Clouds" and the second in Hiram Maxim's Aeroplane."*

Then in one of his perhaps more informed predictions he stated, *"Maxim's Aeroplane is, as you all know, also an unrealised ideal so far as any practical use is concerned. He has succeeded in making it fly, but only under the most favourable conditions, and practically without cargo. Its two fatal defects have been shown by experience to be the comparatively overwhelming weight of the engine and the fuel that he has to carry to develop sufficient power to rise from the ground and progress against the wind, and the inability of the machine to ascend perpendicularly to any required height.*

"Without the power to do this no air-ship can be of any use save under very limited conditions. You cannot carry a railway about with you, or a station to get a start from every time you want to rise, and you cannot always choose a nice level plain in which to come down. Even if you could the Aeroplane would not rise again without its rails and carriage. For purposes of warfare, then, it may be dismissed as totally useless."

This section may have come right from Maxim's own mouth, from his interview with Griffith, but it would not be proven to be true until Maxim's flight trial, which did not take place until the following summer. On July 31st 1894, for the first time in the history of mankind a winged flying machine would take flight at Maxim's country estate flying under its own power carrying its engine, a boiler, fuel, water, and three people. It had the astonishing total wingspan of over 200 feet. Its propellers were eighteen feet in length and were driven by 363 horse-power and the entire ungainly monster weighed-in at almost four tons! At somewhere between 36 and 42 miles per hour, running along a static rail, it actually left the ground momentarily before it collided with a set of retaining rails whose sole purpose was to stop the vehicle from actually becoming airborne. It was such an unwieldy aircraft Maxim had little faith in its ability to actually survive a real flight and subsequent landing. Once it hit the retaining rails it crunched back to the ground and disappeared forever into the history books. Modern day historians now dismiss Maxim's accomplishment as an aberration with little significance, since he never followed through and built anything of real use. However, Maxim's real importance may lie in the fact that he was a famous and respected inventor who firmly subscribed to the notion that engine power was the solution to the conundrum of flight, something not generally accepted in 1894. He also unquestionably inspired the 35 year old George Griffith who would himself go on to inspire others through his spectacular fiction.

Griffith understood that once his fictional airship was airborne it could remain aloft by pushing an adequate volume of air below the wing surfaces. His description almost sounds suspiciously like the *Bell X-22* tilt-rotor that used the downdraft from rotating fans to lift off vertically before the engine power was redirected horizontally for forward thrust. It was a similar idea to that which had appeared in 1886's *Robur the Conqueror* by Jules Verne.

Once Griffith got underway with his story he used the military might of his airships to devastate the armies of Europe and Russia. The book reads like a Victorian Tom Clancy novel, replete with jingoistic overtones. The French and the Russians are allied against the poor Anglo-Saxon axis of England and Germany. (While Griffith was writing his story William II of Germany had managed to alienate the Russians who had formed an alliance with Germany's ancient foes in France.) Griffith then mobilizes a hidden army of disgruntled citizens around the world to overthrow the power brokers in both Europe and America.

Science fiction historian Sam Moskowitz suspected that Griffith's novel, along with his other books, were not released in America because of some blatant anti-American rhetoric. It is a reasonable assumption, although this particular story is equally contemptuous of Germany, France, England and Russia. The terrorists ultimately round-up the Russian royal household and march them to a gulag in Siberia, the Kaiser is reprimanded and told to renounce his armies or be destroyed, while the bulk of the US Senate and Congress are arrested for perpetuating the endless cycle of war (through arms dealing) and are exiled to an island off the coast of Alaska. In another startling episode of clairvoyance he actually predicted that the British monarch would abdicate the throne, although under duress rather than for love. (It would be four decades later that King Edward VIII would abdicate, and during the general mayhem that followed, Germany would invade the Sudetenland.)

Perhaps Griffith's postulations, regarding the trafficking of armaments from America to Europe, were a little close to the bone, not to mention his 1896 diatribe expressing disgust with the *Monroe Doctrine's* impact on Panama. In his later travels across America, en route to Australia, (chronicled in his book *In An Unknown Prison Land*) he made the following remarks which would seem to utterly negate Moskowitz's position that he disliked Americans:

"My own experience certainly is that the Americans are the politest people on earth, or, perhaps I ought to say, the most courteous, because anyone can be polite if it pays him. Only a gentleman can be courteous. They have learnt, apparently at the hands of Mother Nature herself, that subtle blending of politeness and dignity which we call courtesy."

In *The Angel of the Revolution*, he also gave the Americans due credit when he describes how the convoys from America and Canada are used to sustain England during a siege by the combined French and Russian armies; a process which would indeed save England fifty years later. (In Griffith's future universe it is the Russian fleet that breaks out into the North Atlantic and wreaks havoc on the supply shipping.) He also recognized the strategic importance of Gallipoli and describes a 48 hour battle at the infamous location. Toward the end of the book he has the French navy deploy a small fleet of submarines to devastating effect. Primitive submarines had been around since the early 17th century but it would not be until five years after Griffith's novel that the American engineer Simon Lake would deploy a true ocean-going submarine. Once again Griffith was looking ahead to the implications of these new contrivances in future war.

Toward the end of this remarkable novel we are treated to a brilliantly descriptive chapter wherein the Russian army is advancing on London. One cannot read this without immediately recalling the same episode in H.G. Wells 1897 masterpiece, *The War of the Worlds*. Instead of Russians, Wells used Martians, but the locales and the prose are remarkably similar. Griffith's assault on the Imperial Palace in St Petersburg is also uncanny in that it sounds exactly like the subsequent assault launched by Lenin and his Bolsheviks two decades later. During the armistice at the end of his future war, the treaties are signed at St Paul's cathedral, which is one of the only buildings left mostly intact, again, exactly as the real cathedral was at the end of World War II. As a final episode he has the newly formed anti-war government deliver an ultimatum to the Moslem armies of Asia, telling them to lay down their arms or be destroyed. The final air assault on the Moslem armies is quite uncanny and evokes images of the air assaults launched by the NATO alliances in the Middle East during the 1990's. Almost insurmountable air power deployed against enormous man-power, armed with little more than muskets.

Another, undoubtedly important, contribution to the book version of Griffith's story were the amazing drawings. The original version of the serial was devoid of illustrations, the cheap broadsheet was simply not a suitable or financially viable place for expensive halftones. When the story was elevated to book status by Tower Publishing, it was to be accompanied by no less than 17 pictures. They are some of the earliest and most remarkable drawings to grace the pages of a Victorian novel. Airships are seen floating above the helpless enemy. They are cigar-shaped and equipped with considerable firepower. Anyone seeing these pictures today would immediately assume that they were looking at some kind of UFO story. They represent some of the earliest such pictures and are without doubt one of the best marriages of text and pictures from Victorian science fiction. What is perhaps even more remarkable is the story of the illustrator. His name was Frederick Thomas Jane and at that time he was 28 years old. He had been interested in ships and naval warfare since he was a teenager so, by the time he was hired by Tower to illustrate Griffith's novel, he had some experience in drawing ironclads.

In February 1896 Jane was hired by Pearson to illustrate a short story by George Griffith called *War on the Water*. It was subtitled *An Attempt to Portray the Incidents of an Engagement between Two Great Fleets of Ironclads*. The pictures by Jane vividly depicted the possible future of naval warfare. The following year Jane would be recalled by Pearson to illustrate another story of the sea, Kipling's *Captains Courageous*. Then in 1898 Frederick Thomas Jane would illustrate his first major work, *Jane's All The World's Fighting Ships*. He would even turn to writing science fiction, with at least one story, *The Violet Flame*, featuring what seems to be a nuclear weapon. Before his untimely death in 1916 Fred T. Jane launched a publishing empire based upon his uncanny ability to accurately render ships and aircraft. Today this company still exists and is the most respected publishing house in the world for books on all things military, and even on all things Space. *Jane's Defence Weekly* is used by almost every government in the world as a source of information on weapon systems. His work with George Griffith was one of his first conspicuous appearances and undoubtedly contributed considerably to his notoriety.

There is no doubt that Griffith was a writer of great skill. Some scholars believe he became the envy of his much more famous counterpart, H.G. Wells, and echoes of his "*Angel of the Revolution*" can be heard as late as Well's 1935 novel "*Shape of Things to Come*". This following excerpt from Griffith could easily have been spoken by Wells' hero Cabal, *"We have waged war in order that it may be waged no more, and we are determined that it shall now cease for ever. The peoples of the various nations have no interest in warfare. It has been nothing but an affliction and a curse to them, and we are convinced that if one generation grows up without drawing the sword, it will never be drawn again as long as men remain upon the earth."*

But Griffith was far from finished with his future war. Barely pausing for a rest, a sequel would begin serialization in *Pearson's*, starting the week of December 30th 1893 and ending on August 4th 1894, just four days after Maxim's experimental flight. The new story was called "*The Syren of the Skies*" and it would surpass its predecessor at every level and elevate Griffith to the top rank of British writers. It saw at least a dozen editions.

Griffith' sequel is even more compelling reading than its precursor. It may unnerve the casual reader at first glance, due to Griffith's unfortunate choice of names for his heroes—Aerians. The name invokes the bigotry and eugenic lunacy of the next century, but in his defense it was chosen simply to imply a non-descript race of people who have conquered flight with their airships (i.e. *not* Aryan). Although there are prejudices apparent, which were fairly typical of his time, the story does have heroes from many different races and countries, and the Sultan of the Moslem world is portrayed as an honorable victim. The story constantly overemphasizes the folly of war; especially with the aerial weapons of mass destruction in the hands of both sides. In deference to a great influence Griffith dedicated the story to Hiram Maxim.

This second adventure is set over 100 years after the conclusion of *Angel of the Revolution.* A détente has existed on Earth since the insurrection—imposed by the formidable air power possessed by the Aerians. This time the villain is a descendant of the discredited Russian royal family who uses her overwhelming natural charms to take possession of an airship. She then resolves to use its secrets to restore the Romanoff dynasty. Meanwhile, the Aerians have sworn to destroy anyone who may be bent on bringing warfare back to Earth. Griffith wields an array of clever ideas to accelerate his story along. There are some lapses in his writing skills and he jumps right across some events of which another writer might have written an entire book. He relates how the amount of energy locked in coal is considerably greater than that released by simply burning it. His Aerian utopia is navigated by monorail trains whose *"cars ran suspended on a single rail upheld by light, graceful arches of a practically unbreakable alloy of aluminium, steel and zinc…the train ran, not on wheels, but on lubricated bearings, which glided over it with no more friction than that of a steel skate on ice. On the upper rail ran double-flanged wheels with ball-bearings, and this line also conducted the electric current from which the motive power was derived. The usual speed of the expresses was a hundred and fifty miles an hour."* His hi-speed monorails even go from London to Dover in 30 minutes before crossing the English Channel (albeit by a huge bridge rather than a tunnel.)

Once he has his villain (Olga Romanoff) engage in aerial combat with the Aerians it sounds uncannily like the dog-fights of two decades later, with the airships constantly vying for altitude by spiraling up and down. When his airships are strung out in lines of defense he is unfortunately limited to having them rely on hardwired communication with the ground (Marconi would not make a radio antenna work until the following year). He virtually invents the concept of anti-aircraft guns with a blistering description that would not be out of place in a 1940's newspaper. At one point his airships fly at almost supersonic speeds (Ernst Mach had just invented Mach numbers during his studies of shock waves in 1887) and Griffith felt obliged to write a footnote drawing attention to some odd reports from America in which Professor Langley had shown that the faster a vehicle flies the less power is required to keep it aloft. His submarines, which wreak total havoc on shipping, are now equipped with nothing less than sonar, torpedoes, magnetometers and countermeasures.

But even after writing an excellent future-war adventure story Griffith was not yet finished. Just when the reader expects a manmade Armageddon, Griffith has an astronomer use *photo-telegraphy,* a system which uses light waves to replace wires, to communicate with the highly intellectual residents of Mars! (This was a year before Percival Lowell's book *Mars* and three years before Wells' *War of the Worlds*. But it was less than a year after Camille Flammarion had published his book *The Planet Mars* in which he argued that the Martian canals were real.) The Aerians immediately cease the defense of the cities of Europe after being informed by the Martians of a collision between two asteroids in deep space which had occurred many years earlier. The Earth is directly in the firing line of the resulting spray of debris. There is apparently only four months until impact, and so the only thing left to do is to build an underground fortress and to equip it with the prerequisites necessary to support a population of 250 people. The scenes where the Aerians struggle over who survives, and who dies, is almost identical to that portrayed a hundred years later in the movie *Deep Impact*. Near the end of the book, when the Earth has passed through the conflagration, Griffith's description of the aftermath is disturbingly close to the reality of the Tunguska blast that would level an area of Siberia just over a decade later. The finale of the book is poignant and bears a resonance and irony that Edgar Allen Poe would have enjoyed. It would seem that Griffith may have got the idea for his celestial impacter from Camille Flammarion who had written an exceptionally good story of his own that had been serialized in April-August of the previous year and was titled *Omega – The End of the World.*

Almost a year later, on March 12th 1894, George Griffith found himself at London's Charing Cross station having been persuaded to engage in a publicity stunt organized by *Pearson's*. He would attempt to travel around the world and beat the previous record of seventy four days, set in 1889 by a journalist from the New York Herald. It was to be an appropriate salute to his childhood hero, Jules Verne. Griffith was soon recording his exploits as he followed in the fictional footsteps of Phileas Fogg. The following pages are an edited (but not abridged) transcript of Griffith's report of his journey. It is a remarkable snapshot of life on planet Earth in the late nineteenth century, and it has not been published since 1894. It will not take the reader long to determine that Griffith was a product of the Victorian era, complete with all of the patronising overtones of a natural-born member of the largest empire the world had ever seen. His descriptions of his encounters with the people of the world are sometimes disturbing, and at other times overtly insulting, but considering his circumstances, for the most part, he seems to have been a relatively even-handed correspondent. He makes no bones about showing equal contempt for some of his own countrymen. His description of the various places on his journey are, if nothing else, sadly poignant. Hollywood's depiction of Phileas Fogg's exploits could not be further removed from the stark truth of such a journey undertaken in 1894. The counterpoint between Griffith's somewhat elevated position and the many poverty-stricken souls he encountered is a grim reminder of how far we have come, and in many cases, how far we have yet to travel. His encounter with a sea-captain who had survived the most extreme bad luck when his ship had caught fire makes for a harrowing first-person account and a most interesting insight into the perils faced by those who chose to navigate the oceans in the days before GPS and radio communications.

As is inevitable in the undertaking of an express journey through 24 time zones, Griffith never had chance to linger for long in any particular location, so his impressions seem to concentrate on superficial encounters with the struggling porters or denizens of the local streets and docks. Needless to say, from this position he was not likely to be exposed to any of the more worthwhile aspects of each country's culture. On the few occasions when he had the time to explore, he acknowledged the beauty of the location or the architecture, but more often than not he expressed disappointment; his expectations having been unduly elevated by earlier scribes.

In contravention of the modern-day custom of purging manuscripts written by some of Griffith's contemporaries (Wells,

Kipling, Conan Doyle, etc.) and in the interests of historical accuracy, none of his remarks, which will almost certainly be offensive to many of today's readers, have been altered or expunged in favour of modern-day rectitude. This editor has also attempted to include as many relevant pictures from the era to complete Griffith's global adventure story, including documents provided by the Thomas Cook company, who booked the trip for him. This turned out to be a surprisingly difficult undertaking.

The intrepid Mr. Griffith would accomplish his world-girdling goal and actually knock nine days off the standing record and arrive home after only sixty-five days. In another statement of remarkable optimism, he even posited the notion that in the not too distant future people would be able to perform a circum-global run by air in only 65 hours. It is a startling fact of our modern life that less than seventy years later Yuri Gagarin would circle the globe in an hour and a half and by 1973 American astronauts Jerry Carr, Ed Gibson and Bill Pogue would traverse the same distance more than 900 times, aboard the giant Skylab space station, in the time it took Griffith to complete one circuit.

Since Griffith virtually bypassed the United States (favouring the Canadian Pacific Railway as his method of crossing the Americas) his account differs from that of Jules Verne. However, in the following two years he would return to travel through both the United States and South America. In late 1895 he would take his readers across the Peruvian Andes on the highest railway in the world and would visit some of the most isolated and impoverished places on Earth. Since his round-the-world sojourn skipped South America, his reflections on this part of the world have also been included, as they appeared in *Pearson's Magazine* in 1897-8.

During his journey he would visit the Harvard astronomical observatory at Arequipa, almost 8,000 feet above sea-level, a place where NASA still maintains a presence today. Just prior to his arrival the observatory had been ransacked by Peruvian bandits causing a scandal all the way back in New York. He would then go on to scale peaks thousands of feet higher, such as the famous volcano *El Misti*. His descriptions of the ailments precipitated by altitude sickness must have been a sober reminder for those engaging in early flying experiments.

Griffith would also be dazzled by the grandeur of the Incan fortresses lying abandoned amongst the isolated heights of the

Peruvian Andes and he would visit the headstream of the Marañón River which is notable as one of the sources of the Amazon.

One of his later trips to the United States would be documented in his *Snake Dancers of Arizona*. He would use one of his many pseudonyms (Levin Carnac) to relate his impressions of 19th century native American rituals and customs. Mario Moreno's *Passepartout* (abducted by archetypical Hollywood natives in the 1956 movie of *Around the World in 80 Days*) would barely recognise the Americans described by Griffith, but this article does at least give the reader a sense of what the real world had to offer for the intrepid traveller willing to cross into the western United States in 1896. Four years later he would document a railway trip across the United States in his book about Australia called *In An Unknown Prison Land*. In this 400 page tome he would marvel at everything from the squalor of turn-of-the-century Chicago to the beauty and bustling excitement of San Francisco, before taking his reader through Honolulu en route to the deprivations of New Caledonia.

Finally, the one thing most obviously missing from Griffith's sojourn around the globe is the prerequisite balloon voyage. Fortunately, Griffith was not faced with the same problems that forced Verne's adventurer to resort to such desperate measures to win his wager. However, once again Griffith does not disappoint. During the research for this book an article came to light called *To France by Air* which appeared in *Pearson's Magazine* in April 1898. Quite remarkably Griffith undertook a four hour flight on February 8th in a large hot-air balloon from London, England to Agincourt in France. In the late 19th century such a flight would have still presented a hazardous proposition.

This article conveniently fills the void in his adventures with a wonderful tale of flight at the height of the Victorian era, complete with photographs. Later, Griffith, with typical wry humour, was proud to relate that he was "the last Englishman to fall at Agincourt."

All of Griffith's later adventures in South America have also been included in this book, concluding with what seemed an eminently appropriate article called "When Will the 20th Century Begin?" When Jules Verne's hero, Phileas Fogg eventually won the day (and the wager), it was in part because he had circumnavigated the globe by travelling East, eventually crossing the International Date Line and gaining 24 hours. This famous punch-line in Verne's novel is what gives the story much of its charm. On the other hand, Griffith had no such problem understanding the vagaries of international boundaries and time zones. In this last article he opines on the subject of exactly which location on Earth (near to the dateline) will be the first to see a dawn in the 20th century. One hundred years later some people were still arguing over this, and particularly over exactly when the new millenium would begin (2000 or 2001). As you will see, Griffith had no problem figuring it out in 1898.

Shortly after Griffith's round the world sojourn his novel *Syren of the Skies* concluded serialization and his publisher was standing by with another contract. Griffith met Moncrieff on August 8th and a deal was signed for the book publication, which would be re-titled *Olga Romanoff or The Syren of the Skies*. It would receive rave reviews from the press at the time.

In 1897 Griffith would revisit the subject of planetary collisions in his short story *The Great Crellin Comet*. It would be first published in *Pearsons Weekly's Christmas Annual* of November 1897. (For more details of this remarkable story and how Griffith invented the countdown see "The World Peril of 1910" available from Apogee Books' website. http://www.apogeebooks.com) It is perhaps worth noting that this story appeared about three weeks before H.G. Wells comet story *The Star* appeared in London's *Graphic Weekly*.

The next time Griffith would turn his formidable talents towards space would be for another serial which ran in *Pearson's Magazine* from January to June 1900. He wrote it while on one of his many foreign exploits, this time while in Australia in late 1899. It was called *Stories of Other Worlds* and the installment titles were, *A Visit to the Moon, The World of the War God, A Glimpse of the Sinless Star, The World of the Crystal Cities, In Saturn's Realm* and *Homeward Bound*. Once again it is worth taking note of the date of publication, at least five months before Wells' *First Men in the Moon*. When Griffith was ready to send his protagonists out into space it would not be to merely visit the moon, his was a full-fledged expedition of space tourism. He later expanded the story and it was published by Pearson's as a novel in 1901 retitled "*A Honeymoon in Space.*"

In Griffith's major space epic he pulled together all of the familiar accoutrements of his previous stories. Cigar-shaped airships, daring heroes, beautiful acquiescent heroines, elaborate battles and of course innovative technology. It is a long book for its time, over 300 pages, but in the detail there is the usual display of creativity from Griffith. His trio of adventurers depart on a rip-roaring rush around the solar system in a hermetically sealed spacecraft that uses an undefined anti-gravity device for propulsion. Both the serial and the novel include evocative illustrations by Stanley Wood and Harold Piffard. The story takes place in November 1900, a mere 11 months after it was written, so it was intended to be a near-future that his readers might conceivably recognize.

The protagonist, an English gentleman called Lord Redgrave takes his fiancée on a tour of the solar system aboard his extraordinary spacecraft, the *Astronef*. He seals the ship and activates the air-scrubbers before heading out of the atmosphere. During the voyage Griffith explains the effects of low gravity on his travelers before arriving at the moon in a mere 12 hours, where they alight at the crater Tycho. Having landed, they pack equipment for their exploration, which includes a "kodak" and a panoramic camera (something which the Apollo astronauts didn't take, but whose absence was compensated for by taking overlapping still images with a 70mm camera.) Once Lord Redgrave and his companion are ready to embark they don pressure suits. *"The helmets were smaller (than diving helmets), and not having to withstand outside pressure they were made of welded aluminium, lined thickly with asbestos, not to keep the cold out but the heat in. On the back of the dress there was a square case, looking like a knapsack, containing the expanding apparatus, which would furnish breathable air for an almost unlimited time as long as the liquefied air from a cylinder hung below it passed through the cells in which the breathed air had been deprived of its carbonic acid gas and other noxious ingredients."*

The exceptional description continues, *"The pressure of air inside the helmet automatically regulated the supply, which was not permitted to circulate through the other portions of the dress...any air in the dress, which was woven of a cunning compound of silk and asbestos, would instantly expand with irresistible force, burst the covering, and expose the limbs of the explorers to a cold which would be infinitely more destructive than the hottest of earthly fires."*

Griffith can surely be forgiven the inclusion of asbestos in his spacesuit since he could hardly have been aware of the toxicity of the element. Once outside, the story continues with this uncanny portrayal of the surroundings and equipment, *"They were in the shade cast by the hull of the* Astronef. *For about ten yards in front of her was a dense shadow, and beyond it a stretch of grey-white sand lit by a glare of sunlight which would have been intolerable if it had not been for the smoke-colored slips of glass which had been fitted behind the glass visors of the helmets."*

The adventurers see the ruins of an ancient city and Redgrave speculates that the inhabitants may have been driven underground, (an idea dating back to Bernard De Fontenelle that Wells would embellish in his own lunar story later that year.) Redgrave and his companion investigate the possibility of a lunar atmosphere by striking a match, to no avail; a trick employed 29 years later by Fritz Lang in his movie *Frau Im Mond*. The explorers decide to descend into the depths of Newton crater and in this scene the prose is eerily reminiscent of the Millenium Falcon flying into the maw of an enormous asteroid in George Lucas' *Empire Strikes Back*. The Astronef switches on its searchlights and soon settles deep inside the moon where they discover water and an atmosphere. After a disturbing encounter with the local sub-selenian fauna they depart and head for Mars.

The Martians inhabit an ancient and decaying planet. Griffith mentions Flammarion's *Omega* story, a clear sign that he was aware of, and was probably influenced by the great astronomer's story. Redgrave flies his *Astronef* into the Martian atmosphere where he encounters a large fleet of Martian warships. The Martians open fire using shells armed with chemical warheads, but the airtight Astronef protects its daring entourage. Redgrave engages the enemy by ramming a Martian vessel. The accompanying illustration in the book is one of the first pictures to show a space battle. The Martians are caught off guard and *"human figures more than half as large again as men were staring at them through the windows in the sides...in a second the Astronef's spur pierced her, the Martian ship broke in twain, and her two halves plunged downwards through the rosy clouds."*

The Martian ships are portrayed in Stanley Wood's picture as cigar-shaped metal tubes with masts and portholes. Griffith's description of the Martians peering from the portholes, leaves you with the distinct impression that you have just met a full-fledged archetype of a UFO more than fifty years before such things became commonplace.

After beating the Martians, quite convincingly, the *Astronef* departs for Venus. In Griffith's universe it is a beautiful pristine world of snow-covered mountains and silver mists populated by winged humanoids that he describes as angel-like. They are apparently capable of flight due to the fact that they have four wings and a tail for steering and they are supported by an atmosphere two and a half times denser than the Earth's. The encounter is uneventful and so the spacecraft embarks for Jupiter. Another completely remarkable sojourn takes place when the ship diverts to Jupiter's moon, Callisto.

"In another hour or so the Astronef had dropped gently onto the surface of Callisto at the foot of a range of mountains crowded with jagged and splintery peaks, and a mile or two away from the edge of a sea of snow and ice which stretched away in a vast expanse of rugged frozen billows beyond the horizon.

"After this they went and put on their breathing dresses and went for a welcome stroll along the arid shores of the frozen sea after their lengthy confinement to the decks of the Astronef."

A lucky guess by Griffith? Certainly the telescopes of his time may well have detected a bright surface on Callisto and the astronomers deduced a sea of ice, but it would be almost a century before the Voyager probes would confirm the frozen surface of some of Jupiter's satellites. Griffith even explained how Ganymede has an aurora and he could scarcely have had any inkling of Jupiter's intense radiation belt which does indeed suggest such aurora could exist. In this story, Ganymede is populated by a humanoid species who live indoors in glass cities. Griffith describes a series of variable speed roadways that run in parallel throughout the cities, an idea later favoured by Isaac Asimov and others. After some interaction with the Ganymedian population he notes that the Jovian satellite *Europa* has declined into the final stage of planetary evolution and is in the "icy silence of death."

Next Redgrave flies the Astronef into the Jovian atmosphere to take a peek at what lies beneath the clouds. Griffith goes along with Victorian astronomer Richard Proctor's version of the giant planet and describes an infernal and hellish surface of lava and flame constantly remaking itself and completely hostile to life. Later he confirms his familiarity with Proctor when they move on to Saturn and the hero, Redgrave, discusses how the rings need to be navigated with caution because of, *"...Proctor's hypothesis that the rings are formed of multitudes of tiny satellites."* He continues, *"Those are rings of what we should call meteorites on Earth, atoms of matter which Saturn threw off into space after the satellites were formed."*

At last the Astronef turns for home and during the voyage Redgrave demonstrates to his fiancée the benefits of zero gravity. *"Stooping down and taking hold of the chair with both hands, without any apparent effort he raised her about five feet from the floor, and held her there...for a moment he let her go, and she and the chair floated between the roof and the floor."*

This description makes it quite clear that some of the implications of zero gravity were well understood at the turn of the century. On the final journey home the Astronef is subjected to one last hazard. An invisible gravitational anomaly that Griffith calls, *"A derelict of the Ocean of Space, vast invisible orbs, lightless and lifeless, too distant from any living sun to be illumined by its rays, and yet exercising the only force left to them—the force of attraction."*

It's not exactly a *black hole*, but it is close kin, and for the time of writing, 1899, it was absolutely cutting edge. The dark star manages to pull the ship far enough off course that Redgrave is obliged to rethink his trajectory. He decides to fly in towards the sun and use Venus and Mercury to provide gravitational boosts to slingshot the Astronef back on course and on to Earth where he splashes down in the Pacific. This has to be Griffith's tour de force. It is so far beyond anything else in fiction at the time that it really does beggar parallel. About the only one who was writing similar stories with such conviction and intelligence was the Russian rocket scientist Konstantin Tsiolkovsky, but Griffith was certainly unaware of his work since it was virtually unknown, even in Russia, until the second decade of the 20th century. While H.G. Wells great space epic of travel to the moon would not begin to appear in serial form until four months after Griffith was done touring the entire solar system.

H.G. Wells would admit a grudging fascination with his competitor although he would write an unfavorable review of Griffith in the *Saturday Review* in 1895. He would later mention Griffith in his book *The War in the Air* in which he called Griffith's *Outlaws of the Air* an "aeronautic masterpiece."

George Griffith is almost completely unknown today. Part of the reason for this oversight undoubtedly rests in the fact that his publisher, Tower of London, went bankrupt in June of 1896. By October of that year Griffith found himself in court in London trying to stop the receivers from liquidating his copyrights. Ultimately he won the battle (and set a legal precedent doing so) but it must have been costly and time consuming and in the meantime it left him with no publisher for the two Romanoff novels and *Outlaws of the Air;* his most successful early works, .

It seems quite extraordinary that scholars of science fiction have placed so little importance on Griffith's works. He is often the subject of negative comparisons to his more famous counterpart, H.G. Wells. But Griffith was intent on telling a good story, and he took some pains to make sure that the speculation and technology were as up-to-date as he could manage. On the other hand, Wells was always bent on instructing his readers in sociology, using moralistic fables, sometimes with the subtlety of a blunt instrument. The few scholars who even talk of Griffith continue to dismiss him by saying he was unimaginative and that he did little but co-opt the ideas of Wells, Camille Flammarion and others. The Flammarion connection is interesting and clearly acknowledged by Griffith, but the idea of cometary collisions dated back at least as far as Edmond Halley and it seems that Griffith's story is very probably the first to recognize the danger represented *by the kinetic energy* in such an object. It also seems difficult to place any credence on the insinuation that Griffith stole from Wells. Griffith preempted him with a Mars story (Olga Romanoff), a space voyage (A Honeymoon in Space), a comet story (The Great Crellin Comet), an aerial warfare story (Outlaws of the Air) and even his "time travel" story (Valdar the Oft-Born) was published before Wells adapted his *Chronic Argonauts* into the bestseller *The Time Machine* (although admittedly Griffith used reincarnation as his method of travelling through the ages, and not a machine.) Griffith also introduced dozens of visionary ideas for viable new technology, something Wells rarely accomplished until much later in his career. If anything it is much easier to argue that Griffith owes a debt to Jules Verne, but he can hardly be damned for that, since Verne influenced people the world over.

After terminating his long relationship with Cyril Pearson, Griffith corresponded for the *Daily Mail* from South Africa, a location where he had set a future war story about the British versus the Boers, written *before* the war began. His story *Hellville USA* was about a town-sized penal colony, quarantined from the rest of America; a concept taken to its ultimate conclusion almost a century later in the hugely successful John Carpenter movie *Escape from New York*. Master novelist Michael Moorcock would later call Griffith "the first professional science fiction writer" because he produced story after story, on demand, for his editors and publishers.

Griffith would also leave more than just a literary heritage. He had a son, Alan Arnold Griffith, named after the characters in *Angel of the Revolution*. Alan Arnold Griffith was one of the most talented minds in the history of aeronautical engineering. In 1926 he proposed a new concept called an "axial compressor" in his paper *The Aerodynamic Theory of Turbine Design*. It would not be possible to build such a device until the late 1930's, but it would ultimately revolutionize the thrust-to-weight ratio in jet engines. As a result of these new ideas, aircraft manufacturers around the world began investigating the possibilities of vertical take-off aircraft using the downward thrust of these new high powered engines. In 1952 A.A. Griffith was working for Rolls Royce, at their Hucknall facility in England, when work began on his awkward new flying machine called the "Thrust Measuring Rig." (A similar vertically mounted contraption had been tested the year before by Ryan aircraft in America, their version would be underpowered, but would soon be equipped with the Griffith designed Rolls Royce *Avon* axial engine and would become the *X-13 Vertijet*.)

The basic principle was to mount a jet engine in an ungainly frame of piping with its exhaust nozzle pointing down towards the ground. Some of the exhaust (about 10%) was diverted through a series of pipes to an array of outriggers that were then connected to the pilot's rudder pedals and control column. The redirected exhaust was used to balance the vehicle in a vague semblance of control. It was nothing less than a primitive reaction control thruster system. The XJ-314 experimental thrust measuring rig became known as the *Flying Bedstead*. It first flew free of restraining cables on August 3rd 1954.

Later that year, on November 16th, Bell Aircraft Company of Niagara Falls, New York, tested their own vertical take-off plane, known as the Bell ATV. It used jet engines on swiveling joints. Instead of using one engine for the downward thrust and an array of primitive reaction control thrusters like the *bedstead*, the Bell ATV simply rotated its main engines down for take-off (exactly as described by George Griffith in 1893) and then swiveled them hor-

AA Griffith's 1954
Flying Bedstead

izontally to fly forwards. The Bell ATV was soon abandoned in favor of an adaptation of Griffith's redirected exhaust system which had by then been labeled *vectored thrust*. Bell would continue on with their research and in 1957 they would fly the X-14, a small vertical take-off aircraft powered by two British engines. In Britain Griffith's *flying bedstead* ultimately evolved into *Project P.1127*, later known to the world as the Hawker Harrier VTOL, the world's first successful VTOL fighter plane.

In late 1959 Hawker sent designer Ralph Hooper to *Bell* in Niagara to check out the X-14 and by the early 1960's NASA were sending Langley test pilots, such as Jack Reeder, to England to test-fly the Harrier. Less than six months after Hooper's visit, Bell engineers made a proposal to NASA for a free-flying vehicle that could be used for training Apollo astronauts to land on the moon, to be powered by the General Electric J-85 engine using Griffith's axial compressor. (This engine still has one of the highest thrust-to-weight ratios of any engine in the world and was used by Burt Rutan's White Knight mothership to launch SpaceShipOne.) At this point Bell had a lot of experience in VTOL, but it would be an advanced version of Griffith's design that would be the key to unlocking the secret of vertical take-off and landing. Four years later, in April 1964, two bizarre looking conglomerations of tubular aluminium were shipped to NASA's facility at Edward's Air Force Base. They used a single large jet engine which used downward thrust to remove five sixths of the vehicle's weight (to simulate lunar gravity) and a string of outriggers with peroxide rocket thrusters for stabilization. Take-off thrust was provided by rocket engines. Its name was the *Lunar Landing Research Vehicle,* but it was soon nicknamed the *Flying Bedstead* after its predecessor of a decade earlier. Later it would have a rudimentary cockpit attached to it that simulated the cockpit of the Apollo lunar module, this version was called the *Lunar Landing Training Vehicle*. It would be used by Neil Armstrong and many of the other Apollo astronauts to prepare for landing on the moon.

Alan Arnold Griffith is barely remembered today as one of the fathers of the modern jet engine, but he became the chief scientist at Rolls-Royce where he did some of the earliest work on stress and

NASA's 1964 *Flying Bedstead*

metal fatigue. His work on aeronautics led him to cite his father's friend Hiram Maxim in a letter to *Flight* magazine in October 1910. He also wrote at least one paper, two years before Sputnik, about re-entry heating problems. On his retirement in 1960 the newspapers referred to him as a "shy genius" and "the man behind jet history." He once said about himself that, "there is no doubt that my father's vision and imagination touched off my own interest in flying." He received a CBE in June 1947, along with the Blériot medal, the Louis Breguet Trophy and other recognition from the aeronautical community before dying in 1963.

His father, George Griffith, is also a forgotten titan of his era. His legacy is not merely a wealth of extraordinarily prescient futuristic fiction. He also inspired a son who would go on to make contributions in the struggle to place humans on another world. After an extraordinary run of thirteen years, during which he wrote no less than 45 books and countless articles, George Griffith died in relative obscurity at Port Erin on the Isle of Man, on June 4th 1906. He was 49 years old.

A Fred T. Jane illustration from 1893 of George Griffith's "tilt-rotor" vertical take-off airship.

George Griffith's Legacy to Real Science
The career of A A Griffith

George Griffith made a lasting contribution to the development of science fiction, showing remarkable insight in some of the devices he foresaw. However George had a son, Alan Arnold Griffith, named after heroes of his novels, who was to make equally striking contributions to the real world of science and engineering. Alan was born Alan Arnold Jones on 13th June 1893 in the Kilburn area of London. His father did not change the family name to Griffith until May 1894, giving as his reason for the change, "Nobody called Jones was ever famous!" As George's success as an author grew the family moved frequently to more fashionable addresses in London and to Littlehampton on the coast, where George could indulge his enthusiasm for sailing. As his popularity began to wane in the early 20th century, to economise he moved his family to the Isle of Man, where his sister-in-law ran a boarding house in Douglas and where Alan's sister, Muriel, had been born in 1895. George had been an unusual father insisting, for example, that the family spoke French and German at meal times. They lived in a cottage near Port Erin where he died in 1906, when Alan was only thirteen and by which time such fortune as had been earned had been spent. By the date of the 1911 census Alan and his mother were living in her sister's boarding house. Alan attended Douglas High School and proved to be an academic high achiever. At the age of eighteen he won the Sir W. H. Tate scholarship to read Mechanical Engineer-ing at Liverpool University. By this time his family were in seriously straitened financial circumstances: it is believed that he managed to save some of his scholarship money to help support his mother.

A.A. Griffith

For most of his life Alan was not known by his first name, but was always "Grif" to colleagues, family and friends

Grif graduated in 1914 and spent a further year leading to a Master's degree. By this time the First World War was in progress. It is thought that Grif, who was very thin, was judged unfit for military service and was sent to the Royal Aircraft Factory (later R.A.E.) Farnborough on war work. At that time Farnborough was a major production facility for warplanes. Grif was set to work in the engineering workshops. These shops operated a piece-work system, in which a job was assessed for the time it should take, and then the workers were rewarded if they could beat the target. For example, Grif would be given a task to make 300 examples of an aircraft part, for which the allotted time was, say, three weeks. To the annoyance of the foreman he would then sit and think for a few days, making no parts. He would then spend a couple of days making a special jig – still no parts. Finally, he would carry out the production run in a matter of days, beating the target by a factor of two and earning far too much money from the piece-rate system. This was considered subversive, so they moved him to the research labs.

In the research laboratories Grif worked initially under G. I. Taylor, an original thinker, who made many ingenious contributions to physics and engineering. They were much concerned with the problems of assessing stress in aircraft components that had to be made very light and stressed to (and too often beyond) safe limits. One of Grif's first contributions was to come up with a method of estimating torsional stress distributions across arbitrary cross-sections. He noted that the equation obeyed by the stress was the same as that governing the shape of a soap bubble blown over a hole of identical shape to the cross-section. Hence blowing such a bubble and measuring its shape solved the equation – effectively an early form of analogue computer, which earned him the nickname "Bubble" Griffith.

Work on stress led inevitably to asking the question "Why do things break?" Although this was a very early stage in the development of atomic models – Bohr had proposed his only a few years before and crystallography was virtually in its birth pangs – it was still possible to estimate the forces between atoms and hence the breaking strain of materials. However, all materials fractured at strains far below, typically twenty times below, what would be expected from interatomic forces. It was this problem that Grif addressed next. He chose glass as a working substance by studying the breaking of glass fibres. He found that newly drawn fibres were very strong, but that they quickly lost this strength with handling. He reasoned that this increased fragility was due to tiny surface cracks appearing. From this hypothesis he developed a theory of rupture. Imagine a fibre being pulled under stress. The tiny cracks will tend to be opened up. To enlarge a crack takes energy to increase the free surface area of the material, on the other hand some energy is won back from the release of strain in the body of the fibre. At some point the rate at which energy is released exceeds the rate at which it is required to enlarge the crack and then catastrophic failure occurs. Grif was able to express this in a formal equation and verify its accuracy by experiment. This he did by blowing a fresh glass bubble, scoring a crack of controlled length on the surface and then measuring the bursting pressure. He published this work in a paper entitled "The phenomena of rupture and flow in solids" which appeared in the Philosophical Transactions of the Royal Society in 1920. This paper remains one of the most frequently cited sources of all time, even now, ninety years after it was written. It is generally considered to be the founding paper for the whole science of Fracture Mechanics and is widely referenced in all works on the physics of materials and the strength of structures. In 1921 Grif was awarded his doctorate by the University of Liverpool.

Grif's work on the rupture of materials could have developed into an immediately valuable tool of practical engineering, but it was brought to a bizarre end. His work was conducted in a hut on the Farnborough field. One day his assistant left the glass-blowing torch alight and burned down the hut. It is not possible to burn down government property without questions being raised. At the subsequent enquiry Grif was asked, "Just what were you doing in this hut?" To which the answer was, " Investigating why glass breaks." This brought the comment, "What use is that to the aircraft industry?" and the work was terminated. Interest in Fracture Mechanics was not revived in any serious way until the early 1950s, by which time it had become all too painfully obvious how important crack propagation was to the safety of aircraft. Grif was moved into engine research.

In the Experimental Engine division of what was now the Royal Aircraft Establishment Grif began thinking of the possibility of using gas turbines for aircraft propulsion. Others had considered this, but such engines generally were heavy and had unpromising efficiencies. As was his now well-established style Grif addressed the fundamental theory of the field. In 1926 he wrote a paper entitled "An aerodymanic theory of turbine design". In this he showed that the blades of a turbine, and those of an axial compressor, must be treated as aerofoils. Care must be taken to ensure that the blades do not operate in a stalled condition, which appears to have been the problem with earlier versions. Given proper design he predicted high efficiencies for gas turbines and potentially excellent performance for aircraft propulsion. His paper appeared three years before Frank Whittle made his first suggestion for a turbine engine. Griffith's initial proposal was for a turbine engine driving a propeller, or ducted fan, whereas Whittle's later proposal was for the jet efflux to be the sole propulsive agent. A further difference was that Griffith proposed the use of an axial compressor from the very beginning, on the grounds of its theoretical efficiency, whereas Whittle adopted a centrifugal compressor.

Following the 1926 proposal to investigate turbine engines the RAE Farnborough soon started experiments by building an axial compressor test rig to verify the Griffith calculations. The results confirmed his predictions, but there was little impetus to support a full-scale engine development. In 1929 Frank Whittle, then a cadet in the R.A.F., suggested a pure gas turbine engine. This differed from the Griffith proposal, which envisaged a turbine-driven propeller. Whittle's proposal was sent to the Air Ministry Laboratory in London, to which Grif had moved as head. Grif pointed out a couple of mathematical errors in Whittle's work and also felt some of his assumptions were over-optimistic. In recent years journalists have tried to imply that Grif deliberately suppressed Whittle's work out of professional jealousy. No one who knew anything about Grif's character could possibly believe this. He never indulged in self-promotion. He hated publicity. He never accepted an invitation to give a lecture. He was always happy to put forward his ideas and allow others to develop them. He did, however, believe in getting calculations correct and could be very critical of mistakes.

Whittle was sent by the RAF to Cambridge University to take a degree and Grif returned to R.A.E. Farnborough after his three years at the Air Ministry Laboratory. From 1936 two engine development programmes started. Whittle formed the company Power Jets and set about making a pure jet engine with a centrifugal compressor. Grif had always maintained that the axial flow compressor was theoretically superior, but it presented difficult technical challenges at the time. Nevertheless the R.A.E. set about developing such a device. Hayne Constant played a significant role in this work. The R.A.E. work led to a fully specified axial flow pure jet project (the F1) which it was intended that Power Jets should make, but the needs of the war intervened and the firm had to concentrate on bringing the centrifugal engine to an airworthy state. The R.A.E continued their own line of Griffith-inspired work developing the F2, engineered by Metropolitan Vickers, which flew in test beds during the war and later developed into the Armstrong-Siddeley Sapphire – a successful engine in the post-war period. The Whittle project led to the first flight by a British jet aircraft in 1941, and towards the end of the war, the introduction of the Gloster Meteor jet fighter. Commercial development of the centrifugal compressor engines eventually fell mainly to Rolls-Royce, notably in their Derwent and Nene engines, but this layout did not progress much further, at least in high-powered engines.

German successes are often overlooked. They started jet engine work in 1934 under von Ohain and had a prototype Heinkel 178 flying by 1939. The Messerschmitt 262 fighter with twin axial-flow jets made a serious impact on allied bombers, but came too late to influence the outcome of the war. Probably the Germans deserve more credit than they popularly receive, but in wartime the victors get to write the history.

Grif had left the R.A.E in 1938. He had always said that if they tried to make him a manager, then he would leave. This they did, so he left. He was recruited by E.W.Hives at Rolls-Royce, who gave him the wonderful job-description, "Carry on thinking". Grif was given a small office of his own in Duffield Bank House, the Rolls-Royce hospitality residence, and provided with a personal designer, Donald Eyre. Eyre was highly skilled in transforming Grif's ideas into working drawings. He also kept meticulous notes of their work from day to day, which have been published as his reminiscences by the Rolls-Royce Heritage Trust. This record shows that a continuous flow of original ideas came from this team. By 1940 they had a proposal for a ducted fan propulsion unit with an axial compressor gas turbine core. In 1941 there was a proposal for jet lift vertical take off and for the use of vectored thrust, as employed by the Harrier fighter 20 years later. Pursuing the line that axial compressors were essential, Grif produced the layout of the engine that eventually became the Rolls-Royce Avon, one of the most successful engines of the post-war period. He also devised a by-pass scheme, which became the Conway. Looking back on the history of the development of the airborne gas turbine it is hard to resist the conclusion that Grif's long-term view was entirely correct. The axial flow ducted-fan engine is now completely dominant in air transport. It was typical of him to insist on aiming for the theoretically correct solution. When Rolls-Royce were having trouble with the prototype Avon engine and this was mentioned to Grif, he simply replied, "That's why we have development engineers!"

In his role as Chief Research Engineer, and later Chief Scientist, at Rolls-Royce Grif's purpose was always to look ahead to the far future. Though he first proposed jet-lift in 1941, it was not until 1954 that the "Flying Bedstead" took to the air. This was a test vehicle that could lift off vertically on the thrust of two Nene turbojets and was stabilised by four outriggers carrying jets of air bled from the engine's compressors. It demonstrated that stable jet lift was possible. The device was a popular sensation and led to Grif being highlighted in the newspapers, which exposure he loathed. He absolutely refused to give press interviews. He did not trust journalists, even though, or possibly because, his father was one. He used to tell a tale that his father was once being sent off on a mission by a press baron of the day who told him, "Now Griffith, always send back a good story. If it happens to be true, that is no problem, but it must be good."

Vertical take-off was tested further by the Short SC1, which had four lift engines and one for forward flight. This demonstrated the transition between lift and forward flight and employed specially designed small high-thrust engines intended for the lifting process. Grif had envisaged large supersonic transports with banks of such engines, pointing out that the dead weight they represented would be offset by savings in the undercarriage and in being able to use a narrow delta wing not compromised by the needs of low speed take-off and landing. In the event supersonic transport was seriously hampered by unacceptable noise over land areas and these ideas were never pursued. In the last few years of his life Grif was thinking about hypersonic transports propelled by hydrogen burning outside the aircraft. He retired from Rolls-Royce in 1960, but remained a consultant until his death in 1963. His work had been recognised by his election as a Fellow of the Royal Society in

1941, by the award of the CBE in 1948, the Silver Medal of the Royal Aeronautical Society in 1955 and the Bleriot Medal in 1962.

Grif was a quiet, reserved man, who nevertheless had a wry sense of humour when in the company of friends. Though probably quite unlike his extrovert father, he did on occasion show a small streak of anarchy. During the war people noticed that papers piled on his desk had a padlock placed on top. This was a result of Security telling him that he must keep his papers under lock and key at all times.

It is enlightening to compare the real world of engineering science with the fictional world of George Griffith. In The Angel of the Revolution George Griffith's hero invents a flying machine, builds a small model and, having found a sponsor, constructs a fully operational aerial battleship without seeming to need any development at all, nor running into any teething troubles. Oddly his sequel, The Siren of the Skies, is set a century later, but no significant changes have occurred in the design of the craft and no defences seem to have evolved to counter his war machine. Contrast this with the real world, where aircraft designs evolved rapidly, but often with years of painstaking development and many fatal errors on the way. On the other hand most new weapons (with the possible exception of nuclear warheads) give only a brief superiority to their inventors: countermeasures usually appear with remarkable speed, especially under the pressures of wartime. Grif liked to point out that fictional predictions of the future often missed important developments. He noted that his father wrote his works twenty years after James Clerk Maxwell had laid out the theory of electromagnetic waves and Hertz had demonstrated radio waves experimentally, but authors of the time still had their flying machines communicating by signal lamps. None foresaw radio.

John Griffith
October 2010

HOW I BROKE THE RECORD ROUND THE WORLD

(12th March 1894 – 16th May 1894)
Extracted from Pearson's Weekly

By
George Griffith

Edited with illustrations compiled from the period

by
Robert Godwin

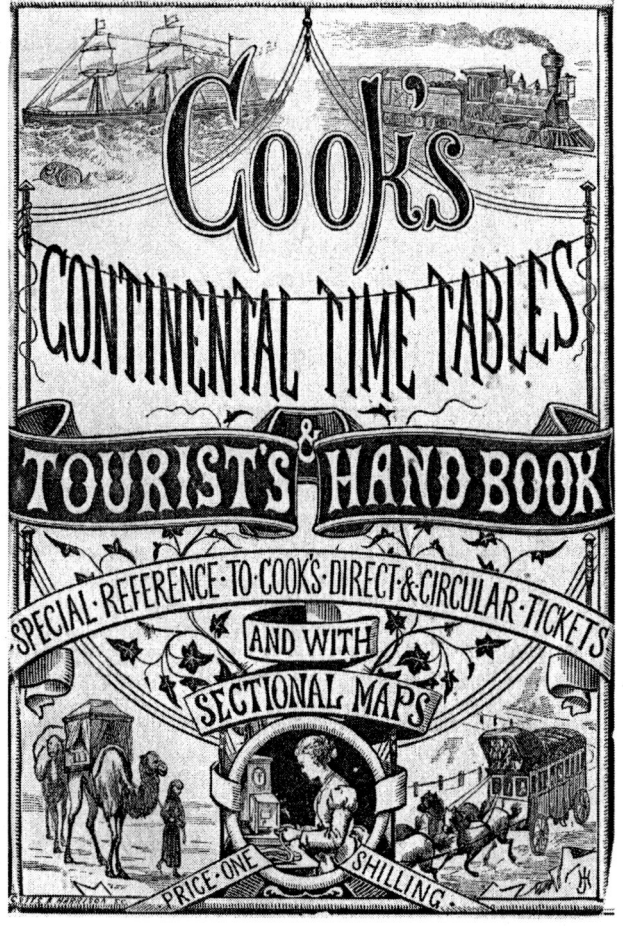

I. — ACROSS EUROPE IN FORTY-FIVE HOURS

TAKE a map of the world, on Mercator's projection, if you have one, and with pencil in hand trace a line beginning at London, crossing the Channel via Dover and Calais, Europe via Paris, Genoa, Rome, and Naples, then strike out across the Mediterranean through the Straits of Messina to Port Said, down the Suez Canal, through the Red Sea, across the Indian Ocean to Colombo, then curve round the island "the Pearl of the Seas," as the Singhali, not without reason, call it—then eastward across the sea and between Sumatra and Malacca to Singapore, then northward to Hong Kong and Yokohama, then strike out north-eastward across the broad Pacific to Vancouver, then eastward and southward over America to Montreal and New York, then north-eastward again across the Atlantic to Southampton, and lastly from Southampton to London—do this, and you will have traced the outline of the picture which it will be the object of this article to lay before your mental gaze.

But as a map differs from a picture, and as a dry, articulated skeleton differs from a human being aglow with life and health, so does the voyage round the world, which I have just had the good fortune to accomplish more rapidly than anyone ever made it before, differ from such a map-tracing as, for the sake of better comprehension, I have asked you to make.

The ever-changing scenery of land and sea, of hill and plain, and storm and calm; the alternations of the beauty of the fairest lands of earth with its most lifeless deserts; of the luxuriance of tropical vegetation with the chilly splendours of mountain uplands clothed in everlasting snow and ice—all these, and more, go to make up the varied glories of the world panorama, nearly 24,000 miles in length, which, as it were, has been unfolded before my eyes since I left Charing Cross only sixty-five days ago.

In such a journey, made at such a speed—for I may as well say here as later on that my actual time of travelling was only fifty-seven days, and that, with the exception of Yokohama and Hong Kong, I spent less than twenty-four hours in any one place—it was, of course, quite out of the question to make more than the most cursory observations. The vast and ever-changing panorama was so rapidly unfolded before me that before one scene had time to make any very distinct impression it was overlaid by another, and often a totally different one. This being so, my articles are not to be taken as a globe-trotter's "vade mecum" round the world. They are a record of what I saw and did, and nothing else, and it must be remembered that I went out to do rather than to see.

Charing Cross Station in London 1890s

Sharp on time at eleven o'clock on the 12th of March last, the special day express steamed out of Charing Cross station, and I was one of the passengers in an alleged drawing-room car, which subsequent experience has led me to imagine was bought by the South Eastern Railway second-hand from one of the American companies. By one o'clock I was on board the Calais-Douvre.

In spite of the Channel being in a somewhat ugly humour, I was able to draw a good augury for my undertaking from the fact that I reached French soil a quarter of an hour ahead of scheduled time. So close had all the connections been cut that when I reached Charing Cross again, and tied the knot in the 24,000 mile girdle that I had put round the world, that fifteen minutes had just grown to forty, and no more.

At seven o'clock to the minute the Paris express pulled up in the Gare du Nord, and here, for to a certain extent I was "personally conducted," an envoy of the ubiquitous Cook met me, spirited my very limited baggage through the barriers in some occult fashion, and placed it in a neat little coupe in which I was rattled through the streets of Paris, brilliant with lights and just awakening for the evening's amusement, to the Gare de Lyon, where I was to embark on the sleeper for Rome.

Gare du Nord Paris

Gare de Lyon Paris

I had two hours in Paris, and out of this found time to eat an excellent dinner of which I stood considerably in need. There was nothing the matter with it but the price. When the bill was presented I mustered the relics of what had once been my French, and told the waiter that I was going on a very long hurried journey, and that I really didn't want the dinner service and the table from which I had eaten. He told me they were not included in the bill as I had thought.

Time was lacking for further argument so I paid up, feeling very much as though I was compounding a felony in doing so. A minute or two before nine I boarded the sleeping-car in which I was to travel without a change across the Alps and over the plains of Piedmont, and down the coast of Tuscany to Rome.

A Wagons-Lit compartment from the 1890s showing the conversion from day to night use.

The "wagons-lits" differ much from the American cars, and on the whole I think they are better. A narrow passage runs down one side of the car instead of down the middle, and out of this open half a dozen compartments not unlike miniature state rooms on board ship. Each of these contains two berths, one above the other, running transversely instead of longitudinally, and the beds are very comfortable, especially if you get one in the middle of the car.

In the daytime the upper berth vanishes, and the lower becomes a sofa. A little table springs out from the side, and the whole compartment is metamorphosed beyond recognition. But for purposes of sight-seeing the International cars are far inferior to the American. You can only see out of one side of the carriage unless you have the door of your berth open and keep dodging backwards and forwards into the passage. Added to this, the windows are nearly always covered with an opaque layer composed of condensed steam and smoke from the engine.

French and Italian engines do not steam, they smoke. They burn block fuel made of Belgian coal-dust, crude petroleum, and other objectionable ingredients, and the product of its combustion has a clinging nature which makes it absolutely detestable. The cars are amply glazed, and as in the hill country to the South of France, there are many tunnels, in each of which the windows acquire an added layer of soot, the result is simply maddening.

You know that you are running along through some of the loveliest scenery in the world, but you have to look at it through a medium which gives it the aspect of London in November. The windows of our car were washed once between Paris and Rome. This was at Turin, after all the finest scenery had been passed through. For my own part I confiscated a duster and did my own window-cleaning when I found that the company did not do it for me.

Culoz station circa 1894

At half-past five on the morning of the 13th I woke up at Culoz, three hundred and forty-eight miles from Paris. Like all my fellow-passengers I wanted breakfast, and discovered to my disgust that there was absolutely nothing to be got on the car. This is a defect which certainly ought to be remedied, and could be very easily. At Aix-les-Bains we were tantalised by the sight of the buffet, but did not stop long enough to be able to buy anything,

Aix-les-Bains station circa 1894

At Chambery they kindly allowed us five minutes in which to scramble for glasses of bad café-au-lait at half a franc each which were brought on the platform, apparently by a speculative peasant woman. This, it must be remembered, was not on a cheap excursion train; it was on one of the "grands exprèss Européans," to travel by which you have to pay express extra fare and nearly £5 above that for sleeping accommodation. After this it is hardly necessary to say the International Company is a close monopoly.

The run from Chambery through the Maurienne district, or Valley of the Arc, to the entrance of the Mont Cenis tunnel would have been entirely delightful if it had not been for that exasperating dirt on the windows. It was early enough for the upper and middle slopes of the mountains which towered up thousands of feet on both sides of the line to be covered with snow, and there were just clouds enough drifting through the valley to add a fantastic charm to the scene without obscuring the sunlight of the Alpine spring morning.

From the plains of Southern France the Mont Cenis line rises till it reaches a height of over four thousand feet in the centre of the tunnel, and the nearer we approached the entrance to the tunnel the wilder and grander the scenery became, until, looking up through the fleecy drifting clouds, I could see the sun shining on peaks of

The entrance to Mount Cenis circa 1894

everlasting snow and ice that towered five and six thousand feet above the line on either hand. The narrow alluvial plain intercepted by the Arc was covered with well-kept fields and orchards looking fresh from their winter snow-bath, and every turn of the line as it rounded the spurs of the foothills brought into view some quaintly picturesque Savoyard village, or the graybrown ruins of some old-world stronghold standing aloof upon its lonely height, with its ragged windows and broken loopholes looking, as it seemed, with a sort of disgusted surprise at the strange smoking, snorting Thing that was so noisily invading its ancient solitude.

A run of about two hours through such scenery as this covered the sixty-one mile climb from Chambery to Modane, the International Custom House and frontier station between Italy and France. We took our baggage into the French end and satisfied the French officials that we were taking nothing out of France that they didn't want to lose, and these then delivered us to the gold-laced, cocked-hatted Italians, whose business it was to see that we were taking nothing free into Italy that they could make us pay anything on.

No luggage whatever is carried free in Italy, and it cost me fifteen francs for the privilege of taking one small portmanteau and a handbag across the frontier. I had not been many minutes in Italy before I saw how badly the money was wanted.

The buffet at Modane is artfully placed at the Italian end of the station, so that it may be impossible for the hungry and thirsty, traveller to employ in eating and drinking the precious minutes of the brief stop, which are wasted in swearing in mixed tongues at officials who seem to think that you have come there for no other purpose than letting them see what you have brought with you at their good leisure and convenience. Happily, in my case, 10d. sterling corrupted a Frenchman into winking at an Italian who for another 10d. took my word for the fiscal innocence of my baggage, and so I just got through in time to buy something to eat and drink on the train. After this came the passage of the Mont Cenis a run of thirty minutes through the bowels of the Alps. As soon as I got my window cleaned at the southern end I got my first glimpse of Italy. Rank blasphemy as it may seem to say so, I am obliged to confess that I was terribly disappointed. I expected to see the paradise so enthusiastically described by poets and tourists, who seem to have allowed themselves quite a poetic licence of description, I looked for a lovely land, soft, and sunlit, and fertile; a land of eternal spring and summer, of vineyards and gardens, of picturesque peasants and still more picturesque habitations.

Instead of this, I saw a land of wild bleak mountains rising from bare, ragged, ill-cultivated plains, dotted with dirty, squalid hamlets and tawdry towns, not ruined enough to be picturesque, only dilapidated enough to be shabby. In the distance, on the opposite side of the valley from the hills along which the line runs, the towns clustered picturesquely about the tops of the foothills, usually surmounted by a church or a convent or the fragments of a ruined castle, and at the distance, which lent enchantment to the view, I was well content to admire.

As the train ran down from the mountains I thought things would improve, but they did not. All the beauty kept at a distance. All that was near was dreary, squalid, and ugly. The people matched the country, and over all lay the disfiguring blight of hopeless poverty. Out of every five men, two wore a uniform, one was decently dressed, and the other two were in rags. "Bankruptcy" was writ large from the Alps to the Gulf of Genoa.

Genoa Harbour late 1890s

I reached Genoa—"La Superba" now no longer, at any rate as far as externals go—just before nightfall, and my first glimpse of the Mediterranean was of a grey calm sea under a cloudy sky as cold and unromantic as the English Channel in November. From Genoa to Rome the run just lasted from nightfall to daybreak. I had a change and a two hours' wait here, so after a commodious wash and breakfast I chartered an open trap and took an hour's drive through the Eternal City.

I found the whole place en fete, flags flying, the military and police in their gayest uniforms, the streets sanded, and everyone in his and her Sunday best. I didn't know that I was expected by anyone but Cook's agent, and as a matter of fact I wasn't. It was the King's birthday, and the Romans were getting ready to celebrate it as though money was no object and national bankruptcy a thing unheard of.

I don't propose to describe Rome from what I saw during that hour's drive, so I shall content myself with saying that the Romans have evidently built the modern part of their city with a haughty disregard of cost that speaks volumes for their confidence in their own borrowing capacity. The contrast between the splendour of the city and the squalor of the country was enough to explain all the eccentricities of Italian finance.

I left Rome at 8.20 on the Pullman for Naples. Although the day was by no means cloudless, and though the Italian sky was anything but the deep sapphire of the poems and prose romances, better weather for scenery seeing could hardly have been made to order. The train ran along under a bright sun nearly the whole way, while the Apennines and the Sabine Mountains on the left and the Alban Hills and Volscian Mountains on the right lifted their highest peaks, often crowned by the ruins of some Roman stronghold or mediaeval abbey or castle, above the cloud banks which lay along their middle heights.

I stood outside on the rear platform of the car nearly the whole way, and enjoyed a rapid succession of such landscapes as could scarcely be matched in any other part of the world, either for natural beauty or historical interest. Running smoothly along a well-ballasted, dustless line at a good forty miles an hour, every two or three minutes opened up some new prospect of hill and valley, mountain and gorge, and every two or three miles took the train sweeping round the base of one of the conical foothills almost covered with homes.

These hill-towns of Italy are epitomes of Italian history in stone and stucco. As you descend their narrow, zigzag streets you go from today through the Middle and Dark Ages back into the old time when Rome was the mistress of the world, and the few broken ruins scattered about the top of the hill formed the pillared walls of a temple sacred to Venus or Apollo, or else the villa of some Roman aristocrat, whose slaves toiled for him on the Campagna below, or hewed wood in the forests of the Apennines or the Volscians.

Sometimes the ruins are those of a round tower or square keep, still strong and massive after a thousand years of sun and storm, but in every case the story is the same, and it is the story of advancing civilisation and increasing security. Age after age the houses come lower, until the modern hotel stands with open doors, and the wary landlord waits to fleece the fatted tourist a few hundred feet below the ruins of the grey fastness, where four or five centuries ago men were robbed in a rougher and readier style. Thus do times change, and men, to a certain extent, with them.

After a glorious run of over four hours across the fertile and fairly well cultivated plain, between a series of ever-changing views each so beautiful that they kept me in a state of constant regret that I could not be on both sides of the platform at once, a grievous disappointment awaited me at the end. As the train ran out to the wide plain which lies behind the Bay of Naples I saw to my intense disgust that Vesuvius had on the biggest and densest of his cloud cape. Only quite the lower slopes were visible, and these, of course, were as commonplace as a Scotch moor after all the splendid scenery through which I had just come.

At Naples I once more became a personally-conducted tourist. A great deal of cheap humour has been indulged in by alleged humourists of the "new" school on this subject, but so far I have found it to be, like a good deal more of its sort, all bosh. Certainly when one is tearing round the world against time it is an excellent thing to be personally conducted, especially if you have just a few hours in a town and want to use them to the best advantage.

I must confess that I was almost as much disappointed with Naples as Oscar Wilde was with the Atlantic. I did not find it "a bit of Heaven fallen down on earth." I never saw an earthier place or earthier people in my life. Of course March is March even in Southern Italy, and that is probably the reason why the famous bay was grey instead of blue, and why the streets looked dirty and the painted houses dingy and tawdry, and the whole town generally out at elbows.

Perhaps, also, I had too lately left the spic and span gorgeousness of Modern Rome. I am, however, more than ever convinced that it is not wise to read too much about a place or to see too many coloured photographs of it before going there. I am sure that my rapid glimpse of Italy would have brought fewer disappointments if I had not known my "Childe Harold" so well, and had seen fewer over-tinted reproductions of its beauties. It is a beautiful land beyond doubt, but the part I saw of it was anything but a paradise.

Shortly before sunset I went off to the *Sachsen*, which was lying a good way out in the bay, and which was to carry me 10,000 miles across the world to Hong Kong. Just as the sun was going down the kindly Fates dissolved the clouds from the summit of Vesuvius; and the truncated cone, with its slender wreath of smoke, stood out sharp against the grey evening sky, divided from its lower slopes by a long horizontal band of dense white cloud, over the upper surface of which the fitful gleams of the half-moon played every time the clouds up in the zenith drifted away from its disc. This was the last and fairest glimpse we got of Western Italy as the *Sachsen* steamed out of the bay and headed south-eastward for the Straits of Messina.

II. — LIFE ON AN EAST-BOUND LINER

A LONG, white-bulled, well-proportioned vessel, of nearly 5,000 tons, straight stemmed and comfortably broad of beam, with two pole masts and a single tall drab funnel, such was the North German Lloyd liner, *Sachsen*, which was to be my floating home for the next month, and which in that time was to carry me across the globe from the old world of the West to the older world of the East, a distance of more than ten thousand statute miles.

The Norddeutscher ship *Sachsen*

With a feeling of unadulterated satisfaction I got to my stateroom, and proceeded forthwith to unpack my extremely limited impedimenta. I had made my first important connection, and now there was nothing to do but to settle down for the month's steaming under suns that would shine ever brighter, and seas that would grow ever bluer and smoother, until the mythical Gates of the Sun were past, and nearly half my journey would be completed.

I may here also say that I looked forward with more confidence than justification to a nice, quiet month of reading, thinking, and writing. The reading was successful while the ship's somewhat limited library held out, and the thinking was an even greater success than the reading. In fact, one had not read many pages of a book before the thinking quite got the better of the reading. Then the book would be closed, and one would go on thinking for the next hour or so—when the next meal would be ready.

As for the writing, it will be some slight relief to my conscience to make public confession that by the time I reached Hong Kong I had actually written about as much as would respectably fill an ordinary day's work at home. The fact is that the life on an Eastern liner, of which I am going to try and give you a more or less distinct conception, is entirely incompatible with anything like serious work.

I have seen active, hard-working journalists and authors, who in temperate climes could hold their own with anyone in producing copy, sit at a table on deck, or under a punkah in the saloon, and gaze in moist and dripping despair at the paper in front of them, whose virgin whiteness was a faithful reflex of the blankness of their own minds. I only saw one man do any work at all in the Tropics, and he was a tall, stalwart, big-brained man of many inches, a wandering correspondent who had been nearly everywhere and done nearly everything.

One day in the Indian Ocean he wrote five pages of copy, and when I congratulated him respectfully on his achievement he gave me a haggard look and made an expressive gesture with his two hands as though he were wringing a wet towel out. Then he said : "Yes, that article had to be posted at Singapore, but it has been just like taking my brains like that and squeezing it out. Just ring for the steward, will you?"

When I saw the state to which tropical journalism had brought a so much stronger man than myself, I concluded that it would not be safe for me to risk it any further, and saw that it would be more prudent to devote myself exclusively to thinking.

To those who have nothing on their minds, very little on their backs, and something in their pockets, life on an East-bound liner is just about as pleasant a state of existence as the apparently inevitable imperfections of terrestrial life permit the average mortal to enjoy. There is absolutely nothing to do, and that is just what you want to do.

Every day at sea has five events. The first of these is breakfast. If you make a good meal you gain sufficient energy to wait for lunch, and speculate on what the run will be. At eight bells—12 noon—you see the captain and the first officer shooting the sun from the bridge, or, in other words, taking the latitude. In about twenty minutes the figures are put up outside the saloon.

On an Atlantic liner this is a moment of breathless interest, because the fate of a very considerable pool usually depends on the result, but in the Tropics the most hardened gamblers find the getting-up of a pool beyond them, and prefer to wait until the comparative cool of the evening, and play nap or poker in the smoking room.

Very soon after the second event of the day comes the third—tiffin—in view of which a judiciously cultivated thirst affords pleasant visions of lumps of ice swimming in cool fluids and clinking invitingly against the rim of the floating bowl. You take out your watch for about the eighth time since breakfast, and put it on from thirty to forty minutes according to the eastward run the ship has made, and you do it with a light-hearted recklessness which some day you may think of with a shudder.

I find, after careful calculation, that between London and London I put my watch on no less than thirty-three hours and fifteen minutes, and yet when we came eventually to that mysterious part of the earth where the next day is the same as the one before it, I only got twenty-three hours twenty minutes back. If anyone can tell me what has become of the other nine hours and fifty-five minutes I shall be very glad to learn. I might want them when my time comes.

Tiffin on the *Sachsen*, and, indeed, on all the North-German liners, is really a midday dinner of five or six courses, with about as many more of those little etceteras which give you such a satisfactory excuse for taking twice as long as is necessary over the meal. This also means getting a double allowance of punkah. All the time you are eating and drinking and chatting the great fans suspended from the roof of the saloon swing slowly backwards and forwards, sending ever-repeated shower-baths of cool air down upon you, making you feel most excellently at ease until you happen to look round and see the poor wretch who is pulling the rope.

Then, if you have not seen it before, you see the sharp, impassable, dividing line which, all over the East, is drawn between those who are served and those who serve. It is practically as rigid now as it was in the days of slavery. On the one side of it are ease, indolence, and a somewhat imperious impatience of all trouble; on the other is constant toil, under conditions which, to European eyes at least, seem to make work an intolerable burden. The man and brother theory has no practical recognition between the 30th parallels of north and south latitude.

After lunch comes the afternoon siesta in deck chair or hammock, and those pleasant dreams born of the gentle motion of the vessel, the warm zephyrs of drowsy air that come stealing in under the awnings, and the musical splashing swish of the water as it rolls away from the sides of the big ship cleaving her way through it at fifteen or sixteen miles an hour.

Between four and five the dreams give place to business, or, in other words, more eating and drinking. The eating takes the form of dainty little confections, fruits and ices, and the drinking of iced tea à la Russe with lemon juice, which can be varied at your own choice, and cost, with diverse cups more or less cheering and re-invigorating according to the ingredients upon which the smoking room steward exercises his skill.

After this the remaining hour or so of the long lazy afternoon may be dozed away until it is time to wonder at the ever-new and ever-glorious pageantry of the sunset, and then the gong goes for dinner. By this time a complete change of clothing has become necessary. Eight or ten hours, in an oceanic Turkish bath, have brought you into a condition in which dry clothing is at once a luxury and a necessity—so you go and dress.

I regret to say that the social servitude of the black coat and the hard-boiled shirt exists to a quite unreasonable extent in the upper circles of Tropical society. One would think that men who, in other respects, show no signs of mental weakness or congenital insanity, would not think it necessary to encase their moist and manly forms in dress suits, starched shirts, and high collars, in order to sit down to dinner on board a steamboat in company with people with whom they will probably never have more than the current month's acquaintance.

The mournful truth, however, is that they do so. I did not, and there was a certain amount of natural original sin in the satisfaction with which I watched the starch and the consistency gradually dissolve out, and the hard and aggressively glazy surface of the social armour-plating melt and wilt under the influence of cutaneous conditions beneath.

Dinner on the Eastern liner, apart from its gastronomical interest, which is very considerable, is not, as far as my experience goes, a very improving function. In the first place, the *Sachsen* was infested with a band of insufficiently restrained energy, and its efforts would have made rational conversation difficult even if it had been conducted in one language instead of five, and as we were all strangers or casual acquaintances the talk naturally averaged small; and small talk in five mixed languages is about as unprofitable as it is embarrassing.

I feel, however, a patriotic satisfaction in recording the fact that, although we were travelling on a ship that was German from stem to stern and truck to keel, the language of intercommunication was English. A German talking with an Italian, or a Norwegian speaking with a Spaniard, invariably spoke English. Forty years ago they would have spoken French, but now English is the world-language. I have even heard a Chinaman and a Japanese arguing out a commercial difference in very respectable Anglo-Saxon.

Paterfamilias has considerable reason in the complaints which he makes periodically in the papers as to the miserably imperfect education of the British youth in foreign languages, and his consequent suffering in competition with the foreigner. But out in the Far East one sees another and more encouraging side to this question. Whatever his nationality may be, the European who sets out to make a living, or to fill an official post in Egypt or India, China, or Japan, has got to speak English and to make himself as much like an Englishman as possible.

In fact the Eastern world is becoming rapidly Anglicised. It will never be German or French, Italian or Russian. The British race has stamped itself permanently upon the world of trade, commerce and politics from Port Said to Yokohama, and those who would succeed in that world must be as English as they can. I noticed on board the *Sachsen* that even the orders given by the officers to the sailors were English, veiled only by a perhaps unavoidable disguise of Teutonic pronunciation.

With such apology as may be necessary for this linguistic digression, I will take up my parable again and go on with a description which may be taken as applying to our every day life on board ship from the West to the Far East, varied only by such incidents as sighting land and going ashore, and sailing away again, after too brief glimpses of places and peoples to be described hereafter in their proper sequence.

Dinner at length over—that is to say, about a couple of hours after we sat down to it—there was a general adjournment to the deck to enjoy the delightful contrast between the coolness of those few precious evening hours and the almost breathless heat of the long burning day.

Now, if ever, a certain amount of exercise was taken. Couples, not usually of the same sex, would pair off, and fair forms, clad in white, fleecy raiment, would go fluttering up and down the broad Promenade deck in close proximity to more or less sensibly or picturesquely attired male creatures, and with arm linked in arm with a pretty affectation of obtaining a support not always necessitated by the rolling of the ship.

The two or three hours between dinner and turning-in time were by far the most pleasant portion of the twenty four hours. There is an atmospheric charm about early night in the tropics which is quite indescribable to those who have never experienced it, simply because there is nothing else with which to compare it. If a man is at all capable of feeling that it is good to be alive this is the time when he will feel it. If not, he can make fairly sure that earth has nothing to give him that is worth the taking.

I need hardly say that no such unfortunate was found, as far as I could see, among the fifty or sixty men and women of divers nationalities who made up the temporary aristocracy of the good ship *Sachsen*. The use of that word aristocracy reminds me that any attempt at description of life on an East-bound liner would be quite incomplete without something being said as to its social aspect.

Nowhere else on land or sea are the dividing lines of social caste so strictly drawn or so strongly marked as here. It is true that the divisions are temporary, and are based primarily on pecuniary distinctions, but while they last they have got to be observed.

Your social rank is for the time being decided by the class in which you are travelling. A suddenly enriched dustman in the saloon could not afford to be on too friendly terms with an impoverished duke in the second cabin, while he in turn would lose caste if he let his possibly lonely heart go out too far even to an entirely worthy person whose pecuniary exiguities obliged him to take passage in the steerage.

Each social rank, too, has its own territory rigidly defined and set apart. The long, broad promenade deck which stretches flush with the top of the bulwarks over three-quarters of the vessel's length amidships is sacred to the aristocracy of the saloon, the captain, and his higher officers. On this no second-class passenger is supposed to set foot from one end of the voyage to the other.

I have heard rumours told with bated breath of such invasion, but I cannot say that I have ever seen one. What would happen to the steerage passenger whose too daring foot should tread that sacred surface of snowy planking I do not dare even to conjecture. In fact I am not aware that the written or unwritten codes of maritime social law contain any provision for such an outrage as this would be. Those who framed them have evidently considered it to be too impossible even to deserve consideration.

So, too, the after or quarter-deck, which in old fashioned ships was the domain of what were then called the cabin passengers, is set apart for the perambulations of the voyagers of the second saloon, while the fore part of the main deck, between the end of the saloon promenade and the forecastle, is the area in which the steerage passengers have to make themselves as comfortable as they can when the decks are dry. When water begins to come over the side, this is the first part of the ship it strikes, and then there is no refuge left but the stuffy discomfort of the 'tween decks.

These divisions of territory, however, only hold good in an upward direction. To the aristocrat of the saloon the whole ship is free; he may invade the quarter-deck at his good pleasure, though it is not considered to be quite good form to do so, and if he feels particularly condescending he is equally free to go and compare at close quarters the spacious luxury of his own temporary lot with the literally "cribbed, cabined, and confined" discomfort of that of his poor and distant relations in the steerage.

And yet there is one spot on the upper works of the ship to which even a first saloon ticket is not a passport, and where even he may not set foot without a special invitation from the autocrat of the floating community. This is the bridge. Here the captain lives, and moves, and has his official being on a lonely eminence that is shared only by the officer of the watch and the man at the wheel. In former times the captain's cabin was under the quarter-deck, but in all new steamers his sleeping and sitting rooms are on the bridge behind the chart room, and most comfortable habitations they are until the ship begins to pitch or roll to any extent, and then their proud elevation begins to tell.

Each of these three classes of sea-going society is of course provided with its own servants. The nobleman in his ancestral home or the plutocrat in his new-built palace is not waited upon hand and foot with more complete and efficient service than is the saloon passenger on an ocean liner, especially if she happens to be a North German Lloyd boat. At the lowest computation we had one steward on board the *Sachsen* to every two passengers, and these white-clad servitors seemed to be the most tirelessly obliging creatures of their kind. Every possible want was either anticipated or satisfied the moment it was uttered.

I suppose they slept sometimes, but throughout the voyage I was on deck at odd times every hour of the day and night, and I remember no occasion when a steward was not on hand to do anything that was wanted. From this fact I conclude that the luxurious ease which we enjoyed had to be paid for by someone. I need scarcely add that this efficiency on the part of these helots of the sea most effectually completed the demoralisation that was commenced by the temperature, and continued by the abject laziness of our lives.

The same state of affairs exists in a lesser degree in the second saloon, but the steerage passengers have but one servant who, by the way, is more of a master than a servitor. This is the cook. The services of stewards are not included in steerage rates, and so they have to be either hired or chosen by rota from among the passengers themselves.

I will now ask you to believe that while I have been indulging in this somewhat garrulous chat and trying to make you feel as far as possible at home on the *Sachsen*, she has been ploughing her way southward through the darkness of the night of the 14th of April from the Bay of Naples to the entrance of the Straits of Messina, where the waters of the Tyrrhenian Sea flow between Scylla and Charybdis into the open Mediterranean. Next week we shall see the sun shining on the snowy slopes of Etna, and take our way across the Inland Sea to the Gateway of the East.

III. — EASTWARD HO!

  IT was nearly noon on the 15th, when a dark mass of cloud enshrouded land looming up right ahead told us that the time had come to take our last look at European soil. The cloud-draped hills were those of the Italian mainland and as we approached them there opened up to the right hand, across a narrow strip of water, a landscape which is perhaps one of the most beautiful in the world. This is the eastern coast-line of Sicily.

From the low green promontory of Cape Faro, past Messina and Taormina to Giarre, the clouds that hung about the Italian hills were prevented by the easterly breeze from creasing the Straits, and the Sicilian shore was bathed in brilliant sunshine, which threw the white walls and red roofs of the houses down by the sea, the greenery of the lower slopes of the mountains, and the bare grey rocks and sombre gorges of the upper heights into strong and picturesque relief.

As we rounded the cape and steamed in between the Rock of the Syrens and the Whirlpool of Charybdis, the whole of this magnificent panorama came into sight at once. Messina, crowned by the Citadel and Fort San Salvador, lay along the sea edge and stretched up the gentle slope of the valley in which it lies encircled on three sides by its splendid amphitheatre of hills.

On the left the white walls and red roofs of Reggio were just visible, and above them, too, rose a long high ridge of hills emerging out of the clouds that we had now left behind. We kept close in to the Sicilian side, and, as we steamed along, valley opened into valley, and mountain rose beyond mountain, always higher and higher, only at last to be utterly dwarfed by the lofty grandeur of Etna.

As we neared the big volcano I kept my glass on the land expectant of my first glimpse of the cone. At first I thought I was going to be carried past without seeing it. I could see nothing but a high mass of white cloud rising far away above the summit. of the ether hill., but as we drew nearer and nearer I saw long diverging streaks begin to appear and dark patches come out here and there over the surface.

Then the seeming cloud-mass took definite shape, and I saw that it was no vapoury cumulus but the solid snows and glaciers of Etna itself. The long radiating lines were ravines and crevasses; the dark patches were great forests of pine and dwarf oak, fighting the snows for existence. The light clouds which rested on the summits of the lower hills, albeit they were nearly five thousand feet high, only stretched in a thin fleecy band midway between the forests and vineyards of the lower slopes of Etna and the giant cone which towered nearly eleven thousand feet up into the clear blue of the Italian sky above.

Woodcut of Mount Etna from the period

After we had rounded the Cape dell'Armi, and were steaming away south-eastward for the Egyptian coast, the crest of Etna, with its snows and ice gleaming in the sun like some daylight beacon hung high in mid-air, was the last bit of Europe that I saw until I was abreast of the Scilly Islands sixty days later, on the early morning of the 16th of May.

Friday and Saturday, the 16th and 17th of March, were spent running across the Inland Sea towards Port Said, before a strong fair breeze which enabled as to derive some assistance from the two topsails and three fore-and-afters. Although these sails of themselves would barely get steering way on a steamer the size of the

Sachsen, they were still of considerable indirect service in steadying the ship and enabling the crew to do more work with the same consumption of coal.

As I shall have something to any later on about the alleged and real speed of ocean liners, I will merely say here that the *Sachsen* all through the voyage averaged about three hundred and twenty knots, or three hundred and seventy-three statute miles a day, which, as she made no pretence of being an ocean greyhound, was very respectable work. Allowing twenty-three hours, thirty minutes to the day, this gives a mean speed of nearly sixteen statute miles, or between thirteen and fourteen knots, or nautical miles, an hour.

At noon on the Saturday I posted my first letter in connection with the oceanic postal system which I kept up all round the globe. In other words, I committed to the waters a tightly corked and sealed bottle containing a letter giving the latitude and longitude, and the name of the ship, and offering a reward of a sovereign to the person who should find the letter and post it to me at the offices of *Pearson's Weekly*.

All in all I committed twenty of these missives to the care of the deep. The first was thrown overboard one hundred and ninety miles north-west of Port Said, another one went into the Red Sea, another into the Arabian Gulf, three more into the Indian Ocean, one into the Straits of Mallacca, two into the China Sea, five into various parts of the Pacific, and the remainder into the Atlantic Ocean.

Judging by results of former experiments of the kind, there is a chance of two out of the twenty coming to hand, but the time of delivery is extremely uncertain. A similar letter dropped into the middle of the Atlantic a few years ago turned up in a Norwegian fjord seven months and a half later. It is within the bounds of possibility that some geologist of the far future will dig one of these bottles of mine out of some yet unformed coast-line in the days when round-the-world record breakers will follow the course of the equator through the air, and do the journey in not many more hours than I took days to do mine.

Soon after six o'clock on Sunday morning we sighted the low shores of Egypt, and before long a few houses and beacons, apparently rising direct out of the water, told us that we were within sight of the Gateway of the East. The houses were the larger buildings of Port Said, and the beacons marked the entrance to the Suez Canal.

Port Said 1894

Between the two outer beacons we steamed slowly into the harbour, an area of 570 acres, maintained at a depth of twenty-six feet by the constant use of the enormous dredgers which are among the most salient features of the Suez Canal. The western pier, which runs out for a mile and a half from the land, is intended to protect the harbour from the influx of Nile mud and sand. There are 25,000 blocks of concrete in the foundations of this structure, and every one of them measures over thirteen cubic yards and weighs twenty tons.

Port Said itself stands on the little strip of land which separates the Mediterranean from the Lake of Menzaleh, into which flows the Pelusian arm of the Nile. It is said to be as unique, geographically and ethnographically speaking, as it is in the number of diversified forms of wickedness which may be found within its borders. With regard to the latter characteristic, I had not the time, and possibly not the inclination, to make any close investigations of an experimental nature.

The harbour at Port Said

The *Sachsen* dropped anchor in the cooling basin about seven, and within a few minutes became utterly uninhabitable until about one o'clock. Her anchor was hardly well down before she was surrounded by great lighters loaded down to the waters edge with coal and swarming with dusty, screaming, gesticulating fellaheen, who proceeded to scrape the coal up into buckets, mostly with their hands, swing the baskets on to their heads, and walk with them up the planks that led to the coaling ports, into which they tossed the contents, raising clouds of dust and showers of grit which speedily drove us off the deck.

They were the most ragged, unkempt lot that I had seen since a year before, I had watched a band of deluded and disgusted kanakas working nitrate deposits on a lonely island in the South Pacific, and yet, curiously enough, every one of those dusky helots, toiling for a few half pence a day, carried his coal basket up the planks with a step and mien so graceful that it seemed to speak of some inherent nobility of race or character that not even centuries of oppression had been able to eradicate. At the same time, I am aware that it might have been entirely due to the almost universal custom in the East of carrying burdens on the head.

Ten minutes after the coal heaving began I had successfully foiled the first, but by no means the last attempt at Oriental swindling, and got landed at Port Said for a fare that was at any rate less than half the value of the boat in which I was conveyed. If I had complied with the first demand of the boatman, about as handsome a young rascal as ever I set eyes on, by the way, I should have come pretty near paying the original price of the craft.

It was the first time that I had come in contact with an Oriental thief. I saw many of them during my five hours' stroll about the burning sandy streets of Port Said, and I confess that I was decidedly impressed. He is endowed with a passionate counterfeit of honesty and sincerity which to unaccustomed eyes makes him look very like an honest man. He has perhaps the most eloquent eyes that ever were placed in a human head; his gestures are insinuating and graceful, and perilously convincing, and his language, even when you don't understand it, carries a certain amount of conviction with it.

Yet he is probably the greatest thief on earth outside the ranks of European financiers. He will lie with an ease and fluency which utterly shames the crude efforts of the coarser Western mind, and he will rob you under your very nose with a grateful effusiveness which almost gives you the impression that he has been obliging you, when in reality he has been swindling you in the most unblushing manner.

Acting on the principle of submitting to the lesser evil to avoid the greater, I secured, on the recommendation of Cook's dragoman, a youthful guide rejoicing in the somewhat composite name of Mohammed Ferguson, who was introduced to me as about the least dishonest of his kind. Mohammed spoke remarkably good English, and of course knew Port Said inside and out, so I was willing to become his prey to a certain extent in return for his information and protection against other swindlers. He kept me on the run for over four hours, and in that time I saw all there was to be seen at any rate of the exterior of Port Said.

Well named the Gateway of the East, this town, which, save for a few of the original Arab habitations, has sprung up from the desert since the beginning of the canal works in 1858, is entirely unique among the towns of the world. It is here that East and West first rub shoulder, if they do not join hands. They meet but by no means mix; nothing can obliterate the line that divides the Occidental from the Oriental man.

This fact is strikingly illustrated in Port Said itself, the European and Arab towns are divided only by a narrow street, but to cross that street is to walk from the Western world into the Eastern. On one side of it are the cheap temporary-looking brick and iron buildings, the half-French half-English shops, and so much of the hurry and bustle of Western business-life as can survive under that fierce Egyptian sun; on the other the shabbiness, the squalor, and the indolent repose of the Orient.

The mixture of races to be found in the streets of these two towns is simply bewildering to strange eyes. Half a dozen strides take you past as many different nationalities, types of face and build, and varieties of costume, from the half-naked Nubian in his leopard skin with his woolly head bare to the sun, to the sallow Turk in his flowing robes, and from the Arab Sheik in his picturesque, if not over-clean, turban and burnouse, to Tommy Atkins in his pith helmet and brown holland regimentals.

To say that such a scene was interesting or picturesque would be uttering the merest commonplaces. All the nations of the earth seemed gathered together in those parched and dusty streets, and it is scarcely necessary to say that the confusions of tongues could hardly have been greater if the town had been peopled straight from the Tower of Babel. In one respect only was it like other towns; the fat brown babies that were rolling naked in the sand and dust when they cried—which was certainly not often seemed to do so in the usual early English.

It was Ramadan, or the Moslem Month of Fasting, and all through the town the True Believers were fasting and thirsting from sunrise to sunset. Islam is a noble creed and worthy to be treated with all respect; but I should say that to go without drinks every day for a month in a furnace of a climate like that of Port Said is an article of faith which takes a lot of keeping.

For my own part, I found lager beer an absolute necessity about every half-hour, and Mohammed stood by and watched me drink it with a respectful condescension in which I looked furtively, but in vain, for any sign of the contempt which he doubtless felt for the self-indulgent unbeliever. For eleven days neither bite nor sup had passed his lips while the sun was above the horizon, and yet he was as alert and cheerful as though he had never heard of fasting.

Even the strictest observance of Lent is child's play to Ramadan in the desert. It is, of course, easy enough to go without food for twelve hours or so; but not to be able to drink even a drop of water under that blazing sun, and amidst the sandstorms that the desert wind are constantly throwing up, is a piece of religious discipline that must be discipline indeed.

Not the least striking feature of the streets of Port Said is the distinction between the Egyptian girls and the married women. The former go about not only unveiled but attired in costumes whose airiness varies from a single long calico robe and a girdle, in the case of the older girls, through various stages of scantiness down to the coating of dust and sand worn by the babies above mentioned.

The married women, however, are shrouded from head to feet in awkward voluminous garments, mostly of black, and are so closely veiled that little more than their eyes can be seen. I don't think that it is generally known that an Arab woman's veil is not at all like what we call a veil in England. It does not hang from the forehead downwards. It is a piece of black cloth or silk passed up over the face and round the head about level with the bridge of the nose.

In the middle line of the face it is joined to a sort of cowl that comes down over the forehead by a spiral of thick gold or silver wire, which keeps it in position. This is called the beruah, and the effect of it is to make every married Arab woman look as if she was squinting with the splendid eyes which look at you out of the two holes on either side of it.

Under these circumstances it is of course impossible at any rate for the married portion of the female population of Port Said to look pleasant. The ultimate object of this disguise is, I presume, to obviate irreverent admiration on the part of male creatures other than these ladies' lords and masters, and this object is completely attained. I don't think the man lives who would be capable of the effort of imagination that would be necessary to admire an Arab woman as she appears in the streets.

The men, or at least those who were of the pure Arab blood, were simply magnificent. No matter whether they were clothed in the scantiest of rags or the full and supremely picturesque garb of the Desert Bedouins, they bore themselves like the royal race that they are. There was no mistaking them, for whatever their social or pecuniary circumstances, they were the aristocracy of the place.

Their type is one of the most permanent in the world, and the men that I saw striding along the streets of Port Said as though they were still the kings of earth that they once were, were identical in face and form and raiment with those who marched with Khalid and Derar to the conquest of Damascus more than a thousand years ago, and those later heroes who broke lances with the mail-clad cavalry of Richard Coeur de Leon.

This permanence is, so far as my necessarily rapid observations carried me, the most saliently distinctive point of difference between East and West. The East never alters; it stands disdainfully or indolently aloof and watches the rushing tide of Western life go hurrying past; but except to steal or beg something from him, the Oriental has nothing to do with the Western.

The centuries pass over him and leave him unchanged in himself and his surroundings. The lath and plaster houses, in which mud often took the place of plaster, and the wood and stone mosques, of which I regret to say I found two in Port Said—one for the rich and one for the poor—are built on just the same plan as they would have been three hundred years ago, and the dwellers in them were wearing clothing just as similar to that worn by their ancestors ten generations ago.

The entrance to the Suez Canal

I saw no exceptions to this rule until I had passed over half the circumference of the globe, and was provoked to an irresistible smile by the sight of a Japanese shuffling along the streets of Yokohama in tight boots, check trousers, a tail coat, and a pot hat. But then Japan is so far East as to be almost West.

Soon after twelve the whistle blew for us to go on board again, and half an hour later the anchor was up and we were steaming at the regulation speed of six miles an hour between the barren banks of the Suez Canal.

IV. — THROUGH THE DESERT LANDS

The moment that the screw began to revolve and the *Sachsen* moved slowly through the Ismail Basin towards the entrance of the great Canal, the dividing line between West and East had been passed, and henceforth for thousands of miles everything would be Oriental, which is the same thing as saying that everything to come would be as unlike all that we had left behind as it possibly could be.

The Suez Canal, common-place as it looks at first sight, is in reality a most fitting entrance to the strange and marvellous world of the Orient. It is only a great ditch of semi-stagnant water about twenty-six feet deep in the middle, varying from sixty-five to one hundred and twenty-five yards in width, and one hundred miles long from mouth to mouth. It runs between sandy banks of almost unvarying yellow monotony, and dreary marshy lakes of bitter water, and yet the whole region teems with memories that reach back into the morning twilight of history, and it is haunted by the shades of those whose genius and whose glory have stamped themselves indelibly upon the destiny of mankind.

For ages the piercing of the eighty miles of sand and swamp which joined Asia and Africa, and separated the Levant from the Gulf of Suez, has moved the enterprise of kings and statesmen, and it has been realised more than once before the opening of the existing Canal.

More than three thousand years ago Evanesce the Great, the Augustus of Egypt, who very possibly worked upon a still earlier plan, cut a canal from Lake Timsah to Pelusium, and through it his merchantmen and war galleys passed from sea to sea. More than a hundred thousand lives were lost in carrying the work through; but they were only the cheap lives of slaves, and the number of them that perished seems to have been recorded with a sort of pride in the glory and greatness of the monarch who could pay such a price.

How long the coast of Rameses remained navigable is not known, but in time the all-invading waves of the ocean of sand invaded it and choked it up. Seven centuries passed, and then Pharaoh Necho cut a channel from the Nile at Bubastis to the Arabian Gulf near Patumos. But before the new canal was ready for navigation, though not before a hundred and twenty thousand more human beings had perished of thirst and overwork and disease in making it, Pharaoh abandoned his scheme at the bidding of certain wise men who told him, in a prophecy destined to be fulfilled long after his mummy had been laid in its granite chamber, that the Canal, if completed, would open Egypt to the barbarians and profit no one but the foreigner.

Nearly twenty-five centuries have passed since then, the Canal has been completed for the fifth time, nearly £20,000,000 sterling of Egyptian money have been sunk in it, and the foreigner possesses it, and with it the practical mastery of Egypt.

Once more the desert asserted its supremacy and undid the work that had cost so much. Then came Darius, the Mede, who conquered Egypt, and again a canal was cut, almost on the lines of the present one, from sea to sea, and it was through the remains of this water-way that in after years Cleopatra tried to take her ships to Suez after the disaster of Actium. After the Persian came the Roman in the person of the great Trajan, and once more opened the water route to the East, and again the years brought the sands from the desert and choked it.

Five hundred years later the Saracen was ruling in Egypt, and he too renewed the work and carried his grain by water from Fostat to Suez. Long after this canal had become unserviceable the Venetians dwelt lovingly on the idea of re-opening the water-way with a view to recovering their lost trade round the Cape of Good Hope by means of a short cut to the East, but the project never passed into realisation. If it had done, the destinies of Europe, and perhaps of the world, might have been changed.

Louis XIV, Sultan Mustafa, the contemporary and admirer of Frederick the Great, and Napoleon himself all three in turn looked longingly at that narrow strip of sand and marsh, and dreamt of doing again what the Egyptian, the Persian, the Roman, and the Saracen had done before them. But nothing came of their dreams save surveys and estimates, and then came the financial magician who worked off on Said Pusha, the Viceroy of Egypt, after whom Port Said is named, the most bare-faced, and at the same time perhaps the most magnificent, of the swindles of the world, and accomplished the work which made his now tarnished name immortal.

These are some of the memories which people the Suez Canal and the gray-brown wilderness through which it runs. From first to last that long narrow ditch has been the grave of not less than a million men, while the amount of treasure that has been sunk in it is simply incalculable. Some idea of the colossal difficulties under which the work, even on the present Canal with all the resources of modern civilisation at command, was carried on may be gathered from the fact that for the first four years 1,600 camels were employed every day in carrying water in casks to the workmen at a cost of over £300 a day.

The Suez Canal shortly after opening in the 1860s

Until the steam dredgers and excavating machinery were imported in 1863, the work was carried on by the forced labour of virtual slaves, ill-fed, under-paid, and over-worked, and driven to their toil by the hippopotamus-hide whips of their task-masters. Of course they died in thousands, just as the slaves of Rameses, and Pharaoh, and Darius had died at the same work before them, so slowly does humanity advance in the direction of mercy when it is a question of dividends and cheap labour.

As soon as the *Sachsen* left the Basin she entered the first section of the Canal, which runs in a perfectly straight line for about thirty miles between the brackish waters of Lake Menzaleh on the right hand, and the reclaimed land on the left, a low, level, grey-bound wilderness, behind which you can see the low sand-bluffs which mark the outline of what was once the coast of Arabia.

A steamer on the Suez Canal

Long ago, in the days of the canals of Rameses and Pharaoh Necho, the scene was very different to the dismal lifeless prospect that we could see on all sides from the high promenade deck of the *Sachsen*. The wilderness on the left was the land of gardens and vineyards, and on the right stretched one of the most fertile districts in Egypt, and therefore in the ancient world.

Below the light green shallow waters of the lake lay a sandy sedgy bottom, which had once been the dry desert, and beneath that again were lying the remains of the buried villages and towns whose inhabitants, ages ago, dwelt in a fair and fertile land where now there is only a wilderness of sand and weeds and water, possessed by flocks of pelicans and silver herons, and a few herds of half-starved cattle.

About five hours' steaming brought us to Kantara, and here the banks rise to a considerable height, for at this point the Canal pierces a ridge, called in Arabic Kantarat-el-Khazneh, or Bridge of the Treasure, which formed a natural bridge between Africa and Asia, over which passed the caravan route between Cairo and Mecca. Another half hour took us through the pass and into the Balah lakes, and here the dreariness of the desert landscape was suddenly transformed and glorified by the splendours of an Egyptian sunset.

In no other regions of the earth is the difference between day and night so absolute and entire, or the transition from the one to the other so splendid to the sight and so delightful to the senses as in the desert. This was the first sunset that I had ever seen on the Egyptian wilderness.

I have read, I suppose, hundreds of descriptions more or less eloquent or laboured as the case might be, but one and all fell short of the reality—so short, indeed, that I recognise the utter hopelessness of conveying any adequate conception of what I saw and felt to anyone who has not passed through the same experience.

All the afternoon the bank of the Canal and the desert beyond them had lain grey and bare and parched beneath the blazing sun. The air, surcharged with heat, lay heavy and motionless above the parched land and the bitter, stagnant waters of the lakes. Everything near stood out hard and sharp in outline, with light and shadow sharply contrasted without any graduations.

Everything at a distance was distorted by the burning medium through which you saw it; heights looked entirely different from what they really were, and mirages, constantly floating about the horizon and ever changing their form, made the whole scene look so unreal that it seemed rather like a landscape seen in a nightmare than a portion of the world of reality.

But as soon as the sinking sun approached the rim of the wide desert plain the mirages melted away, objects stood out in their true proportions and at their true distances, a tinge of ruddy golden haze floated up into the hot grey-blue sky, and a delightful softness and coolness began to supersede the harshness and heat of the daytime.

Vapours that were hardly clouds gathered along the western horizon and began to glow and blaze with a hundred shades of gold-and crimson. The grey of the sand and the harsh brown of the rocks were covered and softened by a swift flood of tinted light, the sun's disc rolled down behind the edge of the vast sandy plain that stretched out to the westward, the last level beams faded out, and then, like a veritable veil of enchantment, the cool softness of the twilight fell down over land and lake, the stars twinkled through the rosy flush of the afterglow, and then, as this faded, shone out brighter and brighter, and the moon which, happily for us, was almost at the full, rose over the eastern sand-bluffs, and changed the water to molten silver, and the gray sand to the whiteness of driven snow.

The moment the sun set there flashed out from the bows of every ship in the Canal the white dazzling rays of an electric search-light. Every ship is compelled to carry one of these between sunset and sunrise, and, as may well be imagined, the effect produced by them is by no means the least beautiful feature of what was now a strange and really beautiful scene.

For miles ahead and astern we could see the brilliant points of white light constantly appearing and vanishing as the ships carrying them passed between banks of different heights, while our own, sending out its broad fan of rays ahead, made it appear exactly as though we were steaming between an endless succession of morning snow drifts.

Night scene on the Suez Canal

About an hour after nightfall we stopped for a few minutes off Ismailiya to land a few tourists for Cairo, and then entered Lake Timsah, or the Lake of Crocodiles.

A short time after we entered the Canal on the other side we steamed past the lower slopes of a low grey hill which stood out clearly in the moonlight on the right hand. This was the Gebel Maryan, or the Mount of Miriam, where, according to the Arabian legend, Miriam, after she had been smitten with leprosy, "was shut out from the camp seven days," when the people of Israel were journeying from Hazeroth through the wilderness of Paran.

From Tusun the Canal runs in a straight line through the cutting that takes it through the rocky barrier of the Serapeum, and here the search-lights revealed a village pleasantly situated among pretty shady gardens, quite an oasis in the desert, which owes its existence to irrigation from the fresh water canal. A little way to the east lie the ruins of a Serapeum, or Temple of Serapeus, and near to these, nearly buried in the sand, lie some blocks of limestone which once formed the pedestal of a monument which Darius the Mede erected on the bank of the vanished canal which once bore his name.

At the end of the straight stretch the channel of the Canal runs out into the great basin of the Bitter Lakes, which are generally believed to be identical with those Waters of Marah of which "the children of Israel could not drink, for they were bitter," when they had come out from the wilderness of Shur and found no water.

The low, flat banks of the Waters of Marah were almost indistinguishable in the half light from the deck of the ship, but the moonlight shone clearly on the rugged slopes and rocky heights of the Geneffeh range to the southwest. I remained on deck, enjoying the strange fascinations of the scene, until we had crossed the Bitter Lakes and entered the last stretch of the Canal, which runs in an almost straight line from here to the head of the Gulf of Suez. Then Nature asserted herself and I had to go to bed.

About three hours later I was awakened by the stopping of the screw, and went on deck to find the *Sachsen* lying in the basin off Suez. I was glad to see that the sun had not risen, and so, with the beauty of the sunset still fresh in my mind, I prepared to enjoy the, if possible, still stranger beauties of the sunrise.

To the west, behind the shabby, squalid town of Suez, towered the bare, rocky pinnacles of the Ataka Mountains standing out sharp and clear against the pale blue sky, and on the east arose the somewhat lower, but almost equally picturesque, summits of the Asiatic coast range. As the sun rose, its first rays touched the pinnacles of Ataka a few minutes before they lit up those of the lower range, and for the moment it was possible to indulge in the strange illusion that two suns were rising at once, one in the east and the other in the west.

A sunrise in the clear dry air of the desert is, as may well be imagined, somewhat different from one in the moister atmosphere of the temperate zone. The light flashes out clear and instantaneous, the transition from dark to light is almost imperceptible, so gradual is it up to the moment that the sun appears above the horizon. Then in an instant the world is flooded with light; objects seem to spring suddenly out of the semi-obscurity, and stand in bold relief of light and shade; and then the delightful coolness of the night departs, and the heat of the long burning day begins.

The *Sachsen* only remained off Suez long enough to report and send her search-light ashore for the use of the next Lloyd liner that came up from the south. Then she steamed round the curve to the channel that leads from Suez to Port Ibrahim, which is the true southern end of the Canal, and thence out into the Gulf of Suez. And now, in the cool of the early morning, we were carried through a region which in historic interest is, after its kind, unequalled in the world. Here the two great continents of the ancient world frown at each other across the narrow seas from stern forbidding heights of bald black rock which rise like barren islands from the ocean of sand whose wind-swept waves run in long grey tongues far up into their lower valleys.

As an eloquent German has said: Asia and Africa here seem to confront each other across the Red Sea "like wrestlers who have divested themselves of their garments and are on the point of entering the lists to fight a fierce battle for the sovereignty of the world." Few similes are better borne out than this is by those huge mountain masses of naked rock which stand up there out of the sand, bare and gaunt, with their sternness unrelieved by either a scrap of herbage or the trace of a human habitation.

We had only been sixteen hours coming through the Canal, and had escaped the unpleasant and too-frequent experience of having to "tie-up," or, in other words, moor in one of the sidings or passing places in order to allow another vessel to go by, in obedience to the fiat of the presiding genius of the Canal, who sits in his room at Port Said with a model of the Canal in front of him, and passes every ship through in miniature duplicate, stopping the real vessels and passing them on again by telegraphic orders, transmitted from an instrument at his side.

As the passage of the Canal varies anywhere between sixteen and sixty-five hours, according to the state of the traffic, the *Sachsen* was in luck, and we got out into the Red Sea a good fifteen hours ahead of schedule time.

I thought it had been hot at Port Said and in the Canal, but the temperature there was mild and balmy in comparison to that of the Red Sea. A wind, heated to suffocation point by passing over the burning rocks and sand of the Egyptian desert, blew almost in our teeth the whole way down to the Straits. Every mile that we made to the southward took us farther and farther into the furnace, and even at night there was little or no relief.

Wind scoops were fitted into the open ports of the state-rooms, but their only effects were to pour floods of super-heated air into the room until one could only lie in the berth and gasp and perspire, and vainly try to go to sleep and dream of icebergs and snow storms.

Awnings were of course rigged everywhere over the ship until she looked like a huge floating tent. Every garment that decency could do without was discarded, and I noticed the whole ship's company looked a good deal thinner the first morning in the Red Sea than they had done in the Canal.

The consumption of iced liquid sustenance increased with almost demoralising rapidity, but even now the punctilious gentleman to whom I alluded in my second article, persisted in suffering at dinner in evening dress. One or two appeared in white clothes of the orthodox evening cut; this is the dining uniform of most Europeans in the East. I can't say that I admire it, it makes a man look too much like a whitewashed waiter.

Thus, with moist skins and throats which persistently remain dry, however diligently they were irrigated, we steamed on down the Red Sea, ever hotter and thirstier, in the midst of a universal lassitude of spirit and dissolution of the flesh, for four scorching days and suffocating nights, until the morning of Friday, the 22nd, brought us within sight of a long range of serrated mountains stretching away to the eastward and southward, at the end of which rose the bald and rugged peninsula of Aden, the coal-hole of the East and the Tophet of Tommy Atkins.

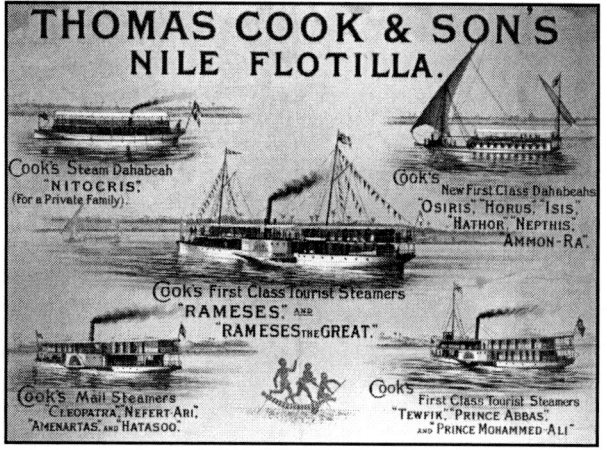

V. — FROM ADEN TO EDEN

The hot head wind which had struck us in the Red Sea freshened up somewhat, both as to strength and temperature, after we had passed through the Gate of Tears, as the Arabs, with considerable reason, describe the narrow channel that leads into the Arabian Gulf.

It will be a long time before I forget that wind. The Red Sea is a villainous place, and the wind was thoroughly characteristic of it. In a place of shelter you broke out into a violent perspiration, and the moment you exposed yourself to the wind it dried your skin up until it felt rough and crackly like old parchment.

As we turned to the eastward after clearing the Straits, it cooled down slightly, as I say, but, if anything, increased in force. The result was that we lost almost four hours of the advantage we had gained by the time that the *Sachsen* steamed up under the lee of the peninsula, and dropped her anchor near to a group of other ships, flying the flags of half a dozen nationalities, which were lying in the bay.

Aden in the 1890s

The scene presented by the anchorage of Aden that morning would have been an instructive one for a politician of the Little England school, provided that he could have looked at it with intelligent eyes. Scattered about the spacious anchorage there were nearly a hundred men-of-war, merchant steamers, and smaller craft. The Frenchman lay by the German, the Russian between the Austrian and the Italian, but of coarse the majority of them were British—eighty-six out of every hundred vessels that go through the Suez Canal, by the way, fly the British flag—and there in the midst of them lay a big, white-hulled British battle-ship, a fitting symbol of the pax Britannica which ever has been and ever must be based on the ability to hit hard and straight.

A British battleship typical of the era

The white ensign hanging from her stern was matched by the Union Jack floating from the tall flag-staff on shore, and under the shadow of this there dwelt in peace the representatives of all the great Powers of earth on a barren rock whose purpose in the scheme of creation seems to have been to prove the endurance of the longsuffering Briton, and to show how bad a place he will take hold of and live in, ignoring all other conditions save the fiat of imperial necessity.

Although Aden, called Adana or Athana by the Greeks and Romans, was one of the most important trading places in the

Eastern world of the ancients, and was for a long time the capital of Yemen, and the great trade emporium for the products of Eastern Africa and Southern Asia, it had been degenerating into insignificance for more than three centuries when the British took possession of it in 1839.

In less than sixty years the little settlement of eleven square miles of rainless and barren rock and sand, with less than 600 inhabitants, has become one of our most important eastern possessions, and, in addition to being the great coaling-station of the middle Orient, does a seaborne trade of between five and six millions a year, and maintains a population of about 40,000 people. It was practically the first that I had seen of the long line of British posts that stretches unbroken round the world, a sort of imperial sentry box placed by the highway to the Greater Britain of the Tropics.

As the *Sachsen* was apparently intended to make as quick a passage as possible to Hong Kong, the captain could only afford us between three and four hours to disport ourselves on shore, hence we were unable either to visit the town of Aden proper, which lies on the other side of the peninsula from the anchorage, or the celebrated, but, as I was told, greatly overrated, water tanks up in the hills.

A pull of about a mile and a half took us to the landing-stage, and here we made the acquaintance of two important factors in Eastern economics—the Oriental Beggar and the Depreciated Rupee. The former followed us persistently in a half-naked crowd of importunate humanity wherever we went, and the latter was introduced to us by financiers so scantily attired that their clothing was barely sufficient to wrap their capital up in.

It was somewhat curious to see these men, whose whole attire would have been insufficient to raise the smallest loan in an East-end pawnshop, produce, apparently from nowhere, handfuls of rupees looking like bright two-shilling pieces. They offered to sell them to us at fifteen for a sovereign. If we had not been already aware that the bank exchange was about sixteen and a half they might have done a decent trade. On our refusal to purchase they first lied with true Oriental eloquence and fluency on the subject of the bank rate, and then offered to earn a more honest copper by showing us the way to the bank.

The portion of the peninsula on which we landed may be called the official and business portion, in spite of the fact that the Government House is in the town. A very good level road runs along the shore opposite to the anchorage, and along this are scattered, with a magnificent disregard for space and convenience, the post-office, police station, coal wharves, and naval stores.

At the northern end of this road is quite a respectable crescent, composed of hotels, consulates, telegraph offices, and shops which you have to go into before you find they are shops. The sun of Aden makes it impossible to display goods in windows; they would probably melt or take fire.

When you get inside it is not long before you begin to feel something like the fly after it had accepted the invitation of the spider. All Oriental shopkeepers are thieves, more or less, those of Aden seemed mostly more. I really wanted several things, but after I had wasted what breath and temper I had to spare in argument about the prices I went without them rather than take away with them, as I must have done, the uncomfortable conviction that I had been swindled by the unbeliever.

Most of the trade of Aden is in the hands of cross-bred Arabian Jews, who look upon all itinerant Christians as fatted calves brought out by the mail steamers for their special benefit. So far as my examination of their wares took me I should say that what they offer as Eastern goods are mostly imported from Birmingham or made in Germany.

Their pure Oriental silks are liberally adulterated with Manchester cotton in the looms of Nottingham and Leicester; their Chinese and Japanese goods are chiefly frauds, and can be bought much cheaper in London, and their ostrich feathers—or, at any rate, such of them as were shown to me at exorbitant prices—would have excited only the derision of the best girl of a Whitechapel coster.

These remarks, which are no more ill-natured than I feel justified in making them, may be taken as generally true of the native traders in all the ports of call along the route to the Far East. The casual buyer will not go far wrong in taking them for liars and thieves to a man. As a rule, the traveller who buys alleged curios from them to bring home is simply re-importing European goods to Europe at a heavy loss.

The thieves of Aden we were able to get rid of by the simple process of taking ourselves off their premises, but with the beggars it was a very different business. The Oriental mendicant is, I should think, the most incorrigible of his kind. He won't take no for an answer; in fact, he seems to be rather encouraged by it than otherwise. Our crowd at Aden followed us about steadily for three solid, scorching hours without getting a copper, and yet they yelled "Backsheesh" at us from the pier as we pushed off to return to the ship with every bit as much vigour as they put into the yells with which they greeted us.

There is, however, one really entertaining way of bestowing backsheesh at Aden, and this is to pitch the coins into the water from the ship's side for the Somali boys to dive after them. These black-eyed, bright-skinned little water-imps come off in dug-outs, which they manage, with wonderful skill with a single rude paddle. The craft is a tiny affair just about enough to float them, and it usually has about three inches of water on board, in the midst of which they sit. When they get too much water on board, the boys splash furiously with their feet, and literally kick it into the sea again.

Diving boys on the decks in Aden

They come alongside yelling out their invariable chorus: "Hi! Hi! Have a dive, have a dive!" This yell, by the way, is a sort of shibboleth with which you are greeted at almost any port you may call at from Aden round to Singapore. This is to be interpreted as an invitation to spin a coin into the air, so that it may fall into the water.

You spin the coin, then you see several pairs of brilliant black eyes gleaming up at it, and as many sets of shining white teeth grinning in anticipation of the plunder. Then, as the coin touches the water, there is a huge splash; in an instant the canoes are empty, and mostly upside down; the water is churned up into foam; in the midst of this you see a wild waving mass of brown legs and white footsoles; these disappear, and the water calms down.

You wait for results, and presently black heads begin to bob up out of the depths, the black eyes and white teeth gleam again, and in one brown paw you see the coin triumphantly held aloft. Then it is stowed away in its captors mouth, and, after a moment's interval of aquatic gymnastics, the dug-outs have been turned right side up, and their owners are sitting in them yelling for more backsheesh.

These Somali boys are certainly the most wonderful divers I have ever seen—at any rate so far as regards quickness and precision. It seems to be a matter of absolute unconcern to them how long they remain under water. I don't suppose they can breathe there; but if they can't, they must be able to stand an internal pressure of wind that would blow an ordinary European swimmer to pieces before he got back to the surface. Their business is to get the coin, and they got it every time. Of all the scores of coins that were thrown from the deck of the *Sachsen* not one touched the bottom.

One of the water imps, a lad of about fourteen, climbed up on to the top of one of the boats, slung in the davits above the promenade deck, just as the ship was moving off. A sixpence was thrown into the midst of a swarm of canoes, and it had scarcely touched the water before he shot through about forty feet of air and plunged after it. Just as he started he yelled out a collection of syllables which some time ago were the plague of London, and they came out with a purity of pronunciation that was absolutely disgusting. I daresay he thought it was a kind of British war-whoop.

Nemesis, however, followed hard on his heels, for just as he was rising with the captured coin the *Sachsen* spurted a dense flood of mingled hot water and ashes from her cinder port, and be bobbed up right in the middle of it. The speechless astonishment and disgust on his face as he splattered the ashes from his mouth and rubbed them out of his eyes was among the most vivid memories that I took away with me from the Aden anchorage.

It was half-past one by the time the anchor was up, and we steamed away with a feeling of thankfulness from the spot, which, I think, I have been quite justified in describing as the Tophet of Tommy Atkins. I was told by a soldier, who gave it Tophet's other name, that every regiment coming back from India has to spend a year at Aden, presumably for their sins and the glory of the British Empire, but, bad as Aden is, it is not quite the worst Eastern station that Tommy has to occupy.

Out of every regiment that stops there a company has to go on to Perim, a desolate, barren, and burning island in the Red Sea, swept by almost constant hot winds from the desert, and generally supposed, to be the nearest approach to purgatory that one can get into without dying. It is to be hoped that the most sinful company gets sent there, and that the Recording Angel takes their sojourn duly into account.

The wind, though still ahead, cooled down delightfully as we got out into the Gulf of Aden. By noon on the 23rd we were off the north of the Island of Socotra, with less than 2,000 miles of ocean between us and Colombo.

Every day now the sea grew bluer and brighter, and the sky lost more and more of the white-hot look that it had above the desert; but still there seemed to me something lacking which made me compare both sea and sky unfavourably with the well-remembered glories of the southern sea—a comparison which was somewhat unfair to the Indian Ocean, considering the fact that I had seen the splendours of the Sea of a Million Isles with eyes which were nearly fifteen years younger.

The nights in the Indian Ocean would have been delightful almost beyond description, if it hadn't been for the social necessity of wearing clothes, but the days grew hotter and hotter as our southern course sent the sun higher and higher in the heavens. Under the

Southern Cross, that most over-described and disappointing of constellations, it was possible to "feel good," as our American, passenger put it, when the last possible article of clothing had been discarded, but in the daytime there was neither rest nor peace, save just at the moment when something in the shape of iced fluid was being swallowed.

Seven days' steaming carried us across the Indian Ocean and at two o'clock on the morning of the 30th the *Sachsen* slowed down, and I went on deck to find her gliding into the smooth harbour of Colombo, through a crowd of ghostly ships and small craft, some lying at anchor and some gliding about as silently as phantoms in the dim light of a somewhat hazy morning, illumined by the waning moon and one great solitary planet, which hung high above the looming mass of land and cloud to the eastward—Venus waiting for the rising of her lord the Sun.

Unfortunately the clouds hung right over the centre of the island, and so I lost the nocturnal spectacle of Ceylon, and one of the most beautiful sights in the East, Adam's Peak seen from the sea by moonlight. Still the delightful change from the desert lands through which we had passed a few days before to the tropical paradise that we had now reached, was enough to compensate me for the loss, especially when added to the satisfactory knowledge that, thanks to good luck and the *Sachsen*'s engines, I had reached Colombo in a little over seventeen days from London, and was nearly forty hours ahead of my schedule.

VI. — A GLIMPSE AT THE PEARL OF THE SEA

As I said in my last article, we reached Colombo nearly forty hours ahead of schedule time, and this being so we naturally expected that we should have at least a day at our disposal on shore. The authorised stopping time for the German Lloyd steamers at Colombo is twenty-four hours. Considering how far we were ahead, the passengers, both in the saloon and the second cabin, were unanimous in their desire to have, at any rate, half the regulation time in the island.

Even I, who was certainly in a greater hurry than anyone else on board, could not refrain from agreeing with those to whom time was little or no object. Given twelve hours at Colombo, and I should still start with more than a day in hand, and a good prospect of picking up another between Ceylon and Japan. This being so, I felt justified in putting my view of the case before the captain and joining my request to that of my fellow passengers.

Colombo Ceylon circa 1890

I am sorry to say, however, that the Autocrat of the Bridge did not see his way to meet our views, and I must add that very considerable displeasure was excited by his refusal to keep the ship more than six hours in port. I cannot help thinking that this was anything but good policy from the point of view of the company. It was one of two features which marred an otherwise most luxurious and enjoyable trip, and, as it turned out, nothing at all was gained by a refusal which annoyed and disappointed nearly every passenger in the ship.

Everyone who has a day or so ashore in Ceylon spends it in a journey to Kandy, the ancient capital in the centre of the island, and this is what we wanted to do. The train leaves Colombo at half-past seven, reaches Kandy at 11.13, leaves again at 2.5, and gets back to Colombo at 6.0. Thus the *Sachsen* could have sailed at seven in the evening of March 30th, well ahead of her time, as she was not scheduled to arrive there before the 31st.

Picture of Kandy in the 1890s

If this arrangement could have been carried out I should have been able to describe here the seventy-four mile run to Kandy from the sea-level to nearly two thousand feet above it, through a country whose diversified surface and wealth and variety of colouring and vegetation has hardly an equal in the world.

But the captain's fiat had gone forth, and there was no appeal, so I had to take all these beauties for granted, even as I have to ask, you who are accompanying me round the world to do, and content myself with a stroll about Colombo and a drive to Mount Lavinia and back.

It was still quite dark, or at least as dark as it had been all night, when a couple of compatriots and myself got a boat and were pulled from the anchorage to the landing-stage underneath the Custom House. Of course, we didn't get out of the boat without the usual row consequent on the inevitable attempt to swindle us.

As I have before hinted, the Oriental boatman is possessed by a rooted conviction that whoever uses his craft, even for the shortest time, ought to buy it at one end of the journey and give it back to him at the other, consequently every time you engage his services you have either to be robbed or else to struggle with this conviction and overcome it. Fortunately our boatmen made so much noise in putting their view of the question that they attracted the attention of some official on the landing-stage, who came with a lantern and a thick stick and ended the argument in our favour with promptness and despatch.

Going ashore at Colombo I can only describe as walking into a vast open-air hothouse. I know the expression is paradoxical, but the description is fairly correct. If you can imagine the Tropical House at Kew with its roof and walls taken away, its size indefinitely expanded, its contents multiplied, and its temperature kept about the same, then you will have a fairly distinct idea of my first impression of Colombo. Of course, there will be the white-walled and deep-verandahed hotels, shops, and public buildings to be added, and with them, too, the few dusky-skinned and mostly scantily-clad natives, who were loitering about like so many Oriental Micawbers, apparently waiting for something to turn up.

There was something almost unreal in the strange beauty and charm of the scene. Everything looked so spic and span and clean, from the white walls of the houses to the reddish-brown surface of the broad, beautifully-kept road. The strange forms and brilliant colouring of the trees and shrubs, the half-light, half-dark of the sky, out of which a few stars were twinkling palely, the brightening of the fore-glow in the East, and on earth the dimness of the heavy, languorous air, laden with a thousand scents, produced the impressions rather, of fairyland than of the workaday world of reality.

It was then a little before five o'clock, and Colombo was still asleep, save for the few loiterers before named and the clerks on duty at the telegraph office. But by the time I had despatched my cablegram home, and we had taken a short and very leisurely walk past the lotus pond and the racket court, and heard the matutinal chorus of the frogs among the broad floating leaves, Colombo or at least the helot portion of its population, began to wake up.

A few days ago, I was abroad early in a manufacturing town in the North of England watching the crowds of mill operatives and foundry hands going clattering in their iron-bound clogs over the wet pavement towards the mills and iron works which formed not the least ugly features in one of the ugliest towns to be found, even in Lancashire.

By force of contrast, my mind instantly went back to the. street-scene that I had witnessed in Colombo a few weeks-before. The dull, dirty, red brick houses, the hard, grimy pavement, and the tall smoke-crowned chimneys gave place to white walls gleaming through thick clustering foliage, to smooth grass-lined and tree-shaded roads, and to towering palms waving their crests above the housetops in the scented morning wind. The rough-clad iron-shod operatives gave place to dusky turbaned coolies clad in cotton garments of all shades of colour and many degrees of scantiness, and they moved their bare feet over the smooth roads swiftly and silently, like an ever-increasing crowd of phantoms.

Yet in all the wide dissimilarity which separated the Indian ryots from the Lancashire operatives, there was just one touch of Nature that seemed to make them kin. Both had the same set seriousness of face, the same distinct and yet indefinable stamp which hard physical toil sets upon its sons, and both went to their work, either in silence or conversing in short jerky monosyllables. In a word, both, according to their lot and locality, were the helots of society, those who do the hard manual labour of the world and whose fate it is to keep their shoulders to the wheels of the coach on which a more fortunate section of their fellow creatures ride so comfortably.

These Colombo coolies are chiefly importations from India; they are members of a race and a caste that has furnished slaves for ages, and slaves they are still, to all intents and purposes. In fact, slavery in some form or another seems to be essential to getting any work done in the East. The ruling race or class furnishes the brains, the directing force; the motive power can only be furnished by the muscles of the helots who can toil for the merest trifle and the most beggarly subsistence under atmospheric conditions which make physical toil almost impossible to Europeans.

And yet, strange to say, amidst that motley crowd of dark-skinned, brilliant-eyed, black-whiskered coolies striding along with the free graceful step that no toil seems to cripple, I saw, shuffling in thin broken shoes and tattered European clothing, an unmistakable British tramp, going to work with the rest of them. Only his own evil genius could explain his presence there, but there he was, tenfold forlorner and more degraded than his brethren of the road in Europe and America, for the white man who has sunk to the level of the Eastern coolie has about touched the bedrock of human degradation.

The Grand Oriental Hotel in Colombo

At six o'clock we learnt the welcome tidings that the hotels were open, and that iced drinks were once more obtainable. With one accord we turned our unanimous footstep, towards the Oriental Hotel at the seaward end of York Street, and there I made my first, but by no means my last, acquaintance with a kind of glorified lemon squash, which is made with limes instead of lemons, and includes a most delightful variety of acid and sub-acid flavours.

Of the many fluids that I sampled, from the miserable decoction which is called tea in China and Japan, to the subtly-fascinating varieties of the American cocktail, I think the lime-drink of Colombo is, when drunk under proper atmospheric conditions, the most delightful.

A street scene in Ceylon

When we had swallowed as many of these as a somewhat extended discretion permitted, we hired a hackerry, a sort of double dog-cart on four wheels, with a white awning and curtains of oil-cloth that can be lowered when it rains, to drive out to Mount Lavinia, for breakfast. I was interested, if not much edified, by the way in which a policeman, with an unmistakable brogue, gave directions to our driver. The man had certainly done no wrong during the two or three minutes that he had been in our service, and yet that policeman talked to him as though he had been a convict with a new ticket-of-leave.

Whether or not this was necessary to frighten him out of a possible swindle that may have taken shape in his mind, I don't profess to say, but I must confess that this was the only occasion during my run through the East that no attempt was made to defraud me. Possibly it may be necessary; certainly it seems to be the only custom of the European in the East to address the Oriental as a slave or an animal.

In this particular case our hackman took his bullying with a gentle equanimity, which showed that he was pretty well accustomed to it, and made me feel rather ashamed of the official who, with possibly the best intentions, had administered it on our behalf.

From Colombo to Mount Lavinia the distance is about seven English miles, and, after clearing the town, you drive first along what is called the Galle Face, which is to Colombo what Rotten Row is to London and Orchard Road and the Esplanade are to Singapore. It is a broad, beautifully-maintained road, running along the seaward edge of the military reservation, which, being kept for ever open to the breezes from the sea, is rightly supposed to contribute not a little to the general healthiness of Colombo.

At the end of this we turned sharply to the left, and then to the right into the Colpetty Road, which runs in an almost straight line to Mount Lavinia. This road is, I should think, one of the prettiest and most interesting in the East. The part of it towards Colombo is lined with handsome bungalows, some of them amounting almost to mansions, standing in ample gardens, any one of which would stock a score of English hot-houses.

The road to Mount Lavinia, Ceylon

After these come a long succession of native houses and shops, with every now and then the brilliantly painted roofs or gilded cupolas of Buddhist temples peeping out of the luxuriant vegetation that rose in a wall of greenery on both sides of the road. I am by no means botanist enough to attempt to describe with anything like scientific accuracy the almost infinite variety of trees which rose out of the plantations on either hand, and interlaced their upper branches many feet above our heads.

Tree-ferns and tamarinds, jaks and mangoes were interspersed with hibiscus, and tall grasses. The splendid dark green scalloped leaves of the bread-fruit contrasted with the green and cream-coloured foliage of the cabbage-tree, and above these rose the tall straight stems of the cocoa-palms, crowned with their spreading crests of leaves and their bunches of nuts, while over all the orchids and Burmese creepers ran in long, flowery festoons that hung from tree to tree, and made triumphal arches of greenery and flowers mile after mile along the road.

Of course we should not have been in the East if our hackerry had not been followed by troops of lithe, agile boys and girls, who, in spite of the respectable pace of the lean, sinewy animal between the shafts, kept pace with us for hundreds of yards, and still retained breath enough for constant repetitions of the Singalese form of backsheesh.

"Master, master, give me money!" was their echo of the universal cry of nineteenth-century humanity, and a pretty persuasive echo it was when accompanied by appealing glances from the most magnificently dark eyes I have ever seen, and the smile of red shapely lips, which disclosed every time two perfect rows of the whitest teeth.

The difference between the rising and the falling generations I found to be more striking than agreeable. Nearly all the boys were handsome, well-shaped, lithe-limbed fellows, and there were very few of the girls that had not some claims to prettiness, while some of them were perfect pictures of dusky grace and beauty, and I must really confess that their charms came somewhat expensive in the way of small coin.

With a weakness natural to my sex I bestowed it on the prettiest of the girls and they, with a penetration natural to theirs, very soon detected my weakness, and of course took advantage of it to the last coin I would part with. I don't think I am far wrong in saying that some of those black-eyed supple-limbed little damsels earned more that morning than their parents would make by a hard day's work.

One of them, I think she was the prettiest of them all, a not over-clad maiden of some seven summers, at length influenced my susceptibilities to the extent of half a rupee. When she got it she stopped, stared at it for a moment, and then held it aloft with a cry of delight that it was worth the money to hear. The next moment she was surrounded by a crowd of all ages and the next the whole of that crowd was tearing at full speed after the hackerry. That, combined perhaps with the emptiness of my pocket, spoilt the backsheesh business for the day so far as I was concerned.

It seemed almost incredible that the really beautiful children that followed our chariot would one day, and that not a distant one, grow into the men and women who scowled at us at the footways and from the windows and doors of the houses and bazaars on either side of the road. Saving only the unquenched splendour of their eyes they were the most uninviting set of Orientals that I had so far seen.

They ranged from the tolerably ugly to the absolutely repulsive, and among them were the thinnest specimens of humanity I had ever set eyes on. They were literally nothing but animated skeletons covered with tightly drawn brown skin. Every vein and bone stood out perfectly distinct beneath it, and every time they moved their arms and legs I found myself listening for the creak of their joints.

A good many of them, too, indulge in the disfiguring practice of areca-nut chewing. This turns teeth and gums and lips so red that their mouths look as if they were constantly bleeding. The contrast of this with the brown skin and black hair and eyes may easily be imagined in all its repulsiveness. As for their costume it ranged through every degree of plentitude and scantiness from the flowing robes and high-crowned hats of the Parsee merchant lolling in his carriage to the carved metal fig-leaves of the smaller children toddling through the dust of the road, or paddling in the mud of the ditches.

Mount Lavinia hotel in Ceylon

We found Mount Lavinia a handsome hotel perched on a rocky promontory that formed one horn of a wide shallow bay that streched in a graceful curve northward to the Galle Face, a long narrow stretch of clean yellow sand lying between a blue calm sea and a thick belt of cocoa-palms, some of whose tall trunks lean in so far seaward that their gently-waving leaves were reflected in the water beneath them. Here we had a bathe and breakfast, and of the latter, ample and dainty as it was, by far the most salient feature was the curried prawns.

The curried prawns of Mount Lavinia are a gastronomic revelation to him whose fate gives him the naturally unrepeatable privilege of tasting them for the first time. I don't know whether they are to be obtained in equal excellence elsewhere, and perhaps I can best describe their effect upon my palate by saying that if not it is almost worthwhile going to Ceylon to get them.

By the time breakfast had been followed by a digestive smoke on the shady verandah over-looking a splendid stretch of sea dotted by craft of strange forms and many-hued sails, it was time to re-embark in the hackerry and drive back to Colombo, which we did, thinking hard things of the apparently unreasonable decree which curtailed our stay in Ceylon to a period that was only long enough to enable us to see it as the Peri at the Gate might have caught a glimpse of Paradise through the half-open wicket.

We got back to town with about an hour to spare, and this was taken up by the making of a few purchases, the absorption of more cooling fluids, and in my case, the holding of a Press levee, composed mostly of rival knights of the pen. I have since had the not unmixed pleasure of reading some of the results, and they have convinced me that interviewing en masse is not quite a satisfactory form of journalism. Perhaps, too, the high pressure at which the levee was held, together with the height of the mercury and the prevalence of cooling fluids, are in some measure responsible for the curious results produced.

A few minutes after two the *Sachsen* was under weigh again and steamed out to sea on her way round the southern end of the island, and then, after three days' steaming over an almost motionless and breathless sea, we sighted the island of Pulo Brasse, at the entrance to the Straits of Malacca, where the length of this instalment compels me to take leave of you for the present. Next week we shall run through the Straits and spend a day and a night in Singapore.

VII. — THE CITY OF THE LIONS

The way from the Westward to Singapore—called in Malay "The City of the Lions," either because there are no lions there, or because Singha or Sinha is used indiscriminately for lions and tigers—lies between the Island of Pulo Brasse on the right hand and that of Pulo Way on the left.

It is nowadays a pleasant and peaceful run over usually smooth waters, which gradually change from the deep blue of the open ocean to the somewhat dirty green of the narrow seas. Land, richly wooded and picturesque in form, is always in sight, and the almost constant appearance of sail or smoke-cloud tells the traveller that he is traversing one of the busy seaways of the world.

In former times these narrow waters were anything but as safe and peaceful as they are now that the Pax Britannica has been proclaimed throughout their length and breadth. Dutchmen and Englishmen, Spaniards and Portuguese, Chinamen and Malays, with now and then a wandering Frenchman or Venetian, disputed fiercely for the possession of the fertile lands which formed their shores, and here were enacted some of the most terrible of the tragedies which made the name of the Malay pirates of the Straits a word of terror to the traders of two or three generations ago.

Even to this day the lighthouse on Pulo Brasse is guarded by soldiers, for more than once the Malays have extinguished the light in the hope that some ship coming through would miss her bearings and run ashore on one of the many rocks and islands, there to fall a prey to plunder and outrage.

Shortly before lunch on the 2nd we passed Acheen, Sumatra, and got a far-off glimpse of the Dutch settlement lying on the low ground in the centre of the bay. Behind it rose the mountains of the interior, which I looked upon with all the more interest because I knew that, although European ships had passed and re-passed for nearly four centuries, only one European had crossed the land behind them, and got out alive at the other side.

Sumatra is not very large, say, in comparison with Darkest Africa, yet it can still boast the distinction of having resisted the blessings of civilisation far more successfully than the now freely-exploited wildernesses of the Dark Continent.

Outside Acheen there is a lighthouse and signal station perched on a rocky islet, and here the German said "Good Afternoon" to the Dutchman in a hoarse and throaty whistle, which sounded like an attempt to talk Dutch by steam power. During the afternoon we ran along the northern coast of the island to Diamond Point, quite close in shore, and so in full view of the rugged, picturesque country, with its low, fertile hills running down to the sea-line, and its dark mountains rising from four to eight thousand feet in the background.

Some day, when the Westward course of Empire has carried it once more to the East, there will be some very eligible building sites and town lots for watering-places along this beautiful shoreline, backed as it is by thousands of square miles of inexhaustible fertility.

After a good deal of quarrelling and bickering between the Dutch and the British, during which we just missed being turned out of the Archipelago altogether, an agreement was made in 1824, which gave the Dutch the lion's share of the territory and ourselves the best trading positions. If the wooden-headedness of Downing Street and the jealousy of the Indian Government had not been successfully counteracted by the enlightened patriotism of Sir Stamford Raffles, the creator of Singapore, the Dutchman would probably have owned a big colonial Empire in the East by this time.

On the other hand, if Downing Street and the Indian Office had been as enlightened and as patriotic as Sir Stamford, a magnificent commercial and agricultural area would now be pouring its wealth into the lap of British Commerce. As an example of what one really capable man who knows his own mind can do even when thwarted at every step by bunglers in authority, I may say that when Sir Stamford Raffles hoisted the British flag on the 6th of February, 1819, over the original settlement of Singapore, the population was under two hundred human beings. A year later it was five thousand, and in 1822 it was ten thousand. It now has a population of 184,550, and the value of its imports and exports amounts to over 260,000,000 dollars, or at the present rate of exchange about 26,000,000 sterling a year.

Where seventy years ago the jungle came down to the water's edge, and the tigers were almost undisputed masters of the situation, there is a busy populous city, fronted by an anchorage where the flags of every nation that owns a ship are reflected in British waters. In a word, Sir Stamford was one of those Empire-makers who would have gone near to making the world a British planet if politicians and alleged statesmen at home had only let them.

On the night of the 2nd we ran into a real tropical thunderstorm, and enjoyed one of those displays of celestial fireworks, which, perhaps fortunately for them, are never witnessed by the temperate regions. The next morning we passed the isolated verdure-clad pyramid of Gharra Island, and another day's steaming through the narrowing waters brought us to the Borneo Wharf; where we tied up for a twenty-four-hour stay.

It was now between eight and nine on the morning of the 4th. We had made a capital run of four days twenty hours, allowing for easting, and I was now forty-eight hours ahead of time. The kindly Fates had been more than ever propitious, for, although there had been a stiff current running westward through the Straits less than a week before, it had disappeared just as we started from Colombo, and given pace to a sea as motionless as a mill-pond. I got ashore about an hour later, and had my first experience of the universal Rickshaw.

This, it is perhaps hardly necessary to say, is what its full Chinese name, "Jin-rickshaw," implies—a manpower carriage. It is something like the back half of a perambulator multiplied by four and running upon two large, light wheels. Two long shafts run out in front, joined by a cross-bar, behind which the human horse runs, half-pushing, half-pulling, the vehicle.

At the top of the lane, leading from the wharf to the main road, I was surrounded by a swarm of stalwart, stumpy, thick-legged Malay Syces, or Rickshaw men who picked up their shafts and rushed at me regardless of collision, and shouting, "Rickshaw! Rickshaw!" with an eagerness that seemed hardly justified by the ridiculously low fares that they are compelled to charge.

I did not hire one—at least not just then—and I must confess that the reason why I did not do so was due to a lingering remnant of the Man-and-brother theory, which put me against the idea of using a human being as a horse. It is about two miles from Borneo wharf to the town of Singapore, and I thought I would walk it.

I started out to do so. In two hundred yards the remains of my Western prejudice had literally melted out of my constitution. One of the Syces evidently knew that it would, for he followed me, and, just as Nature gained the victory over prejudice, dropped his shafts invitingly beside me. I got in, and from that moment I walked no more under Eastern suns than I could help.

Rickshaw travelling is an extremely pleasant mode of locomotion—to him or her who is sitting on the seat—but for all that it is strongly suggestive of slavery, especially when you see a burly Briton or a pair of fat Chinamen being hauled up a hill by a panting human draught-animal who lays an appreciable proportion of the dust through which he trots.

There are two roads from the wharf to the town, and, as I had a horse who knew the way, I allowed him to choose his own. He took me by the inland one, which, although it is less pleasant, is a good deal more interesting than the one which runs along the sea. It is lined by the closely-packed houses and shops of Malays, Hindoos, and Chinese, but chiefly the last. The houses were mean, dirty, and odoriferous beyond description, and were, of course, fairly matched in these respects by their inhabitants.

The dirt and shabbiness were also brought up into strong, if unnecessary, relief by the blue-and-yellow wash with which the outer walls are daubed, and the glaring vermilion hieroglyphics, looking mostly like redhot gridirons badly struck by lightning, which form the Chinese substitute for sign-boards. As Chinese is written up and down, the sign-boards have to be hung that way too; consequently a Chinese business street looks like a manufactory of vivid hieroglyphics with the goods hung out to dry.

This was evidently one of the lowest quarters of the town, and the men, women, and children lounging about the shop-fronts and the doorsteps of the houses, and loitering about the roadway, exhibited every shade of yellow and brown, and every degree of dirt and undressedness, that could be imagined.

After half an hour's trot through the elongated Eastern slum, I was agreeably surprised when the road turned into the town proper, and found it to be quite a metropolis of the Tropics. The native town, which lies at the back of the European town, is composed of substantial verandahed houses and shops, ranged in good wide streets, and this gradually merges into the European settlement fronting the Bay and the Anchorage.

Victoria Dock in Singapore

Colombo sank into comparative insignificance before the beauties of European Singapore. The breezy anchorage, swarming with shipping and gay with flags, the inner bay dotted with all kinds of strange-shaped, queerly-navigated Oriental craft, broad streets of tall white houses, under the cool shade of whose verandahs you found shops that would not discredit Oxford Street, and away to the left, as you faced the sea, a splendid sweep of level turf, close-clipped and brilliantly green, flanked on one side by the sea-beach and on the other by a long, curving tree-shaded road, and behind that again a mile or two of churches, public buildings, hotels, and bungalows, standing in the midst of spacious and splendid gardens, with the green heights of Signal Hill rising behind it all—that is a fair reproduction of the mental photograph that I took of what I may call the West-end of the City of the Lions.

The roads of this part of Singapore have been compared by more than one traveller to the leafy lanes of Devonshire, but I am afraid that not even my admiration for my native county would lead me so far from the straight and narrow way of verity as it would be necessary to go to endorse the comparison, Devonshire is beautiful, but not with the beauty of the Tropics. In addition to the magnificently-varied vegetation and the wonderful colourings of foliage and flowers, the splendours of sun and sky, and the indescribable charm of the soft, scented, languorous air, make it quite impossible to truthfully liken anything in the Tropics to even the most beautiful scenery in that region of the earth which is afflicted by the British climate.

I spent the couple of hours before tiffin in Rickshaw riding and very leisurely wandering afoot through the streets of the town. I thought I had seen a fairly varied assortment of humanity at Port Said, but in the streets of Singapore I learnt that there were a few more varieties to be added. As a matter of fact, those who ought to know say that there are more differences and blendings of races to be seen in the City of the Lions than in any other spot of land on the globe.

Orchard Road in Singapore

Just as the Anchorage is a naval cosmopolis, so the town is a focus in which all nations and languages are concentrated. It is said that there is no European nation which is not represented, and in addition to these you see Chinese, Malays, Hindoos, Sikhs, Japanese, Burmese, Siamese, Tamils, Singalese, Arabs, Jews, Parsees, and negroes. Personally I did not come across any Esquimaux or Fuegans, but there is no reason for concluding that they were not there. I did, however, meet with one or two savages apparently hailing from the East-end of London.

After tiffin I got a carriage very like the Colombo hackerry, and after a considerable expenditure of eloquence and perspiration got it for the afternoon for a dollar, or 2s. 2d. English. This would have been cheap but for the exertion consequent on getting the man down to a reasonable figure. He began by asking me ten dollars, or something over a sovereign, and yet when I paid him the dollar at dinner-time he took it with a smile that left behind it an impression that he had still managed to get the windward of me.

I employed the hot part of the afternoon driving out along the Orchard Road—an even more beautiful thoroughfare than the Colpetty Road at Colombo, though not quite so interesting to a student of human nature and after a lazy and lovely drive came in due course to the Botanical Gardens. These are considered to be a great ornament to Singapore, but I must confess that I found them a trifle superfluous.

Where the whole earth is a garden such institutions lose a good deal of their interest to the eye of the average person, and as I did not go out to see with the eyes of a botanist, I shortened my stay in favour of another drive. One reason for my readiness to leave the Gardens may have been the fact that I had to walk about them while I could ride about the roads.

When I got back to the town I climbed Signal Hill, and was well repaid for the exertion by the splendid view over the island and Anchorage, and the delightfully cool breeze that was blowing across the top, Singapore has one of the most perfect climates in the world. It really is a climate, and not a series of ill-assorted atmospheric samples. The weather is practically always the same, and nearly always fine.

Sumatra stands between it and the storms which sweep over the Indian Ocean, while the islands of the Malay Peninsula protect it from the typhoons of the China seas. It also lies outside of the curving volcanic belt which runs from Japan through the Philippines and westward by Java and Sumatra. It is therefore free both from the hurricane and the earthquake.

There is a fairly heavy rainfall, but it is so evenly distributed over the whole of the year that it resolves itself mostly into a series of refreshing showers of warm rain, which don't do anybody any harm, and endow the vegetation with the freshness of an eternal spring. The burden and the heat of the day alike end between four and five o'clock, then the shops and offices shut up, and all Singapore turns out to ride about in Rickshaws and otherwise arouse itself.

It was about this time that a select company of the voyagers on the *Sachsen* might have been seen by a reader in the confidence of the late G. P. R. James resting itself from the fatigues of the day on the broad, shady terrace of the Hotel de l'Europe, and restoring its evaporated energies with an assortment of fluids almost as cosmopolitan as the population of Singapore.

As the afternoon wore on, and the atmosphere became fresher and cooler, the scene from the verandah grew more and more interesting. The broad, tree-shaded road in front is the Rotten Row of Singapore, and it rapidly became crowded with every kind of passenger and vehicle, from the powdered, silk-clad Japanese anonymous riding in couples in their Rickshaws to English clergy in British barouches and Anglo-Oriental dandies in dog-carts and buggies.

Every language that ever was derived from Babel was being spoken within a radius of fifty yards, and on the other side of the roadway the green tennis-lawn were busy with the unquenchable energy of the athletic Briton of both sexes.

When dark fell we went into a singularly indifferent dinner, which made us think regretfully of the tiffin at Mount Lavinia and the generous cuisine of the *Sachsen*, and then certain permanent and temporary bachelors of the party started out, under competent guidance to explore the night side of Singapore, an experience which the present chronicler will take permission to leave to the intelligent imagination of his readers.

At varying hours, large and small, through the night that party got back to the Borneo Wharf, and the next morning we rose creditably betimes, all things considered to find, not without regret, that the time had come to begin the last stage of our long journey on board the *Sachsen*.

VIII. — THE HEATHEN AT SEA

One reason for our early awakening on the morning of the 5th was an ear-piercing, dream-dispelling chorus of yells, screams, laughter, and many-voiced chattering as of a multitude of articulate cockatoos that rose wildly from the wharf along the whole length of the ship.

My first half-awake thought was one of Malay pirates, Chinese junks, stink-pots, and massacre, but as soon as I got across the border that separates the Land of Nod from the world of work I remembered being told that we were going to take on a lot of Chinese passengers for Hong Kong and Shanghai, and concluded that they must be coming on board.

For all that, I found later on that the ship really had been boarded by Chinese pirates in the early morning, and that they and their victims were responsible for most of the row that was going on. The reader who here expects a harrowing description of rapine and bloodshed must, however, prepare for disappointment. I shall have a little story of real Chinese piracy to tell later on, but this is not it. The piracy that was being enacted on board the *Sachsen* was of that purely commercial sort which is not conducted by means of lethal weapons.

The modern Chinaman is, before all things, a man of business, and so smart and acute and subtle is he that, for my own part, I believe the Americans don't want him chiefly because they think he could play them at their own swindles and beat them. There is literally nothing that a Chinaman will not make money out of, from the tombs of his ancestors to the refuse that is thrown overboard from a steamboat.

If you or I were starting on a sea voyage we should not expect anyone absolutely unconnected with the steamer or her owners to be able to levy a tax upon us before we could get a comfortable berth; yet this is exactly what the pirates who had taken possession of the steerage of the *Sachsen* did to their compatriots who were going to travel by her, and the way they worked the swindle was as follows: —Coaling and other operations were going on more or less all night, and the pirates took advantage of the bustle to walk quietly and stolidly on board, armed with mats and bogus luggage, just as though they were passengers.

As it would have cost much more trouble to keep them out than it ultimately did to get rid of them, no notice was taken of them. Once on board they proceeded to occupy all the best, most comfortable, and most sheltered positions in the steerage and on the foredeck. There they spread their mats, arranged their spurious impedimenta, and squatted with the imperturbable stolidity which makes a Chinaman at ease, the nearest approach there is to a graven image endowed with the power of coming to life at will.

In due course the real passengers began to arrive on the scene, and then the fun began, They had already paid their fares-five or ten dollars, or a little over one or two pounds sterling, according as they were bound for Hong Kong or Shanghai—and now they had to buy their places from the pirates in possession, and great was the expenditure of gutturals and gesticulations involved in the process.

The passengers could do one of two things—bid against each other for the best places, or wait until the ship's whistle gave the pirates notice of summary ejectment. Some paid, others waited, and were hustled about by the crew and the stevedores, to the great discomfort of their persons and the apparently hopeless mixing up of their luggage, which mainly consisted of seemingly identical tea-chests and oblong mahogany boxes, almost as much alike as the Chinamen themselves. A third lot kept up the bargaining to the bitter end.

In due course the third whistle blew, and then, as they say in the States, "the circus began." About half the pirates had got on shore, and the other half were too much engrossed in bargaining to notice that the gangways had been removed and the ship was sheering off from the wharf. As far as I could see, no notice beyond the whistles had been given them.

Just as we came up from breakfast a wilder yell than usual came from the wharf, and was answered from the fore-deck. By this time about two yards of water separated the ship from a long baulk of timber that floated against the piles, and this distance was slowly but surely increasing.

Then there poured up from the 'tween-decks a wildly excited crowd of Chinamen, with pig-tails flying and loose garments flapping, and mats and bogus luggage clasped convulsively to their bosoms. They swarmed on to the bulwarks and up the shrouds, and then a rapid hail of boxes, mats, and shoes rained from the ship to the wharf. Some fell in the water, others were caught with yells of triumph and a perfectly amazing amount of gesticulation by their friends on shore.

Not a man of them tried to get ashore before he had hurled his luggage and his slippers on ahead of him. The water between the ship and the wharf was soon covered with flotsam of various descriptions of piratical property, and then the pirates themselves made a start.

A crazy old boat that might have held some half-dozen with safety was pulled by its rashly-enterprising owner through the flotsam with a view to salvage and ferrying. Long before he could state his terms a good score of Chinamen had dropped, jumped, scrambled down ropes, or fallen into the boat. Then another yell went up, and she went down, and left owner and passengers struggling frantically in the water.

Meanwhile, the ship was steadily sheering off. The strip of water was becoming wider, and the chances of getting safely ashore were getting narrower. The time had come for desperate measures, and the remaining pirates took them. In a rapid stream of pigtailed humanity they flopped overboard, deliberately jumping on the heads and shoulders of the struggling wretches in the water, and using their bodies as floats from which to get a purchase for a spring to the baulk.

It was a fight for life, in which the bottom dog had little or no chance. I particularly noticed one fellow drop softly on to the struggling crowd, put his hands on the heads of two gasping, spluttering wretches who were almost *in extremis*, and calmly push them under, in an attempt to reach the baulk, which, I regret to say, was completely successful. The other two, as far as I could see, did not come up again. How many were drowned no one knew, and no one seemed particularly to care.

The Chinese passengers looked on with visible twinkles of amusement and satisfaction in their eyes, and the officers and crew had something else to attend to. The only two persons on board who seemed to show any sympathy with the pirates, who were thus caught on the barbs of their own sharpness, were a very charming American lady, (the wife of the stalwart journalist heretofore alluded to, who had come on board at Colombo, and who had not yet learnt the value, or lack of value, which Chinese human life is appraised at) and an ancient opium-dried Chinaman.

The charming American—when American women are nice, they're entirely delightful—pleaded almost, but not quite, irresistibly for the lives of callous heathens, who would have watched her drown without moving a muscle of their faces, and the old Chinaman showed his sympathy by having an epileptic fit, of which he subsequently died.

In spite of the fact that life was being lost, the comic aspect of the scene, for the time being, quite eclipsed its graver side, and, right or wrong, I must confess that, until the scramble was over and graver thoughts came, I laughed till the tears rolled down my face, and I was by no means the only one who did so.

One reason for this feeling certainly was the Chinese own absolute callousness to this human suffering and death. They saw their fellow creatures drowning, or in imminent peril of their lives within a couple of yards, and yet they stood and looked on, and did not stretch out a hand to save them. This is perhaps because the Chinese are said to believe that it is a "bad pidgin," i.e., unlucky to save life.

He is a fatalist, and he thinks that when a man's time has come it is better to let him go. To save him is to interfere with the course of Fate, and make himself directly responsible for all the bad luck that may befall the man he saves.

In spite of this, I must do them the justice of saying that their presence added a very decided element of interest to a voyage which, so far as the *Sachsen* and her company were concerned, had been rather indolently luxurious than stimulatingly interesting.

The Chinaman of all men on earth, not even excepting the Englishman, is the most unaffected by his environments. He is the same today as he has been for ages past, and will probably remain the same for ages to come. Wherever he goes he takes his little bit of China with him, his mats, his grass-corded boxes, his chopsticks, and his opium fit-out.

The fore deck and steerage of the *Sachsen* were no exception to the general rule, German everywhere else, she was Chinese there from the moment that they established themselves to the moment that they left, and we had only to glance over the fore railing of the promenade deck to look into China whenever we wished.

Chinese troops on deck in the 1890s

In one way the scene reminded me of the story about the five families in the single room in a tenement house who were comfortable enough until the people in the middle took in a lodger. Families consisting usually of papa, mamma, and two or three babies, which look like twins and triplets of different sizes, put down their mats, arranged their tea chests and boxes, and made themselves stolidly and completely at home either above or below deck, as they had happened to find a lodging, one never moved save when the sailors turned the hose on them in washing decks. Then they scattered quietly but no doubt thinking a considerable amount of Chinese profanity, crowded below decks till the storm had passed over, and then came back to exactly the same places and went on as usual.

I ought also to add that their babies were absolute models of infantile propriety, and sweet, if perhaps somewhat savoury reasonableness that the most exacting old bachelor could expect. During the five days that I was shipmates with them, I never heard one of them cry, nor did I ever see one of them spanked. From this I concluded that any natural inborn cussedness of the Chinese does not develop until comparatively late in life. In this he differs widely from the noble Briton.

The feeding arrangements were undertaken by a Chinese contractor, who ladled out the weird and forbidding messes in china and wooden bowls to each family and each company of bachelors, who literally messed together three times a day,

In connection with this feeding, I regret to say, that a long cherished illusion was ruthlessly dispelled by the logic of facts. I, like a good many others, had been under the impression that a Chinaman using his chopsticks practised a kind of gastronomic legerdemain, which transferred his food from his plate to his mouth in a series of deftly projected morsels something in the same way as a juggler tosses his balls or his knives.

The reality was very different. The chop-sticks were two thin strips of bamboo, which they held between their first and second and second and third fingers. Any particularly toothsome morsel they picked up with these, as with a pair of elongated tweezers, and put into their mouths in a most commonplace fashion.

The bulk of their chow-chow—the pidgin English for all kinds of food—they ate, or rather devoured, by putting the edge of their dish to their open mouths and literally shovelling it in with their chop-sticks. The process of swallowing went on all the time, and the chow-chow passed in a continual stream from the dish to their stomachs as long as it lasted. Another opportunity I had was that of seeing how opium is really smoked. By no means all Chinamen are opium-smokers, and only a comparatively small percentage of our passengers indulged in the drug, about which such a colossal amount of nonsense is talked and written by excellent people, whose emotional credulity is far in advance of their analytical faculties.

One enterprising heathen invested a dollar in inducing one of the quarter-masters to clear out a pig-sty, and this he lined comfortably with mats, then he set up a comprehensive opium-smoking fit-out, and soon had a small opium den in full blast, for admission to which he charged ten cents a head, and did a roaring business in what the anti-opium enthusiast would call the demoralisation of his fellow creatures, I didn't see any demoralisation.

A quieter set of debauchees I never came across in my life.

A Chinese opium installation consists of two or three pipes, a little pot of opium, two or three long bits of steel like darning needles, and a little oil-lamp, covered with a glass dome that has a hole in the top. All these are contained in an oblong box of dark polished wood, upon which the smoker rests his head when he lies down for a smoke.

The pipe has a thick stem of perhaps three-quarters of an inch in diameter, and twelve or fourteen inches in length: sometimes there is a mouthpiece, sometimes not. The bowl is fixed about a couple of inches from the other end, and is made of red clay, smoothed on the top and pierced by a small hole, which runs into the bone of the stem. The opium, which is about the consistency of treacle, is dipped out of the bowl on the end of one of the darning needles, and rolled about until enough of it adheres.

This is then held over the flame of the lamp. It swells up and puffs out into little bubbles; then it is rolled upon the smooth surface of the bowl till it takes on a pasty thickness. This operation is repeated two or three times until the connoisseur is satisfied. Then, just at the right moment, it is rammed into the little hole in the bowl, another dip is taken and treated in the same way, then the pipe is ready.

He holds it over the flame and takes a long pull, and blows out a considerable cloud of blue pungent smoke, which will either make you cough or feel sick, according to the range. If he has filled his pipe well, he gets five or six of these whiffs out of it, and, if he is anything of a novice, this is about enough for him, but I saw several old seasoned smokers who got away with pipe after pipe of the alleged intoxicant, and then got out and went about to see if anyone would lend them a fill of tobacco.

The tobacco-smoking, by the way, was about as absurd a performance as one could expect from such a generally level-headed person as the heathen Chinese. Their pipes held about as much tobacco as would half fill a very small-sized thimble. The back of the pipe was a receptacle, out of which they took a pinch with a pair of metal tweezers. This they stuffed into the bowl, and then lit with a slow-match. Three puffs exhausted it, then they removed the movable bowl, blew the ashes out, replaced it, filled up, had another couple of puffs, and so on hour after hour. The passage had ended before I discovered whether the arrangement was intended for getting satisfaction out of tobacco, or just wasting time.

Gambling, of course, went on all day, and, for all I know, all night too, The games had apparently evoluted for ages, and picked up complications about every generation, Chinese whist, for instance, is played with two or three hundred cards, more or less, distinguished by the most fearsome hieroglyphics, and apparently flung down quite casually. The utmost intricacies of chess would, I should think, be the merest child's play to it.

The simplest game played was fan-tan; and this consisted in betting on the number that would be left out of a lot of counter's covered by a bowl. When the money was staked, they were counted out in fours, and the punters won or lost, according as there were one, two, or three left over.

Judging by the piles of dollars that were won or lost, and the persistent conscientiousness with which the game was played, I should say that when that particular company of heathens got to their journey's end, they would be divided into paupers and comparative millionaires. This, I believe, is the usual result of a voyage to the Chinaman at sea.

Thanks perhaps to our new passengers, and certainly to two most interesting acquaintances that I had made, of whom the American lady was one, and her husband the other, the run from Singapore to Hong Kong was the most interesting portion so far of my shipboard experiences. Unhappily we just missed the light outside Hong Kong, and as it is not usual for large vessels to go through the dangerous channels in the dark, we were obliged to waste nearly twelve hours at anchor outside.

IX. — THE TOWN OF THREE NAMES

ACCORDING to schedule time we were due at Hong Kong on the morning of the 12th of April, but, although we started nearly forty hours ahead of time from Singapore, we, as I said at the close of my last article, missed the light outside the harbour on the evening of the 10th, lost nearly twelve hours at anchor, and therefore did not arrive at our berth at Kowloong; opposite the Island of Victoria, until the morning of the 11th. Thus about twenty hours of our advantage were lost.

Hong Kong harbour 1890s

This was the first real set-back that I had had, but it was destined to be a great deal worse before I got finally on my way again. As further bad luck would have it, we happened to arrive at a very bad time both for sight-seeing and health. There had been a persistent drought for about four months, and then for two days and nights it had rained with a vigour and volume that had converted the whole island into what Mr. Mantalini would have been thoroughly justified in calling "a demmed moist unpleasant place."

Earth and air were saturated with moisture and steaming with heat. The upper part of the island, which reaches heights of from 1,500 to 1,800 feet, was robed in dense white mists, and the drains and gutters smelt as only those of a mainly Chinese town can smell.

From the nasal recollections that I have brought away with me from Hong Kong, I am not at all surprised at the plague breaking out in the Chinese quarter, I should rather be inclined to wonder at their ever being without it.

Chinamen, though usually scrupulously clean in their persons, in accordance with the laws of Confucius, are dirty in their dwellings and often disgusting in their habits. Added to this they have a whole-souled, deep-rooted hatred of sanitation, which makes them abhor it above all the other abominations of the Barbarian. If a pestilence cannot be extirpated by the burning of joss-sticks, the banging of gongs, and the scattering of highly-coloured pieces of paper, they prefer to let it kill them, provided always that they can't run away from it.

According to the information given us, the transference of cargo for Yokohama from the *Sachsen* to the Nürnberg, the auxiliary ship in which I was booked to travel to Japan, would take about twenty-four hours, and this would enable the Nürnberg to leave on the 12th, twenty-four hours ahead. We therefore got ashore as soon as possible for a long day on the island, uninviting as the prospect looked, and took the steam ferry from the wharf at Kowloong across the splendid harbour, crowded with shipping of every description, from British, American, French, and Russian men-of-war to Japanese junks and Chinese sampans, to the Praya, a granite quay, some three miles long, which fronts the town towards the Anchorage.

In Chinese, Hong Kong is represented by a couple of characters which look not unlike the two wheels of a safety bicycle might do after a very bad smash. These can be literally translated as "Fragrant Streams" —a rendering, one sense of which I was able to heartily endorse before I had been five minutes ashore—"Renowned Anchorage" or "Fragrant Lagoon."

Renowned anchorage it certainly is, for not only is it one of the finest harbours in the world, but it is claimed that a larger percentage of tonnage passes through its waters than through those of any other port in the world, Liverpool and London only excepted. Yet a fourth interpretation of the name is derived from the Heungkong, one of the many perennial streams which has made the island a favourite watering-place for ages.

It did not take me long to get enough of the atmosphere of the lower portion of Hong Kong, or, to be more correct, the City of Victoria, so I decided to take a trip above the clouds. This I accomplished by taking my passage on the elevated tramway, a cable line which runs straight up the side of the hills to the Gap, and lifts you some fifteen hundred feet in fifteen or twenty minutes.

If it had only been a fine, clear day, I should have had some magnificent views of sea and land, mountain and shore from the ascending car. Even as it was I got some lovely glimpses through the momentary breaks in the drifting mists that came sweeping like the soundless billows of some shadowy sea across the middle and upper heights.

Although forty years ago the island of Hong Kong was little better than a wild and treeless waste of steep slopes and barren peaks, it is now, thanks to the same tireless British enterprise which has made it the Liverpool of the East, planted with thousands of trees, from the pines of the upper slopes to the tree-ferns, palms, aloes, and hibiscus of the Public Gardens, the cemeteries, and Garden Road.

The middle and upper heights of the seaward slope, up which the tramway runs, are plentifully sprinkled with bungalows, most of them standing in finely-planted gardens, where the wealthier classes of European residents live, and up on the Peak itself, nearly 1,800 feet above the sea, there is a fine hotel, which must be a delightful stopping-place, in fine weather. Judging from the fleeting glimpses that I got from its terrace, it must command some of the finest all-round views in the East.

When I got back to the Gap, where the terminus and engine room of the tramway are situated, I found I had a few minutes to wait for the return car, and spent them in conversation with the head engineer. No sooner had I told him that I had come out by the *Sachsen*, than he jumped to a correct conclusion and said:

"Then I suppose you are Mr. Griffith, who is going round the world for *Pearson's Weekly*?"

"That's me!" I replied, with more satisfaction than grammatical exactness, not a little pleased to meet, as this gentleman told me he was a regular reader of P.W. on the peak of Hong Kong, a good ten thousand miles from Henrietta Street.

I had not been a quarter of an hour back in the town before it began to dawn upon me that I had done an exceedingly foolish thing in travelling so quickly from the almost stifling heat of the shore into the chilly mists of the upper regions.

My head began to ache and burn as though my sun helmet had been one of the hot-pots of those unamiable savages whom the author of "She" evolved out of the luridness of his inner consciousness. My skin went alternately hot and cold and dry and wet, and my joints felt like those of a badly-articulated skeleton. Add to this a raging thirst and a general swimminess and nausea and there you have the variety of malaria which is locally known as Hong Kong fever.

All other desires; save one, speedily faded out of my mind. I wanted to lie down before I fell down, and I just got to the Hong Kong hotel by the Praya, and was shown to a bedroom in time to substitute the one process for the other. That was between eleven and twelve, as nearly as I remember. I told them to call me at four, and when the "boy"-i.e., the Chinese room-servant or male chambermaid knocked me up out of a sort of afternoon nightmare, which was my nearest approach to getting to sleep, I had considerable difficulty in either remembering who I was or where I had got to.

At length, with curious clearness, came the fear that if I collapsed again some doctor might get hold of me, swear that I was unfit to travel and make me miss my connection with the Nürnberg the next morning. That supplied the necessary stimulus, and though I was somewhere about an hour, more or less, getting into my boots and jacket, I managed to get out and on board the ferry-boat.

My only reason for believing that I got back to the Nürnberg was the fact that I woke up in my berth on board her the next morning free from fever, but with a very decided head on me. I breakfasted on mangoes, bananas, and two cocktails, and although the physic was hardly such as a regular practitioner would have prescribed, it did me so much good that I was quite ready for another run ashore.
The usual notice had been posted that the Nürnberg would sail at twelve noon, but three o'clock was now substituted, and so, as the

day was much finer, I didn't need very much pressing to join my friend the journalist and his wife in a second trip to the Peak and an exploration of the Chinese town. The former was a little more satisfactory than on the day before, and was followed by no malaria; the latter was almost as interesting as it was odoriferous, which is saying a good deal.

The Chinese part of Hong Kong may be divided into two portions—a Regent Street and a Whitechapel. The former is the Queen's Road, and the latter rises behind it in various degrees of steepness and stuffiness up the hillside, and also spreads down towards the eastern part of the Anchorage. This is the locality where the plague has just been raging.

Hong Kong district where the plague outbreak occurred

The Chinese shops in the Queen's Road differ from most others from the fact that they have glazed windows. There are two reasons for this concession to the ways of the Barbarian: the wares displayed in them are often of very considerable value, and the Chinese shoplifter has a wonderful knack of apparently accidentally entangling things on the hook at the end of a long bamboo pole and vanishing with characteristic slipperiness.

These shops, some twenty feet deep, and with a frontage of about half as much, are not very unlike those of Europe, and, what with their brilliant contrasts of colouring, the profusion of gilding and silvering, and the quaintness and beauty of the wares on sale, they were decidedly attractive, not only to the eye, but also to the contents of the pocket. As these shops are specially set out for the attraction of the Barbarian, most of them, in addition to the pendant hieroglyphics I referred to before, possess some remarkable essays in imitation of English sign-boards.

For instance, one gentleman styled himself, "Dealer in Tailor and Draper, Manilla Cigar all kind, a Silk Handkerchief outfitter." Over the door of a cook shop of an aspect more curious than inviting, one Wong-Foo announced that he

"Always has any France
Pastry Dinner Lunch Supper
All kinds of foreigners cakes
For Sale."

Hong Kong English district

A little farther on a local Carter Paterson told the passer-by that he was in the habit of despatching "All sort goods, Many merchandise in Steamer, not seldom anywhere and safe." Simplest of all, but somewhat lacking in precise information, was a very small sign stuck out at the side of the tea-shop, which bore the almost pathetically-brief legend, "Ah Chan—up-stairs."

As you go west from Queen's Road you get into the more purely Chinese quarter, and the shops almost entirely change their character. With that singular extravagance, and I might say mendacity, of nomenclature which leads the Chinaman to give his shop such efflorescent titles as "The House of Increasing Profit," "The Hall of Brilliant Light," "Celestial Advantage," and "Great Felicity" — this latter is the title of a small barber's shop in Hong Kong—the locality rising above the Queen's Road is called Tai-ping-shan, or "Hill of Great Peace," in spite of the fact that it is one of the worst districts in the East. This is possibly done on the same principle that the equally enlightened owners of metropolitan slums usually call a row of hovels, or a court in which no self-respecting dog would be found dead, Paradise Row or Prospect Place.

The better class of the shops are very curious little shows, and display an interesting blend of theology and business. They are dimly-lighted, poky, and characteristically odorous places. In the darkness at the back you see a little lamp burning before a diminutive Joss, or god, of singularly hideous physiognomy, and round it are paper flowers or little pots of narcissus. Scrolls hang round the walls, and these, I was informed contain extracts from the Chinese scriptures and classics, extolling the dealings of honest tradesmen, evidently not intended to apply to transactions with the Barbarian.

Small tables of carved black wood often hold a little tea-service or water-pipes, commonly called kubblebubbles, for the refreshment of the purchaser, who often takes as long to make up his mind as an English lady on bargain-day.

The counter runs down one side and sometimes along the back, and it is perfectly wonderful what exquisite pieces of merchandise, from silk to silver ware, you can buy in these dingy little holes if you have either a callous disregard for the value of money or unlimited patience in beating the proprietary thief down to a reasonable price.

Not less curious than the shops are the restaurants. These are divided into several classes, and the higher the class you wish to patronise the more flights of stairs you have to ascend, and the more unappetising scenes you have to pass. If you have any appetite left when you get to your destination, it will be either tempted or killed, as the case may be, with the weirdest assemblage of mysteriously-concocted confections that ever tickled a Chinese or puzzled a European palate.

Of course you will have tea, or at least what they call tea in China. We had some, and, as I was trying to drink it, I pictured the sort of wash that would be made by rinsing out the tea-cups and tea-urns after a Sunday-school tea-fight, adding hot water and straining off.

I regret to say that I was also weak enough to carry, with great care and greater anticipation, a pound of alleged best tea from Hong Kong to Japan, across the Pacific, over Canada and America, and across what certainly proved to be " the mournful and misty Atlantic," only to find that the friends to whom I offered it thought I was placing off a feeble sort of practical joke on them.

Bargaining in Chinese shops suggests a subject which certainly deserves a passing mention, and this is the language you use in doing so, Pidgin English is perhaps the queerest tongue on earth. It is an *olla podrida* of Portuguese, English, and Chinese, which contains about four hundred words, and suffices for all business purposes.

To talk Pidgin English you have to turn r into 1, v into b, stick double e on to nearly all the words, and use "savey," "piecee," "number one," "first chop," and "pidgin" as often as you possibly can, throwing in by way of ornament "chop-chop"—quickly; "chin-chin" —good-day, how do you do? good-bye, or here's towards you! "belongee," "hab got," and "topside"—upstairs, or best quality.

Thus the Pidgin English for "today is Christmas Day" is "Today belongee number one Heaben Joss-pidgin-day." "There are too many Chinese in Hong Kong" is "Hongkong side hab got too mucheo piecee Chinaman."

The late King of the Sandwich Islands was once staying in a Hong Kong hotel. His rooms were on the first floor, and a Consular Agent went to pay his respects to him. He asked the "boy" in the vestibule if His Majesty was in. The "boy," without taking the trouble to go and see, went to the bottom of the stairs, hailed his confrere on the landing, and scandalised the visitor by singing out: "Hi, boy, hab got one piecee king topside?"

Even more characteristic of the language is the story told of a griffin, a "new chum," in Hong Kong. While he was looking for a house he accepted the hospitality of a married English friend, who may here be called Smith. One morning his "boy," after coming in, and after calling him and making ready the accessories of an Eastern morning toilet, remained standing looking at him with an intelligent twinkle in his oblique orbs.

"Well, Johnny," said the griffin, "what's the matter? Got any news?"

"Missy Smith hab got one piecee small cow chilo," remarked Johnny in a mechanical monotone, and turned and walked out.

Not until he got down to breakfast did the guest learn the meaning of his boy's intelligence, and then his host told him that his wife had just presented him with a daughter.

By two o'clock we had made our purchases, and got the taste of a Chinese restaurant out of our mouths with lunch at the hotel. Then we went round to the Lloyd office and learnt that the Nürnberg was not to sail till five, so we hired palanquins, and were borne on the shoulders of coolies for an hour or so about the prettier parts of the town, and at length crossed over to Kowloong to find that the ship was not going to sail at five, but possibly at six.

Six o'clock came, and the cargo was still coming across the wharf. We had dinner, then went on deck again to say hard and think harder things about the bungling, which was not only wasting all the time we had to the good, but, for lack of precise information, had deprived us of the chance of making a most interesting journey, which we could well have taken if the authorities of the *Sachsen* had only told us at once how long we were going to be in port. This was a run by steam launch up the Canton River to Canton, the Venice of the East.

Eventually the Nürnberg got away from the wharf at 11.45 p.m.

19th century Chinese palanquin bearers

The captain very kindly put to sea at once in spite of the darkness and a threatening fog, but it was no use. In the narrow Li-ee-Moon Pass, which forms the western entrance to the harbour, the fog came down in a dense grey mass, and to my disgust I heard the anchor chain rattling through the hawse holes. We remained there until an hour or two after daybreak, and so nearly every hour of the advantage that we had picked up on the long run from Naples was lost when I once more got on my way.

X. — THE SKIPPER'S YARN

 HALF a dozen of the *Sachsen*'s company were on board the Nürnberg, bound for Yokohama. Sorry and all, as we were at first to leave the luxurious quarters in which we had travelled so far, we soon settled down very comfortably on board the auxiliary boat.

As we were not more than a dozen all told in the long, narrow, old-fashioned saloon, with the staterooms opening out on either side, as was the vogue before promenade decks and ships of three storeys came into fashion, there was plenty of elbow-room, both below and on deck.

Forward in the steerage we had a few scores of Chinese passengers, similar to those I described in a former article, but I saw very little of them, as it was not considered advisable to show much familiarity just then. Only a few days before, a daring piece of piracy had been achieved on the Canton River, and the relations were a trifle cold in consequence.

The latest and perhaps the only form of Chinese piracy now surviving is exactly illustrated by what took place on the Canton River while we were at Hong Kong. A passenger steam launch, plying between Canton and Whampoa, was carrying between eighty and ninety Chinese passengers, who were going to perform their annual worship at the graves of their ancestors.

All the pilgrims save seven were fairly well provided with money, to be spent in offerings. The seven exceptions had plenty of Joss paper and Joss sticks, as well as other things, which they produced when about half the passage was over.

Suddenly flinging off the outer garments of respectability and devotion, they produced kreases and revolvers, and, firing the latter into the air, ordered the passengers to go aft. Meanwhile one of them covered the captain and another the engineer, and while the boat was kept at full speed the other five cleared the crowd out of every cent it possessed, under the pain of immediate shooting.

The pilgrims panned out at between 1,000 and 1,500 dollars, then the pirates looted the steamer, made the captain steer her into a quiet little creek, where their friends were waiting for them in a boat, disembarked, and vanished, leaving the plundered pilgrims and the disgusted mariners to take their feelings with them to Whampoa and get back into a religious frame of mind as best they could.

This exploit was achieved not on the high seas, or even upon out-of-the-way waters, but on a crowded, busy river which may justly be called the Thames of China. Up to the time of my leaving the East not one of the pirates had been caught or a cent of the plunder recovered. This dodge of disguising themselves as passengers has enabled the Chinese pirates up-to-date to bring off two or three very considerable tragedies within recent years, especially on steamers carrying few passengers and small crews, and consequently the line between the steerage and saloon is pretty rigidly drawn, and the Chinese are kept strictly to their own part of the ship.

The five days and a half run from Hong Kong to Yokohama was absolutely eventless, and therefore I should betake myself direct to the Land of the Chrysanthemum were it not that I am tempted to pause by the way to tell again a true tale of the sea which we heard on the fourth night of our passage from the skipper of the Nürnberg, a genial, grizzled, weather-beaten son of Neptune, and the most thoroughly sailor-like-looking man I've ever seen whose native language was not English.

It is not very often, in these days of ocean liners, running with the regularity of railway trains, that the casual traveller meets a man who in his own person has experienced the worst misfortunes of the old days of sailing packets, and has seen with his own eyes the last awful extremity of the famished castaway so near that a few more hours of thirst and starvation might have made it a fearful reality.

But Captain Hugo Walter, of the Nürnberg, was such a man, and the story which follows here is a faithful rendering of the one that he told us that night of his shipwreck in the Indian Ocean, and his thirty-four days' voyage of nearly two thousand miles in an open boat.

"It was on the 18th of September, 1868, that I sailed from Bremerhafen as first officer of the *Adele*, a full-rigged clipper running in the East Indian trade. We had a crew of seventeen men all told, not counting Othello, the captain's poodle, who was considered quite as much a member of the ship's company as anyone else, and kept watch and watch with us until the last. On the 18th of December, having rounded the Cape far to the southward, we passed the islands of St. Paul and New Amsterdam, which lie far out in the Southern Indian Ocean, about half way between South Africa and Australia.

"Three days after that, on the 21st of December, a smell of burning was noticed in the hold, and as part of our cargo was coal it was at once examined by thrusting long' iron rods into it. When we drew them out their ends were quite hot, and there was no use shutting our eyes to the fact that the worst misfortune that comes to the sailor had befallen us—the Adele was on fire.

"The hold was at once closed up, so as to stop any fresh air from getting to the fire, and then, as it was certain that sooner or later we should have to abandon the ship for we were much too far from land to think of running her ashore or into a port—the boats were got ready, and provisioned, everything that we should want to take with us brought up on deck, and we headed the ship for Australia before a stiff sou'-west breeze, so that she might carry us as far as possible towards land before the fire drove us out of her.

"But the coal had apparently taken fire spontaneously in several places, and the fire made such headway that before the next evening a brown, acrid, pungent smoke began to force its way from the hold into the cabin and forecastle. When a ship takes fire like that, an explosion of gas is not at all uncommon, and so we made everything ready to leave her at a few moments' notice. To make matters worse, she began to leak badly, and though we set the pumps to work they were so often choked with coal and ashes there was no hope of getting the leak under.

"That night it began to blow hard from the south, with small, driving rain, and as the ship ran on through the mist and the darkness no one would have thought that she carried a raging furnace in her hold, and even we found it a bit difficult to recognise that the wet decks under our feet were all that separated us from a mass of red-hot coal,

"We held on to the old ship as long as we could, but about three o'clock on the morning of the 23rd the terrible cry of 'Fire!' was raised and we knew that it was time to say good-bye to her. The gases that had gathered in the hold had blown out the pump-buckets, and two long tongues of fire were creeping up behind the mainmast. The ship was at once put before the wind to keep the flames forward, and the carpenter managed to plug the barrels of the pumps and drive the fire once more below.

"We had three boats, one long-boat and two gigs. The captain and sail-maker, with seven sailors and our only two passengers, took the long boat, the second mate, with the cook, two sailors, and a boy took one of the gigs, and I with the carpenter, two sailors, and another boy took the other.

"While I was busy getting the long-boat ready, the carpenter came to me and asked if he could push off, as the second mate would not wait any longer with his boat, and the roughness of the sea put them in danger of being stove in against the ship's side. I told him to take his boat round to the lee side, and stand off till I hailed him to take me off. Of course, it was much easier to launch the two smaller boats than the big one, and that is why I waited to help with her. At last we got her clear. Her crew shouted out their good-byes, and in a minute or two she was lost in the darkness.

"Then I sang out for the carpenter, I listened for the answering hail, but none came. I got the speaking-trumpet and shouted again and again, but no sound came back out of the darkness, and then the dreadful conviction came home to me that I was alone on the burning ship.

" I couldn't believe that my shipmates had deserted me, but there was the fear that once clear of the ship, they might have been driven away too far to see her in the darkness until the flames at length broke out, and then it might be too late, I tried to go into the cabin to get a lantern, but I was driven back by the thick volumes of smoke that were now rolling out of the burning hold, so there was nothing for it but to wait for day, and that might be too late.

"While I was vainly shouting for the boat, I felt something rubbing against my leg/ It was poor Tello, as we called him for short, with his tail between his legs, his body trembling with cold and fright, and his intelligent, face looking up at me as if to ask me what was the matter.

"There was no time to be lost, and so I set about making a little raft that I could launch and float on till the boat picked me up, if ever it did. While I was busy with this, the day broke grey and dreary, and I stopped my work to have another try to hail the boat. Poor Tello seemed to know what I meant, and he lifted up his voice too, and let out a long shrill howl, and as if in answer to this, I fancied I heard a faint hail come back.

19th century woodcut of ship foundering at sea

"I listened, and it came again, this time there was no doubt, and I soon saw the welcome sight of the boat coming towards me out of the misty darkness. It was half an hour before she got alongside, and I can tell you that half-hour was a little eternity to me, but at last she came and I got a rope out to her. I saw that she was overloaded, for the men had taken far too much of their own property with them, but I had got ready a little cask of drinking-water and a half barrel of cabin biscuits to take with me on my raft, and I was determined that these should go, whatever else went overboard. As it turned out in the end, they just saved us from starvation or perhaps something worse than that.

"The saddest thing of all was leaving poor Tello behind, but it had to be done. We didn't know how far we had to go or what hardships were before us. Tello would want food and water and we had none too much for ourselves. They might be matters of life or death to us, and there was no choice, so I saved Tello the torture of a death by fire with a shot from my revolver.

"We were all dead tired with the ceaseless work and anxiety of the last night and day, and it was all that we could do to pull the boat clear of the ship through the heavy sea. We succeeded at last, and then lay to, just keeping the boat's head to the sea, by seven o'clock the flames burst out all over the ship's waist, first the mainmast, and then the mizzen went, but the foremast held on for nearly four hours longer, and at last a huge cloud of smoke and steam rushed up, showing that the ship was burnt to the water-line, and that fire and water were fighting for this the last of her. The foremast fell into the middle of this, the cloud floated away, and all that was left of our poor Adele had disappeared.

"The captain had given orders that the three boats were to keep together if possible, but the sea was too heavy for this to be done. We spoke to the other gig once, and then we lost sight of her over the big seas, and neither we nor anyone else ever saw any more either of her or the longboat.

"The first thing I did was to order everything that was not absolutely necessary to be thrown overboard to bring the boat into proper trim; then I examined the water and provisions, and found that we had two sacks of biscuits, a ham done up in sail-cloth, eight tins of preserved fruit, six of soup and meat, the half barrel of cabin biscuit that I had brought, two small casks of water holding together about sixty pints and ten bottles of red wine. That was what we had to choose our Christmas dinner out of, the third day of our voyage.

"Fortunately, the weather had become a bit warmer, though we were still constantly wet through with the spray coming over the boat. We had water for fourteen days, and food for three weeks, though unfortunately all our biscuit in the sacks soon got wetted through with salt water. The first allowance of water was one pint each in twenty-four hours, and this was not enough to keep our tongues moist during the heat of the day and leave anything like a drink for meal time. But as the days went on and no sails were sighted, I was forced to reduce the allowance first to half a pint, and then to one cupful a day.

On the 3rd of January a black cloud rose to the East, and came slowly towards us. There was no wind, so we put oars and pulled towards it. For the moment we forgot our thirst and our weakness; all we thought of was to get under that cloud and let the water that it contained fall on us. Then the oars came in, arid the sail was spread out on them, and down the water came in a regular deluge. Every drop seemed to bring us new life with it, and only anyone who has been as thirsty as we were then can know how we enjoyed the first long unrestrained drink that we had had for nearly a fortnight. Better than this we got three days' supply into the casks from the sail, and this was three days more life to us.

"On the 5th of January I gave up the search for Keeling's Island, which I had so far been trying to make, and shaped our course for Sumatra. We had already travelled over a thousand sea miles, and this was about seven hundred farther, but I had great hopes of falling in with some of the ships that would be coming from the East with the north-east monsoon.

"After cutting the rations down to the lowest possible amount I reckoned that we had still food for more than a fortnight, and water for ten days. So far hunger had not troubled us much, but thirst was a different thing. Our mouths and throats were dry, and our tongues black and swollen, and the tiny drop of water that was all that we dare take just saved us from going mad. There wasn't enough of it to relieve the torture of the thirst.

"As it was above all things necessary to keep the men employed, I hit upon the idea of increasing the sail power of the boat. Everybody gave something towards making the new sail, for we had no sail-cloth. One gave a flannel shirt, another a stocking for thread, another a coat made out of what had once been bed-ticking, and so on until we had a very respectable gaff-topsail and jigger.

"With these our boat made very good way on her course until the 8th of January, and then the wind fell to an utter calm. Day after day for nine miserable days we endured the heat of the sun as best we could, and at night rowed the boat in spells, which gradually got less and less as our strength left us. On the 17th of January we only rowed eight miles.

"Our food was nearly all eaten or else spoilt by salt water and heat, and our last little water-cask was only three-quarters full. On the eleventh day of our voyage we had opened my tub of biscuits. Forty pounds of bread doesn't sound much, and yet we five men managed to live on it for twenty-two days. It only came to a third of a pound of bread a day for each man, with a teacupful of water, so you can imagine how little strength we had left for rowing.

"Now and then a sea bird would perch on some part of the boat with no idea that it contained starving men, and some of them were caught. You can imagine what a state we had come to by the fact that the man who caught the bird had the right of drinking its blood.

"At last, on the night of the 22nd of January, we heard the sound of distant thunder, which, as it turned out afterwards, was echoed from the high mountains of Sumatra. We were now so weak that, after a short spell of rowing, we would drop off the seat, and scarcely have strength enough to get on to it again after a spell of rest. Our water was gone, and we only had food for two days.

"At two o'clock the next morning I thought I saw something on the horizon that looked more solid than a cloud, but we had been deceived so often that I said nothing about it till daybreak, and then I roused my poor fellows, who were by this time half dead with hunger and thirst and over-work, by singing out 'Land oh!' as loud as I could, and that was not very loud, I can tell you; in fact, it was little more than a whisper.

"It was wonderful to see what new strength the sight of the land gave the poor fellows. The oars went out, and they pulled the boat at twice the speed they had done during the night. The land was not Sumatra, but a high, wellwooded island, on which we found, when we landed on it twelve hours later, good water, cocoanuts, and bananas.

"We found it to be uninhabited, and so we didn't know where we were until the next morning. As we were running along the southern coastline we saw a high mountain towering up into the sky to the eastward, which I knew from its shape to be Indrapura, one of the highest peaks of Sumatra. When the sun rose on the morning of the 26th we were close to the coast, and by eleven o'clock we saw smoke rising from a fishing-village.

"This was the end of our troubles, for we found here a Malay fisherman, who guided us to Fort Anna, and there the hospitable Dutchmen did everything they could to make us at home. We were the only ones saved out of the Adele, nothing was ever heard of the other two boats, and if our voyage had been two or three days longer, or if we had had any bad weather towards the end, when our strength had given out, I don't think anything would have been heard of ours either.

"And now, gentlemen," said the skipper, as he finished his yarn, "it is time for me to turn in if I'm to have any sleep before we make the coast. Those who are up first to-morrow will get the first sight of Japan."

XI. — A GLIMPSE OF LILLIPUT

DAY had scarcely well dawned on the 17th before the skipper's prediction came to pass, and the Land of the Sun was in sight. In fact some of the coast lights had been sighted as three or four outlying islands passed during the night.

The coast-line along which we ran for the greater part of the day reminded me strongly of that of Sicily, with its green-wooded foothills running out, and forming the horns of charming little sheltered bays, backed by the rugged crowded mountains of the interior, jumbled up together as though there were hardly room for them all, and therefore divided, not by valleys, but rather by deep narrow gorges and ravines.

The likeness to Sicily, of course, recalled the snow-clad cone of Etna, and Etna at once suggested Fuji, improperly called Fujiyama, which is at once the sacred mountain and the salient feature of Central Japan. The affix "yama," I may say in passing, merely means "mountain," and while there are many "yamas" in Japan there is only one Fuji in the world, and one has not got to be very long in Japan before one learns that fact beyond the possibility of forgetting it.

19th century postcard of Mount Fuji

The Mount of Fuji is the only mountain in the world of over 12,000 feet which stands by itself, and rises symmetrically from the plain on which it stands; consequently Fuji looks a great deal bigger even than it is—at least, so I was told by those whom I had no reason to disbelieve. All that I saw of Fuji myself was a glimpse through more than eighty miles of atmosphere of white cloud, delicately tinged with opal, far away up in the sky, and only distinguishable from other clouds by the fact that it never changed its shape.

If it had not been for the bungling at Hong Kong we should have escaped the fogs, and gained another twenty four hours, and this would have given me time to have, at any rate, attempted the ascent of Fuji, and I should have done so, although it was still winter on the summit. The old Nürnberg had done her work so well that it was now a certainty that we should get into Yokohama on the evening of the 17th, instead of noon on the 18th, as she was scheduled to arrive; therefore, as the Empress did not, after all, leave on the 19th, as I had been informed in England, but at noon on the 20th, I should have had time to, at any rate, get a good view of the sacred mountain, even if I had not been able to get to the top of it.

As a rule, the presence of Fuji is rather pervasive, not to say aggressive, in the province of Tokaido you can't get away from him. Wherever you are out of doors, there, too, is Fuji, rearing his great cone up into the sky, dwarfing everything else, and giving you a feeling of absolute insignificance which those who knew told me gets somewhat irritating in time. This did not happen to me, for my first glimpse of Fuji was my last, and he remained persistently robed in envious clouds until I had seen the coast of Japan sink into the sea from the promenade deck of the Empress.

Night had fallen when the Nürnberg's anchor had found its resting-place in Japanese mud, and as I had been suffering all the passage from a persistent insomnia, which afflicted me the whole way from Hong Kong to London, I decided to try and get a long night's rest on board instead of going ashore, and possibly succumbing to the temptation of spending half the night in sampling the dissipations of Yokohama. The night's rest proved a failure, and what I heard in the morning from those who had gone ashore over night made me somewhat regret the choice.

I was, however, ashore betimes in the morning, and my first impressions of Japan, although in some respects pleasing, were not unblended with disappointment. Japan, more than any other country in the world, has suffered exceedingly from the unrestrained eloquence of certain scribes, who seem to have injudiciously trusted to its distance from Europe, and spread themselves over it with an expansiveness of imagination and a fertility of invention which makes the unwary traveller expect a terrestrial paradise inhabited by the politest of men and the daintiest of women, where he really finds an entirely commonplace country.

Like, I suppose, everyone else who lands in Japan for the first time, I went ashore expecting to find myself in a sort of flowery fairyland in miniature, where everything would be dainty and pretty, if now and then a trifle grotesque, and where at every turn the aesthetic sense would be tickled by some fresh surprise. As a matter of fact, I found in Yokohama what was practically a Continental town with an Oriental suburb.

Prettiness there was none, and of quaintness there was very little. The Japanese houses and shops fell far short of the representations, pictorial and literary, that I had seen and read, and there was a great deal more positive ugliness than I could have believed possible in the native-land of Mademoiselle Chrysantheme.

Photograph of Yokohama harbour, 1890s

In Yokohama, at any rate, the Japanese, no doubt inspired by the European residents, have sacrificed the quaint and the pretty, and have merely achieved the commonplace in exchange. Squat, awkward, and plain as they certainly are in their own garments, still those garments become them, and, at any rate, they don't look caricatures, but when, they get, into European costume, as far too many of them in Yokohama do, they look not only ridiculous but dirty.

There are really no cleaner people in the world, for, not content with constant tubbing, they half boil themselves to boot; but for all that, when their complexion, dirty-yellow or muddy-brown, as the case may be, gets into combination with a badly-cut black coat, a collar that is usually too tight, a tie of lurid hues, and a pair of trousers apparently reached down by hazard from the shelf of the slop-shop, the effect conduces to the idea that the clothes have been slept in for about a week, and that their owner has not washed for a similar period.

The women are happily here, as elsewhere, more conservative. I saw one or two of them afoot and some half-dozen of them in carriages, wearing what they no doubt believed to be the latest Paris modes. If you can picture to yourself an over-sized and not particularly well-made doll, with a dark complexion, high cheek bones, or the waxen, equivalent thereof, slanting slits of eyes, and coarse, abundant black hair, dressed for a provincial Sunday-school-sale of work, you will have a very fair conception of the Japanese woman masquerading in the habiliments of the West.

In their own costume they possess at least the merit of looking as though they had just stepped out of the centre of a lacquered tea-tray—and that's about all that I can honestly say for them. Anything approaching grace of carriage or movement is absolutely destroyed by the ridiculous foot-gear that both men and women wear. Their stockings—always white when they are not dirty—are divided so as to give the great toe a compartment to itself, and this division gives them their sole means of keeping their sandals on.

Two grass cords form two loops, running from one point at the front of the sandal to one on either side of it, and the united cords in the front are held between the great toe and the others. The sandals themselves consist either of one thick block of wood, ungainly enough not to be unlike the Japanese foot in shape, or else of a flat piece of board with two cross-pieces fastened edgeways to it.

On one of these varieties they slouch with a slippery-slop sort of movement, and on the other they totter. When they get European boots on they almost invariably get them too tight, and then they limp. The result is, the only members of the Japanese community who can move in a natural, and therefore graceful, style are the rickshaw men, the palanquin coolies, and the outrunners of fashionable carriages. Sometimes, but happily not often, they combine the European costume with the native footgear, and then the effect is painful beyond description.

19th century painting of Japanese girl

There is very little to be seen in Yokohama that is at once interesting and possible of description in the columns of a respectable paper. There have apparently been some morals imported ready-made from the West along with the new constitution, but they are such a palpable misfit that, like the Sunday coat of British respectability, they are obviously only worn for appearance sake. Morals, in our sense of the term, are not indigenous to Japan, and they don't seem to take transplanting kindly.

From the commercial point of view, however, Yokohama is distinctly interesting, Thirty years ago it was a little wood-and-paper built fishing village, in the middle of a marsh, now it is a busy seaport, with a fine protected anchorage, and a good substantial town of about 75,000 inhabitants, with handsome hotels, public buildings, gasworks, hospitals, and daily newspapers.

Most of the hotels, and especially the Oriental, where the company of the Nürnberg stayed, are built with a lavishness of space, and a consequent airiness and coolness, that is characteristic of nearly all European hostelries in the East. This spaciousness, by the way, reminds me of a piece of workmanship which shows what the Japanese can do when properly directed.

The dining-room of the Oriental was a lofty apartment about a hundred feet long by eighty wide. At tiffin (one o'clock) on the second day of our stay they had begun to strip the walls; by dinner-time, at half past six, those walls were completely re-papered. I should like to know how long the same job would have taken in the hands of the British workman.

Looked at as an Eastern town, Yokohama appeared infinitely commonplace after the luxuriant beauties of Colombo and Singapore, and the picturesqueness and characteristic, if somewhat odoriferous, Orientalism of Hong Kong. It was neither East nor West, but a blend of the two, which produced nothing that held the eye or awoke the fancy.

After breakfast on the morning of the 18th three of us took train to Tokio, the capital, hoping that there, at any rate, we should find something of that Japan of which we had read so much and seen so little. The train that took us there, like everything else that we saw in Lilliput, was only three-quarter size. The distance is eighteen miles. There are five stoppages, and the time, according to the time-tables, is fifty-five minutes. Sometimes it is more, and very seldom less.

There are clocks in Japan, but no one save the European seems to take much notice of them. The Japanese himself is a most erratic little person, and seems to think that anything within two hours is good enough to keep either a business or a social appointment.

Save in the post and telegraph offices, where they are precise and punctilious to the point of exasperation, the Japanese seem to think that rigid division of time is a mere fad of the Barbarian, and punctuality is one of the few European vices that they don't seem to have struggled to copy.

We found Tokio a good deal more Japanese than Yokohama, and also a great deal dirtier, untidier, and more odoriferous. The streets are mostly narrow, and from morning till night they teem with loitering, tottering, shuffling crowds of undersized humanity, through which the rickshaw men and vehicle-drivers go ahead at full speed without the slightest regard for the toes or the garments of the pedestrians.

There are no side-walks, and there is no rule of the road except "get there"; consequently you see cabs, rickshaws, palanquins, and open carriages, with here and there an imported dog-cart, all going at full speed, and dodging each other from side to side, apparently only escaping collision and disaster by a miracle.

When there happens to be a tram-line running down the middle of the street, as there is in the main thoroughfares, the effect is heightened. There are no bells on the horses, but the drivers have horns, which they toot with unceasing discord. If this doesn't frighten the horses sufficiently, they lash them with whips till the cars obtain a speed something like that of a South-Eastern express.

After careering along for half a mile or so, as if their lives depended on their speed, the drivers will pull up at a street corner, get down, have a smoke and a chat with anyone who happens to be standing about, and wait for the car to fill up. It may take ten minutes, or it may take forty; that makes no difference to them.

Despite all these provocatives to profanity, I must say that I never saw anyone in the slightest degree out of temper. On the contrary, everybody is polite to the point of effusiveness. If a rickshaw man charged into an elderly female and nearly knocked her off her sandals, he would put down the shafts, forget all about his fare, take off his hat, and apologise.

The old lady would pick herself up, accept his apology with what was doubtless intended for a smile, and the pair would go on bobbing and chattering and grinning at each other until it was necessary to smite the coolie over the head to remind him that he had somewhere to go to. Altogether the Japanese struck me as a singularly childish and harmless people, who had got tired of one civilisation and were playing at another.

Of course, being in Tokio, we went to the temples and tea-houses. The former were gloomy, grotesquely built structures, whose enormous roofs, carved and convoluted, and curled up in their deep overhanging eaves, looked heavy enough to crush the whole building to the ground. Picturesque they were from their very grotesqueness, but I doubt if the disciple of any form of Western architecture could honestly have called them handsome, while as for size, when compared with the stately fanes of the West, they were merely eccentrically constructed dolls' houses devoted to the worship of strange gods.

Their interiors, however, were in their way gorgeous beyond description. Nearly all the highest forms of Japanese workmanship, carving, and lacquer and metal work that the curio hunter has left in Japan are now to be found in the temples. The interiors are a maze of gold and rich colours, seen through the haze of the dim religious light.

In the Buddhist temples of Shiba there are gorgeously grotesque idols and magnificently decorated tombs of the Shoguns, or former military and temporal rulers of Japan, but in the Shinto temples we found no idols. I, however, gathered that the Shinto worship probably rested upon a philosophic basis from the fact that the female deity was represented by a looking glass.

With such of the tea-houses as I saw, I must confess that I was disappointed. They are unfurnished dolls' houses, temporarily divided into rooms by sliding panels of wood and paper. If you stretch yourself in them, you must be careful to get into the middle of the room, or to throw all the rooms on the floor into one, or else you're pretty sure to send your fist or your foot through a wall.

The floors are all covered with thick, finely-woven, and exquisitely clean grass mats, and it is etiquette to take your boots off before you go into the house. As I was conscious of a considerable hole in one of my stockings, I felt this formality to be a bit irksome, but as everyone was too polite to notice it, always supposing they did not consider it one of the fashions of the foreign Barbarian, I didn't apologise. I might also add that they wouldn't have understood me if I had, as what conversation we had with the ladies of the houses was conducted in dumb show.

The performance in each was identical with the others. We took off our shoes, went in, knocked our heads against the doorways, and hurt our toes against corners of walls, and the fronts of the stairs.

Then a room was made for us, and cushions were produced on which we squatted as comfortably as circumstances permitted, then the hostess retired, and presently there was a shuffling of grass sandal-shod feet and a small string of little damsels, not unlike the "three little maids from school," only much less engaging, sidled in, squatted in front of us, bobbed their little black heads several times, and proceeded to make tea, and hand round cakes and sweetmeats.

Every time I went through this process, I felt as if we were playing at dolls' houses and tea parties, and that some of us had outgrown the sport. Added to this, the cakes and sweetmeats were indifferent, the tea hadn't the remotest suggestion of Mincing Lane, and the damsels who waited on us were merely animated curiosities in female form, who seemed to possess no other attribute of femininity than their everlasting simper.

We got back to Yokohama in time for dinner. The *Empress* had come in during the morning, and at dinner I was introduced to the captain, who, to my disgust, informed me that the chief Asiatic agent of the C.P.R., Mr. Brown, of Hong Kong, who had promised me that the *Empress* should get to Vancouver on the 1st of May, had given him no word of instruction to hurry up the ship, or to catch the train on the 1st of May, and that more than that, the furnaces were bricked up to save coal, and it would be a twenty-four-hour job to get them ready for steaming at full speed.

I felt sure there must be some mistake, as I could hardly believe that a man in Mr. Brown's position would have made such distinct promises and then gone back on them, so I telegraphed to Hong Kong asking him to confirm his promise. He may not have got the telegram, but if he did, he lacked the courtesy to reply to it, either one way or the other, Captain Archibald was unable to drive the ship without instructions, although I offered to pay for the extra coal, and so I was obliged to be content with his assurance that he would do all he could within his limits, and trust to luck and good weather for the rest.

A beautiful glass window from one of the CPR Empress ships depicting a railway pass. (Vancouver Maritime museum).

A scale model of one of the original CPR Empress ships
(Vancouver Maritime museum)

XII. — EASTWARD TO THE FAR WEST

DESPITE the schedule that I had got in London, the Empress, instead of sailing on the 19th, did not leave until nearly two o'clock on the 20th. Thus not only was the time gained frittered away in doing nothing in particular, but I actually started from Japan twenty-four hours later than I expected to do.

One of the legendary fleet of CPR *Empress* steamers

To add to my disgust, I was also informed by the passenger agent of the C.P.R. at Yokohama, that the Trans-continental train would not begin to run on the summer time of five days from Vancouver to Montreal until the 1st of June, instead of the 1st of May as I had been led to believe. This meant the waste of another day unless I could get a faster route across the States, and so, from all I could see and hear, the ten-minute connection that I had to make at Montreal for New York was going to be a very close thing indeed.

I had not been very long on board the Empress of China before I discovered that a liberally educated imagination plays a not unimportant part in the framing of those eloquently worded advertisements which proclaim every line of ocean steamers to be the fastest, the most luxurious, and the most punctual form of ocean transit in existence. Indeed, I may say that I found this out before I got on board the Empress at all.

Just for the fun of the thing I went into the office of the *Occidental and Oriental* Company a few hours before I embarked on the *Empress*. Their route from Yokohama to San Francisco is about three hundred miles longer than that of the C.P.R. to Vancouver, but the Trans-continental train service is a good deal shorter and about a day faster. I asked the agent whether he could get me to New York sooner than the C.P.R. could, and, with an admirably-simulated air of the most absolute conviction, he said he could.

"If you travel by our route," said he, "we'll have you in New York two days before the Canadian Pacific people can land you there."

"That's good enough for me," I said. "Put it into figures, and I'll forfeit my passage in the *Empress*, and travel by your route."

Then that comparatively truthful man took his pencil and figured out the dates of the route, and promised me that I should be in New York in time to catch a Cunard boat on Saturday, the 12th of May. I thanked him for his trouble, and left, saying I would think about it. Even an American passenger agent has feelings—at least, I suppose he has—and I didn't wish to inflict needless pain by telling him that if the Empress and the Canadian Pacific Railway did their worst, barring absolute breakdown, I should still get to New York on the morning of Wednesday the 9th.

Another reason that I had for saying nothing was the fact that I knew that he knew this just as well as I did. This experience was somewhat of a shock to the small remaining faith that I had in business human nature, and so I went on board the Empress quite prepared for further shocks. If you will take the trouble to consult the advertisement folders, published by the Canadian Pacific Railway Company, you will find, among other statements, perhaps of an equally imaginative nature, the following particulars with regard to their steamers.

"They are uniformly, built of six thousand tons burden, are 485 feet in length, with 51 feet breadth of beam, and are the only twin-screw steamships on the Pacific. They are of 10,000 horse-power, have triple expansion engines, and steam 19 knots per hour."

I confess that I did not measure the Empress of China as to her length, breadth, or tonnage, nor yet had I any opportunity of gauging the horse-power developed by the engines, but I am prepared to take my iron-clad oath that she doesn't steam anything like 19 knots an hour. Allowing twenty-three and a half hours to the day, 19 knots an hour means 446½ knots a day. We had eleven full days' steaming, and the runs were, 243, 311, 360, 366, 363, 345, 330, 354, 367, 376, and 370 knots. From this it will be seen that the average speed is somewhere about 15 knots an hour.

From Yokohama to Vancouver is 4,300 sea miles, therefore a 19-knot boat ought to make the passage in nine days, with average luck. *The Empress of China* had this, and she took eleven days and a half.

I don't give these particulars for the purpose of finding fault either with the ship or her management, I do it merely as a gentle hint to the Company to put some little restraint on the imagination of the gentleman who does the literary portion of their advertising work.

The Promenade deck of an *Empress* steamer

There is no point whatever in saying that a steamer steams 19 knots an hour when her average is a good three knots under that speed, I am quite aware that the Empress boats were built under government contract as convertible cruisers in time of war, with a guaranteed speed of 19 knots, but to say that they steam this speed as passenger vessels is mere foolishness leavened by mendacity. One other word I ought to say in the interests of possible voyagers who may read these lines. Don't take one of the promenade deck cabins even if you have to pay a good deal extra for it.

I had one. It looked very nice; it was spacious and furnished in an advanced style of luxury, with every modern convenience, as the house agents say, but when I got to sea, I found it a creaking, groaning, comfortless fraud, and out of eleven nights at sea, there were only three on which I was able to hold myself in the apparently luxurious double bed; the other nights I made shift to sleep on the sofa.

The Grand Saloon on a CPR *Empress* steamer

For all this, I am bound to say that the *Empress of China* was in every respect, save one, the best-fitted boat in which I travelled. The exception was the smoking-room, and this was quite inadequate in extent, and far inferior in comfort to the one we had on board the *Sachsen*.

Another bad point about the *Empress* was that she pitched and rolled a great deal more than a ship of her size and power ought to have done, considering the weather, and when she was travelling at fifteen knots an hour she vibrated as though she was being driven at nineteen or twenty knots against a head sea. A pair of rolling chocks on her bottom, and a little more attention to trimming, would go a long way towards remedying these defects, and making her the comfortable ship that she ought to be. As she is I must say that she gives only too much provocation to unscrupulous persons, like the scoffer who sat near me at table, and wounded the feelings of Captain Archibald by describing her as a portion of the rolling stock of the Canadian Pacific Railway.

The Library on a CPR *Empress* steamer

As was natural under the circumstances, almost the sole topic of speculation among the saloon passengers was the question whether we should get to Vancouver on the 1st or the 2nd of May. Captain Archibald had promised me that what the *Empress* could do to get there she should do, but with the small coal consumption that was possible a great deal depended on good weather and good luck.

As we were running up from the spring of Japan into the winter of the Aleutian Islands it was not to be expected that the weather would improve. Added to this, it was the season for fogs on the Pacific coast of North America, and to strike one of these in the narrow waters would have been fatal. Captain Archibald, however, kept his word, and good luck did the rest. On her previous passage the *Empress* had only done 160 knots on Antipodes day—the day that is duplicated to make up the time lost in Easting; this time she made 345.

As we approached the coast our anxious look-out for fog was happily disappointed. The air remained clear, the sea became smoother, the wind went round and became fair, and Monday, the 30th of April, was so fine that everyone, from the captain to the youngest missionary on board, expected the *Empress* to make the record run of the trip.

Instead of doing this she disappointed us in a quite unaccountable fashion by only making 370 knots as against 376 on the day before. We had our last pool on the run that day, and the language in the smoking-room among the punters who had speculated on high numbers in view of the fine weather almost produced the fog that we had been dreading all along.

Cape Flattery woodcut

After my eleventh almost sleepless night I was on deck betimes on the morning of the 1st, and there, to my delight, I saw to starboard the white lighthouse of Cape Flattery, and to the left the dark pine-clad shore of Vancouver Island. The water of the Strait of Juan de Fuca was as smooth as a mirror, the sky was cloudless, and the *Empress* was slipping along at a good seventeen knots an hour.

The farther we got up the Strait the finer the view on either hand became. It was almost as though the eleven days' run had carried us from one world to another. The gorgeous colouring and the soft, dreamy splendours of the East had been left far behind, and we were now confronted with the stern grandeur of the far West.

To port lay Vancouver, a sombre wilderness of crowded pines rising from the very water's edge in rounded heights, over which hung long drifting streamers of mist, and above these again rose here and there a snow-clad peak glittering in the sunlight. To starboard the gaunt, rugged mountains of the Olympic Range raised their icy peaks above the cloud-line 8,000 feet from the surface of the Strait, across which Greater Britain and the Great Republic confronted each other.

It was only now that I gained a really clear and definite conception of the colossal size of this British Empire of ours. Since leaving Naples I had travelled some 17,000 miles, and I had called at six ports, four of which were British possessions, while the other two were, to all intents and purposes, emporiums of British trade. At Hong Kong I had left the last British outpost of the Far East, and nearly 6,000 miles of ocean had been traversed since then, journeying always to the eastward until East had become West, and here the first land we saw was Britain still, and Britain it would remain for 3,000 miles more, stretching without a break from the Pacific to the Atlantic.

Cape Flattery postcard (late 1890s)

The run from Cape Flattery to Victoria, and thence to Vancouver, is as fine a day's steaming as will be found anywhere between East and West. Most of the *Empress's* passengers had come in her through the much-advertised Inland Sea of Japan, and there was not one of them who did not agree that this was superior to it.

We reached Victoria, the capital of British Columbia, about 11 a.m., and here I was met by the first news from home that I had had since leaving London. If possible even more welcome than this was the news that the Trans-continental express had been stopped for me by telegraph from Vancouver, so, after all, I should make my connection on the 1st instead of the 2nd of May. We were detained here for about an hour landing about 600 Chinese passengers and, a few score Japanese, who had been stowed away in the 'tween-decks, and had kept themselves so close that only a dozen or so of them had been visible during the voyage. These Celestials, by the way, are a source of very considerable revenue to the Canadian Pacific Company, which clears about £2,000 a passage out of them when business is good.

For this they have to thank the American-Chinese immigration laws, for although the heathen are nominally bound for Canada, most of them manage to find their way sooner or later across the border into the States. Nearly all of them had been very sea-sick, and I never saw a sorrier collection of humanity than they were when they were turned out for medical inspection before going on board the tender.

From Victoria to Vancouver—which, by the way, is on the mainland of America, and not, as a good many people suppose on the Island of Vancouver—is eighty-four miles, and this the *Empress*, steaming her best through the glassy smooth water, covered in four hours and a half, and therefore by half-past four we had turned the sharp corner from the Strait of Georgia into the Vancouver River, and were running at half speed up into the picturesque basin on which the thriving and rapidly-growing seaport and packet station lies, surrounded by the virgin forests of the wild and woody West.

The splendid western scenery had increased in beauty as every mile was left behind. The narrow waters of the Georgia Strait were crowded with an archipelago of wood-crowned islands, with green shores dotted with white wooden house and grey-brown log-cabins. All round the horizon there were mountains rising into the sky, their lower and middle slopes clothed with dark pine forests, and their upper heights laden with snow, and seamed with the long, snaky tongues of the glaciers pushing their way down to the melting-line, where they dissolved in torrents that rolled down through great gaps in the woods, flashing in the sunlight, while dominating all, far away to the eastward, the white cone of Mount Baker caught the rays of the afternoon sun nearly eleven thousand feet above sea level.

Vancouver is a remarkable instance of British energy and Western high pressure. In May, 1886, there was nothing but trees and a few log-huts on the shores of the basin. For three months after it became the terminus of the Canadian Pacific Railway it grew with almost magical rapidity, then at the end of July a forest fire came and cleaned it right out, with the exception of a single house.

It is now a town of 20,000 inhabitants, with great wharves and warehouses, handsome hotels, churches, and schools, miles of good streets, lighted both by gas and electricity, and some meagre and shabby-looking sheds which no one would take for a terminal station of one of the greatest railways in the world.

Vancouver City Hall after the great fire of 1886

It was under one of these sheds that I found the train of cars which, as the event proved, was to carry me without a change over a distance of three thousand miles from the shores of the Georgia Strait to the banks of the St. Lawrence.

Given the connection that had now been made, I had intended to leave the C.P.R. at Pasqua Junction in Assiniboia, and travel to New York via St. Paul and Chicago, but the newspapers which we got at Victoria contained accounts of serious strike troubles along the Northern Pacific Railway, and, therefore, as no connections could be relied on with certainty after I crossed the Canadian frontier, I decided to adhere to my original route and go straight through to Montreal.

As it turned out, I could have got through the States by that route without delay, but not in time to catch a Saturday boat at New York; and therefore as nothing would have been gained in the end it would have been foolish to take any risks.

Vancouver harbour in 1886

Vancouver docks (late 1890s)

As an example, however, of the leisurely way in which the C.P.R. train trundled across the continent, I may say that a gentleman who left Vancouver with us branched off at Pasqua, travelled to St. Paul, spent nine hours there, then ran up into Canada again by the Saulte Sainte Marie line, between Lake Superior and Lake Michigan, and reached Sudbury Junction by the St. Paul and Boston express before we did.

It was six o'clock by the time we had got our baggage transferred from the steamer to the train and had booked our places in the cars. Then the soon-to-become familiar "All aboard!" sounded along the platform, the engine-bell began its monotonous, but not unmusical clanging, and as the long, heavy train pulled slowly out from under the long wood-shed, I threw myself back on the sofa of my section in the sleeping-car and consoled myself for my aching head and sleepless eyes with the knowledge that the last lap but one of the long journey was fairly begun, and that, with luck, another fortnight would see me back at Charing Cross.

In spite of the immense improvement which the more enlightened of the English railway companies have at length found courage to make in their longer trains, it is still true that he who has not taken a long journey in America has not yet learnt what the luxury of locomotion really means. America is still the only country where you can feel at home on board a train.

The great sixty-six-foot cars, nicely balanced on their six-wheeled bogies, run with an easy, swinging motion which is in delightful contrast with the jerky jiggetting of the short English carriages, and the roomy, comfortably-fitted interiors, amply-windowed by day and brightly lighted up by night, make as comfortable a resting-place as could well be imagined subject to the inevitable conditions of travel.

Painting of Burrard Inlet

Our car, the Toronto, was not one of the latest fashion, but it was nevertheless very cosy, and I had not been many hours on board it before I felt that if I could only sleep at night the journey from ocean to ocean would be by no means an arduous undertaking. For the first forty miles the train ran along the shore of Burrard Inlet and the left bank of the Fraser, a broad, smooth river flowing quietly between banks heavily wooded, and sprinkled with villages, mostly clustered round sawmills. Some of the timber grows to an immense size, and trees forty feet in circumference and a hundred and fifty in height are by no means of uncommon occurrence.

The outlook from the car was in such refreshing contrast to the interminable and unbroken range of sea and sky that we had been looking at for the last eleven days and a half, that I was really sorry when the darkness fell and the car-lamps had to be lit.

The interior of one of the only surviving 1890s CPR Pullman carriages still in existence.

(West Coast Railway Heritage Park Squamish BC)

XIII. — A WEEK ON WHEELS

As the Atlantic Express had started nearly four hours and a half late, we had to suffer two inconveniences. In the first place, we had to lose that four and a half hours of daylight running; and in the second place, we got no dining-car on to the train until the next morning, consequently my first meal in the wild and woody West was eaten in a small wooden hotel at Mission Junction, where the train pulled up for half an hour for refreshments.

Snow plough on train at Mission Junction

Considering the suddenness and the extent of the invasion, the limited resources of the weather-board hostelry, though obviously strained to the utmost, responded satisfactorily to the demand. There are no inns or public-houses out West, they are all hotels, from the palaces of New York and Chicago to the little wooden shanties of the backwoods, containing a bar-room, a kitchen, and a couple of bedrooms.

When we got back on board the car David, our porter, an affable and somewhat portly gentleman of colour, who looked after us all with an interest that was almost fatherly, had begun to make up the sections for the night, or in other words, to transform the drawing-room of the day into the sleeping apartments, of the night.

Nothing else looks so unlike itself as an American sleeping-car by day and night. From about eight o'clock in the morning to nine at night it is a drawing-room on wheels, airy and spacious, with comfortable seats and lounges running along each side. After 9 p.m. its interior aspect is absolutely changed. A long, narrow gangway runs from end to end, dimly lighted by the down-turned lamps. On either side is a wall of heavy curtains, and that is all there is to see.

Behind these curtains, where the seats and lounges were, are the broad, comfortable beds, into which they have been somehow transformed, and outside hangs a large tab, bearing the number of the berth in bold figures.

The necessity for this precaution, especially when one is strange to the car, will be apparent from the fact that there are no separate cars for ladies and gentlemen, and consequently a mistake might be disastrous, I may also add that not less wonderful than the transformation of the car by day and night was the way in which we all managed to go to roost and get up again seven nights and seven mornings without once infringing the proprieties in the slightest.

Thus, for instance, I knew that there was a young lady sleeping in the next section to mine, and yet, although we boarded the car on the evening of the 1st of May, and left it on the morning of the 8th, I never saw her either just before she retired or just after she got up. She merely vanished and appeared, and that was all. How it was managed is a mystery which I have no intention of attempting to solve.

As there is always a very considerable portion of the population of Canada and the States living day and night on wheels in this fashion. I suppose use has become second nature, and has developed the necessary amount of skill in avoiding complications which always seem imminent, and which seldom or never come off.

Unhappily for us, we spent the first night of the journey running through the splendid scenery of the Fraser and Thompson canyons, one of the most magnificent stretches of railway travel in the world, and in the early morning we were running over the twenty-mile stretch of line which skirts the Kamloops Lake, a broad, hill-girthed sheet of water which is formed by a widening into Thompson River. We were all ready for breakfast when the train pulled up at Kamloops Station, and the dining-car was hitched on for the day.

Kamloops stands at the junction of the north fork of the Thompson with the Shushwap. It is called "a beautiful spot" in the romantic work published by the Canadian Pacific Company as an itinerary. As a matter of fact, it is a collection of scattered and meagre-looking wooden houses and sawmills, lying in a very commonplace country, whose principal characteristic is a bleakness unrelieved by any pretence at picturesqueness.

For all that, it is a fine grazing country, and, where irrigation is practicable, suitable for agriculture and fruit-raising. As for the town itself, I have seen many a better second-rate bush township in Australia.

A dozen miles from Kamloops we began to get into the scenery of what I think I may fairly describe as the Lake District of Eastern Columbia, and after this, for fifty miles, the line wound in and out along the tree-clad shores of lakes, now broad and now narrow, branching away in all directions, and yet all connected one with the other, while all round the mountains rose tree-clad to their summits, save where here and there an opening between them afforded a glimpse of some snow and ice-crowned monster far away in the distance to the eastward, giving promise of the stern grandeurs that were to come.

The lakes were those of the Shushwap group, and so circuitous is the railway route in consequence of the steepness with which the mountains slope down to the very water's edge, that before the train has traversed the whole district, the headlight of the engine has faced every point in the compass.

These Shushwup Lakes and their enclosing hills must be a sportsman's paradise. The waters teem with fish, and every kind of northern wild fowl swarm in the creeks and bays, and go skimming over their surface, and up on the hills there are big and small game in plenty to keep both rifle and fowling-piece busy.

For less than a season's rent of a Scotch grouse moor, or an English shooting, a real sportsman could go out to the Shushwaps, and shoot and fish to his heart's content for a month with the added advantage of getting real sport instead of slaughter, and that too in the midst of scenery finer than any to be found in the British Islands.

As we crossed Notch Hill, seventeen hundred feet above the sea, and six hundred above the Lakes, the view from the car windows was such that one could simply sit and look at it, and wonder why on earth people who have no necessity to do so herd themselves together in sweltering smoky towns like so many sheep in a pen, and leave such a glorious region as this practically uninhabited.

Hammering the last spike at Eagle Pass Craigellachie in 1885

From Notch Hill the line runs downward to Sicamous Junction, and fifteen miles beyond this is Craigellachie, notable as the spot where the last spike was driven into the last sleeper of the Canadian Pacific Railway, when the rails from the East and West were joined on the 7th of November, 1885.

On from here, the line beginning to climb again, we ran through the wonderful, and quite indescribable, scenery of the Eagle Pass. First we skirted the woody shores of Griffin, Three Valley; Victor, and Summit Lakes, and then ran into the Pass itself. If Nature had set out in the beginning of things to stake a railway cutting on a colossal scale, the Eagle Pass is just what she might have been expected to accomplish.

For over a dozen miles the valley is never more than a mile wide, and more often than not its width may be measured by a few yards, and yet from the narrow bed along which the torrent of the Eagle River goes roaring and foaming on its way, the great mountain masses rise sheer upwards until the pines are lost in the snows, and the white peaks and ridges are lifted so high into the sky, that you can only see them from the platform of the car after you have left them a mile or so behind.

Hunters in the Selkirks (1890s)

The discovery of this Pass is one of the romances of the C.P.R.. The surveying party from the East had spent weeks in searching for a practicable opening through the enormous masses of the Selkirks, and had almost given the task up in despair, when one of the explorers (out on a hunting expedition) happened with a lucky shot to wound an eagle. He followed it up to get another shot, and suddenly the bird disappeared, although it was flying far below the summits of the mountains.

The sportsman at once scented something much more important than game, and pressed on after the vanished eagle, "blazing" the trees as he went. That night he camped out in the mountains, and the next morning he was able to guide his companions to the mouth of the Pass, which is now named after the bird that led to its discovery.

From the Eagle Pass we ran into the Columbia range, got a glimpse of the glaciers of Mount Bogbie glittering far away to the south-east, and crossed the Columbia River on a trestle bridge half a mile long. Ten miles more brought us to Revelstoke, and another dozen brought us to the entrance to the Albert Canyon, a gorge through which the line runs through perpendicular walls of rock, rising sometimes to a height of nearly a thousand feet, and in some places not more than a dozen yards apart.

At Albert Canyon Station, 2,800 feet above the sea, I exchanged my comfortable quarters in the sleeping car for a less luxurious, but more advantageous position in the cab of the engine, a privilege for which I was indebted to the courteous consideration of the conductor of the train, and the driver of "No. 405."

If I could only do justice to the experience of the next four or five hours, there would follow here about the most marvellous piece of descriptive writing that ever was put into print, but, unfortunately for a quite laudable ambition, I am forced to confess that the task is altogether beyond my capabilities of performance. No one has ever adequately described the Alps of Switzerland and Italy; no one has ever written a satisfactory description of an iceberg, and no one has even described the hills of the Scottish Highlands as they really are.

Now, if you will take the finest scenery in Switzerland, add to it the best that Scotland has to show, and then imagine, if you can, glaciers and cliffs, Alpine gorges and Scottish glens, mountain peaks soaring to the regions of eternal snow, and ravines so deep and narrow that the light of day can scarcely pierce them, heaped up altogether in one magnificent assemblage of indescribable wildness and grandeur, you will have something like the marvellous panorama that was rapidly unfolded on either side of me as I ran from Albert Canyon over the summit of the Selkirks in the cab of "No. 405."

From 2,800 feet, the train climbed to 4,300 in twenty-four miles. To look ahead it seemed absolutely impossible that a train could be taken through the snowy wastes and mountains piled on mountains that rose up in interminable terraces in front of us, but just when it seemed almost impossible the engine would swing round the spur of a mountain, often on the brink of a precipice, at the bottom of which a torrent was roaring along a thousand feet below the line. Then a little dark hole would appear in the wall of snow in front, and with a rattle and a roar the train would rush into one of the snow sheds, built up of huge balks of Rocky Mountain cedar to keep the sliding snows off the line.

Running through these snow-sheds was not the least strange part of an experience wholly strange and wonderful. Their low sloping roofs were thickly fringed with icicles; thousands of long glittering spears of ice seemed presented by unseen hands to bar the passage of the engine. Then the smoke-stack crashed in among them, and in the midst of the darkness, relieved only now and then by a ruddy glare from the furnace when the stoker opened it to throw in more coal, they came rattling down on the boiler and roof of the cab like a shower of gigantic hailstones.

These structures are one of the many unique features of the C.P.R. No less than 7,000,000 dollars was spent in putting them up, and they want renewing about every seven years. Strong and solid as they look, they do not always withstand the tremendous impact of the avalanches that sweep over them. One that we passed through had a gap in it about fifty feet wide; it had been put out a few days before by a moving stream of ice and snow and rock which had snapped the huge timbers like matchwood and carried them away down into the gorge below as if they had been so many straws floating on a torrent.

All through the most difficult regions of the Selkirks and the Rockies, the line is duplicated. There is one track for winter and the other for summer. I passed through on the 2nd and 3rd of May, and when I asked where the summer line was, I was shown a bank of snow often rising as high as the roof of the cars—the summer line was under that.

At Ross Peak Station, 8,600 feet above the sea; we crossed the torrent of the Illicilliwaet, pea-green with glacial mud, and rolling and foaming under its rocky ice-bound banks, under the shade of the colossal Columbian cedars, out of whose trunks come the great baulks for building the snow-sheds and the trestle bridges. Far away upward and Eastward was the huge ridge of the Selkirk Summit, a sharp, shining line of pure white drawn across the grey of the afternoon sky, and at one end beyond this the mighty Sir Donald lifted his bare, rock-crowned head a mile and a half into the clear, cloudless air.

"That's where we're going over;" said Driver Allen; of "No. 405," pointing to the white ridge as we drew out of the station.

" Not without flying !" I jerked out with involuntary incredulity.

And, truth to tell, it did look a literal physical impossibility that our great train of nine heavy cars, drawn by the 85-ton iron monster on which I was riding, could possibly get over that mighty wall of snow and ice, which seemed so completely to bar our Eastern way.

"You'll go over without flying;" said Driver Allen, "That's the way up yonder. That's what we call the Loop."

"No. 405" swung round the corner as he said this, and, looking ahead, I saw the result of one of the most extraordinary engineering feats in the history of railway making. The gorge widened out here to a width of about half a mile, and a long curved spidery-looking trestle bridge spanned the chasm at a height of about 150 feet, and plunged into the wall of snow on the other side.

Following its course with my eye, I made out two long, faintly-masked lines along the mountain side, one several hundred feet above the other, I confess that I held my breath a bit hard when "No. 405" rolled out on to that frail-looking structure, but there has never been an accident on a C.P.R. trestle bridge, and there wasn't one this time. The timbers creaked and shuddered with the enormous weight of the train, but that was all.

Still, I let my breath go with something like a sigh of relief when a change in the note of the rumbling roar under us told me that the great engine was once more on *terra firma*. Then we plunged into the darkness of a long snow-shed, and again the icicles came rattling down over the boiler and cab of the engine. For half a mile or so we climbed in the darkness; then a patch of white light appeared in front.

A CPR bridge near Mission Junction

"Look out as we pass there," said the driver, and as the train shot into the daylight I looked out. There was the bridge lying down below and behind us, and in front the great curve of the railway ran sloping up the mountain side, half hidden by snow-sheds, and through these, now in the dark and now in the light, we swung along round the shoulder of the mountain above an ever-deepening valley at the bottom, of which the great pines and cedars looked like little dwarf trees in a Dutchman's garden, and still on and up till we swung round yet another curve, and Driver Allen bade me look out again.

I obeyed, and found myself once more looking down into the gorge of the Illicilliwaet. The bridge, now a little toy structure such as children might have built, spanned a little brawling brook, and half-way down the mountain side was the line of the lower loop, which from below had seemed so impossible to climb.

Once more we ran through snow-sheds and over stretches of open line, suspended, as it seemed, in midair high above the limit of vegetation and beyond the line of perpetual snow, in a white and silent world of chill and awful grandeur, a world of shining, soaring peaks and mighty mountain sides, whose vast plains of spotless snow swept downwards in majestic sweeps and curves for thousands of feet, unbroken by rock or tree.

The higher we climbed the wider grew the indescribable landscape, and peak after peak came into view all round us, piercing the sky with icy summits that no human foot had ever trodden, until the solemn grandeur of the snowy solitudes became almost awful in its chill magnificence.

And yet even this marvellous region, this frigid fortress of Nature throned above the snow-line, had opened its gates at the touch of the iron sceptre wielded by the hand of clay. "No. 405" rushed through it in a most practical, matter-of-fact fashion, panting and throbbing with the stress of the gradient and the weight of the great train behind it, and in that train, warm and comfortable, my fellow-passengers were rolling along as much in their ease as they would have been in their drawing rooms at home.

One more long snow-shed had to be passed, and then the rounding of another curve brought us into the Glacier House Station, where a handsome hotel, built after the style of a big Swiss chalet, stood 4,126 feet above the sea, half buried in snow, at the foot of the Great Glacier of the Selkirks, a mighty field of green gleaming ice as large as all the glaciers of Switzerland put together, flanked by Ross Peak, Cheops, Grizzly Peak, and the naked rock pyramid of Sir Donald rising from its mantle of snow and ice nearly 10,000 feet above the railway.

Engine 374, the first train to complete the crossing of Canada, just seven years before Griffith. (Engine 374 Pavilion Vancouver)

XIV. — THE END OF THE RUN

Two miles from Glacier House Station the long climb up the western slopes of the Selkirks ended, and when we passed Summit Station, 4,300 feet above the sea, I heard for the first time the hissing of the vacuum brake, which told that at last we were going down hill. The pace now quickened up considerably, and as we had over four hours' time to make up, Driver Allen let "405" have her head a bit, and we went bowling along at a good forty miles an hour down the two-thousand-foot slope, which lay between the summit and Donald, the section station dividing the Pacific from the mountain division of the railway.

Rogers Pass - Selkirk Mountains

I may here note in passing that time on the C.P.R. is regulated in four sections of longitude, each representing an hour. Thus the same time is kept from Vancouver to Donald; then the watches and clocks go on an hour, and Pacific time is exchanged for mountain time possibly so called because you run through very few mountains during the period. At Brandon, in Manitoba, another hour is sent to join the past eternity, and mountain becomes central time. Then from Fort William, on the northern shore of Lake Superior to Montreal, you have Eastern time, which corresponds with that of New York.

As soon as we cleared the last snow-shed we ran out into Roger's Pass, a narrow cleft fenced in north and south by two magnificent chains of snow-clad peaks, rising eight thousand feet above the valley, their bases clothed with dense, dark pines, their middle slopes with snow, amidst which the pines grew more and more sparse as they gradually yielded in the struggle for existence, and their upper heights robed in glacier ice, on which the afternoon sun played with indescribable effects of ever-changing colours, while here and there, far above trees and snow and ice, a solitary pinnacle of bare black rock, towered into the sky too steep and bald for even snow or ice to find a resting-place on its hurricane-swept sides.

From Roger's Pass the line ran through a fissure between Hermit Mountain and Mount MacDonald. So narrow is the gorge which separates these two giants that a single big tree lying across the stream completely bridged it from precipice to precipice, and yet at less than a stone's throw from where the line creeps round the base of Hermit Mountain the peak of Mount MacDonald towers in a succession of almost perpendicular precipices for a mile and a quarter above the track.

We had only left this gateway between West and East a few hundred yards behind when the prospect ahead suddenly opened out, and we ran into the broad, deep valley of the Beaver, a huge elongated hollow, lying between immense masses of mountains, along the northern slope of which the line was strung like a double thread of steel on a narrow cutting, with the great snowy slopes rising a mile or so to the left, and to the right falling away for more than a thousand feet almost sheer to the bed of the creek.

Mount MacDonald Rogers Pass

Midway along this valley we ran across Stony Creek Bridge, once the highest wooden bridge in the world, and now replaced by a single arched span of steel. From the metals to the water of Stony Creek the drop is 295 feet, but it looks quite insignificant in comparison with the tremendous fall of the land from the line down to the Beaver.

From Beaver Creek we ran down an incline of 116 feet to the mile, our big iron horse swinging along in rattling style, through the gorge of Beaver Mouth, where the Beaver takes its leap between the crowded bases of the Selkirks and the Rockies into the Columbia River, and then we skirted and twice crossed the big stream of British Columbia, and after a run of about sixty-five miles through scenery to whose splendours no written words could do justice, the train pulled up at Donald.

Here I reluctantly said good-bye to Driver Allen and "No. 405," whose work for the day ended here, taking away with me a crowd of strange and marvellous impressions and a souvenir of the iron steed in the shape of a big blister on my hand, the result of an untoward jolt which threw me against the steam-pipe. I may, perhaps, add that I also took away a perfectly awful cold in the head, which made me feel the whole way from the Rockies to Montreal as though I were breaking the regulations of the company, which forbid the carriage of explosives.

Kicking Horse Pass Tunnel

We had now descended from 4,300 to 2,500 feet, and after a stop of half an hour, which the change of time made an hour and a half on our watch-dials, the train pulled out and began its last and biggest climb of nearly 3,000 feet in sixty miles up the Kicking Horse Pass to the Summit Station of the Rockies at Mount Steven, 5,300 feet above the sea.

The sun was setting behind the Selkirks as we steamed away, leaving their crowded summits bathed in a flood of ruddy golden light—a sight that has only to be seen once to be remembered forever. Then, amidst the falling darkness, we ran along the valley of the Columbia and up into the lower canyon of the Wapta, a huge chasm through which the railway runs with the river as though disputing the passage with it, crossing from side to side on trestle bridges and winding along narrow ledges, cutting the solid rock between precipices only a few yards apart, and yet rising two and three thousand feet as sheer as a plumb-line.

Then the Wapta gave place to the Lower Kicking Horse, and after a sort of breathing space along the Flats between the Ottertail and Beaverfoot Mountains, whose summits were now lost in the darkness, we ran with ever-decreasing speed up to Field Station, where we pulled up a little before midnight.

Here the train began the stiffest railway climb in the world. The distance from Field to the summit is a little under ten miles, and the difference in elevation is 1,250 feet, but nearly the whole of the rise is made in the last five miles.

I am, of course, aware that the Alpine railways make steeper climbs than this, but then the climbs are not made by trains, but only by carriages about the size of a tramcar. Here a heavily-laden train of nine cars and a baggage-waggon, each equal to two ordinary English carriages, had to be taken up a five per cent, grade that is to say, a rise of one foot in every twenty—and this is how it was done.

The train was divided into two portions; in front of the first there was an eighty-five-ton engine. At the rear of this division a 100-tonner was run up, then the rear portion of the train was coupled on to this; and then, last of all, came an iron monster weighing 110 tons. Not very far short of a thousand tons would be the total deadweight that had to be raised through 1,200 feet before the top of the Kicking Horse was reached.

The first part of the climb was easy, and the only perceptible difference was to be found in the deep sonorous chest-notes given out by the two giants who had come to our assistance; but about five miles farther on the real struggle began. The speed slowed down so that I could get off the car-platform and walk along the line over the snow that lay almost close up to the rails.

The three iron Titans sobbed and roared and strained at their work till the earth trembled with the stress of their struggle to drive the great train up the break-neck grade that lay in front of it. Every now and then the driving-wheels of the lighter engines would slip, and the weight would fall on the colossus at the rear, and gallantly did he respond to the call.

The beats of his 24-inch cylinders throbbed like pulses along the whole train, and from his iron throat he belched forth showers of sparks and clouds of smoke with roars of strenuous defiance. Then the other engines would get their grip again, and once more the train would begin to creep upwards.

Once or twice even Colossus himself lost his hold. Then the train would stop, and we held our breath, waiting for the slight backward, gliding motion that would tell that the grade had conquered the engines; then there would come a chorus of roars, mingled with deep-voiced sobs, bursting from the labouring breasts of the toiling giants, the pistons would beat passionately in the palpitating cylinders, and the driving-wheels would rip and tear round and round until the sparks flew from the rails. At last, something would catch; a creaking groan ran along the train, and then, with a steady pound, pound, pound, the giants got down to their work again, the cars moved on, and steam and steel had gained another victory over the force that sought to drag us back into the valley.

I need hardly say that the sight from the banks of the track was absolutely unique. There, in the midst of a wilderness of black gorges, sombre forests, snow and ice, and towering peaks, the long, brilliantly-lighted train crept slowly upwards like a great gleaming snake; and the three mighty engines, roaring and groaning and throbbing with their work, sent showers of sparks flying up into the darkness, while every now and then the stokers would fling the furnace-doors open, and the gloom would be shattered by a long, blinding ray of red light shooting from the fiery heart of the monster far away over forest and snow-field, glacier and rock-peak, until it lost itself in the black sky beyond them.

It was the sight of a lifetime, and one that could only be seen in that one spot in all the world; and, looking back at it now, I can say without hesitation that it was well worth crossing the world to see. At last the giants' task was accomplished, and the train crept into the Summit Station at Mount Steven.

The first thing I did was to leave the car platform, and go and pay my respects to Colossus. I have more affection for machinery than I have for a good many human beings—machinery being more reliable and less likely to go back on you—but I never looked upon a piece of mechanism with admiration so nearly approaching to absolute awe, as I did upon Colossus. I felt as if I ought to take off my cap to him and beg him accept the expression of my profound regard, but as the driver and stoker were within ear-shot, I paid my respects to them instead on behalf of their "baby," as they called him.

Then I visited the smaller Titans, and then I went to bed, as Byron describes the traveller amidst those Italian beauties which I did not see, "dazzled and drunk with beauty," and literally exhausted by the constant strain of attention and admiration to which I had been subjected for nearly twenty hours.

The next morning when I awoke from a fitful slumber, haunted by ghosts of giant mountains with spectral engines tearing wildly across them, and pulled up the blind of my section window, I found we had already reached another world. The glories and the grandeur of rock and forest, mountain and gorge, snow-field and glacier were gone, and the train was rolling smoothly and rapidly along over a boundless level plain of dusty grey-green grass, that stretched away to the horizon all round unbroken by a hillock or a tree.

The Rockies were far behind, some of their white peaks just glittering low down in the sky, like icebergs at sea, and in front of us lay for a thousand miles or more the prairie grass lands of the North-West. All the gorgeous scenery of the Rockies proper had been passed in the darkness, but I had been so surfeited with splendours that I had but little difficulty in reconciling myself to their loss.

The truth is that there is such a vast extent of this mountain country between the prairies and the Pacific that it is impossible so to arrange the running of the trains that the whole of it can be seen by daylight. If you travel westward you get the Rockies; and miss the Selkirks and Cascades, and if you travel eastward you get the Cascades and Selkirks and miss the Rockies.

The best thing for anyone who had plenty of time to do would be to travel from Calgary to, say, Vancouver, take a run by steamer to Victoria, and perhaps down Puget Sound as well, and then return to Calgary by rail. This would give him about as much of the scenery as could be seen from the line.

For my own part I must confess that after that wonderful climb up the Kicking Horse Pass, my interest in the journey across British North America rapidly declined.

For four days and nights we ran across dull uninteresting plains mostly wild waste and unsettled land, dotted at long intervals with towns that were little villages of wooden houses, bleak, scorched, and comfortless-looking, and cities that were towns, and which one always saw with dissatisfaction and disappointment, not because they ought to have been better than they were considering the time they had existed and the opportunities of their inhabitants, but because of the ridiculous over-advertising and blatant misstatement of the descriptions which one reads before one sees them.

Eastward, after about two days' travel, the wilderness of grass merged into a wilderness of forest, but, saving for the towns and villages aforesaid, it was all wilderness, though here and there vast bleak-looking farms, no doubt rich and productive enough, but sadly uninteresting, had been reclaimed from the waste around them.

After Winnipeg, which we ran through on Friday evening, and which I found to be quite a large-sized town composed of respectable, if somewhat variegated, rows of houses and shops, divided by wide streets of swamp with electric tramways running down the middle, we got into the lake country of the East, a dreary, sloppy region of intermingled land and marsh and water now bleak and bare, and now covered with sparse and forbidding-looking woods springing out of undulating rocky ground.

After Fort William, on the shores of Lake Superior—which was still covered with ice—the scenery greatly improved, but still the land was not an inviting one, save perhaps for the really beautiful smaller lakes and the torrents flowing into them, which ever and anon we passed.

This was the land of the Trappers and the Voyageurs, with whom the entrancing pages of Ballantyne, Kingston, and Butler, Fennimore Cooper, and Lord Milton have made every boy, who is a boy, familiar, and, perhaps, owing to the expansiveness of my own boyish visions, I must confess that I was a trifle disappointed with what I saw of it from the railway.

Forest fire caused by train passage in the 1890s

At the same time it ought to be admitted that a great deal of the impression of shabbiness and forlornness that the unprejudiced traveller gets in running through this region is due to the effects of the numerous forest fires which are constantly occurring along the line, owing to sparks from the engines, and which result in a broad belt of ragged land, sprinkled with blackened stumps and prostrate half-consumed trunks of trees.

Really the only notable thing that I passed between the Rocky Mountains and Montreal was a long blue roaring flame at the top of an iron pipe issuing from the earth on the west bank of the South Saskatchewan opposite the township of Medicine Hat. That flame had been burning for over nine years, night and day, and during that time had probably wasted enough energy to have run the alleged expresses of the Canadian Pacific Railway for a year or so. So much for the practical enterprise and mechanical genius of this portion of the Canadian North-West.

Bit by bit we had picked up the time lost at Vancouver, and, considering in what leisurely fashion we did it, I don't think there would have been much difficulty in picking up a day and a night as well. Still, the connection at Montreal that had been promised me by telegraph was made, and, prompt to the minute, the train pulled up in Windsor Street Station, Montreal, after its long journey of 2,906 miles from the Pacific coast.

Montreal's Windsor Station

The Delaware and Hudson Company had kindly promised by telegraph to hold their train to Albany for me, but this was not necessary. The connection which I had expected to be obliged to make in ten minutes was made easily in the twenty that I had to spare, and within that time I had boarded the train of the Grand Trunk Line, and held a Press levée to boot.

Saving the run through the great tubular tunnel-bridge across the St. Lawrence, which seemed specially designed to shut out the scenery of the river, the day's journey from Montreal to New York was in delightful contrast to the four days' run across Canada.

The trim, prosperous fauns, the picturesque heights of the Adirondack Mountains on the right, and the lovely shores of Lake Champlain on the left, with the dark background of the Queen Mountains of Canada on the opposite shore, and then the oft-described but never overlauded beauties of the Hudson River, the Pallisades, and the Catskill Mountains, made up as delightful a day's run as anyone need wish to take in the luxurious interior of a Wagner drawing-room car.

Wagner drawing-room car

New York Central Station

At nine o'clock the New York Central train pulled up in the Central Depot—which, by the way, is the only main line railway-station in New York proper, and half an hour later I was relating my experiences to the representatives of the New York Press in my room at the Grand Central Hotel, Broadway. Then I took a rapid nocturnal run through Gotham, and found it very like Paris transfigured by the breathless hustle of American life.

At nine o'clock the next morning I left Hoboken on board the *Trave*, on the last lap of my journey. I have nothing new to add to the manifold descriptions that have been written of Transatlantic passages, so it must suffice to say that at four o'clock on the morning of the 16th of May I found myself off the Scilly Islands steaming at the *Trave's* best speed up the smooth waters of the Channel. At six o'clock I boarded the tender in Southampton Water, and two hours later I left Southampton in the American special for London.

New York harbour 1890s

Norddeutscher *Trave* steam ship

At twenty minutes past ten I found myself once more at Charing Cross, blinking at the familiar scene with eyes that had not slept for nearly sixty hours, and had not known a real night's rest for thirty nights, but with a satisfactory consciousness that I had successfully performed the task that so many had called impossible, and had circled the globe in my allotted time, with just forty minutes to spare.

COOK'S EXCURSIONIST AND TOURIST ADVERTISER, MAY 21, 1894.

ROUND THE WORLD RECORD.—At the moment of going to press we learn that Mr. Griffiths, who has made a Tour Round the World in behalf of "Pearson's Weekly" (which tour was specially planned and arranged by us throughout), arrived at Southampton on Wednesday, May 16th, in this successful endeavour to beat all previous records. Leaving Charing Cross on Monday, March 12th, Mr. Griffiths travelled *viâ* Brindisi, Suez Canal, China, Japan, Vancouver, British Columbia, Montreal, New York, arriving at Southampton as stated above, and, thanks to a combination of fast steamers and happy sailing connections, made the circle of the globe in the unprecedented time of 65 days.

A RAILWAY BEYOND THE CLOUDS.

By
GEORGE GRIFFITH.

PERU being essentially the country of paradoxes and extremes—as, for instance, the richest and the poorest, the hottest and the coldest, the most fertile and the most barren of the lands of earth—it is perhaps in accordance with the general unfitness of things Peruvian that, having no roads outside the streets of its towns, it should also be the proud possessor of the two most marvellous railways under the sun.

A Bird's-eye view of Lima, from Fort San Cristobal

We in Europe have heard a good deal of late of Alpine railways, up which vehicles like tramcars on their hind legs are, or shall be, pulled or pushed by cables or ratchet-wheel contrivances up a trifle of five or six thousand feet carrying a couple of dozen persons; but this is only a sort of locomotive hop, skip, and jump to what the trains do on the two great railways of Peru. These, too, are trains with heavy locomotives, cars on the Pullman pattern, and baggage-waggons to match. The climbing that they do is quite worth talking about, for on the Central Railway, the one to which this article will be devoted, the traveller starts from the Callao

Station, eight feet above the level of Callao Bay, and when he has travelled 106 miles he is on the point of entering a long tunnel, the mouth of which is 15,665 feet above the Pacific. On the other, the Southern Railway of Peru, he will start from the beach at Mollendo, and cross a wild, arid plain 14,666 feet above sea level, and he may end his journey at the terminus at Puno, on the shore of Lake Titicaca, where the train will run him down on to a jetty alongside a steamer, in which he may make a voyage out of sight of land on a sheet of water whose surface is as high above that of the Pacific as the peak of Monte Rosa is above the waters of the Mediterranean.

Originally, the purpose of the Central Railway was as magnificent as its conception, for it was nothing less than to stretch the iron thread from the shores of the Pacific across the colossal barrier of the Andes, and then down the Eastern slopes to a port on the Amazon, whence a line of steamers would connect the port of Callao with those of the Old World—and, splendid as the conception was, it must be admitted that the most difficult portion of its execution has been accomplished; for the line, as I have said, rises from the wharves at Callao, till it pierces a 3000ft. mountain, at an altitude only a few feet short of that of the summit of Mont Blanc, and then descends again at the present terminus at Oroya, 12,178ft. above sea-level.

My upward journey on the Central line only extended as far as Casapalca, ninety-five miles from Callao, and just a little short of 14,000ft. nearer the stars.

Peru was just emerging from the throes of her last revolution; the upper portion of the line had been closed for six months, and beyond Casapalca there were still earth-slides on the metals and broken bridges that had not been repaired. Through the kindness of the Chief Engineer of the line, I was given a seat on the engine of the first freight train that went up, and I was not disappointed in my expectations that I had before me quite as marvellous an experience as I had some eighteen months ago, when I rode across the Rockies on the engine of a Canadian Pacific train.

Of course, the scenery of the foot-hills of the Cordilleras in the Southern Tropics is as different as can well be imagined from that of the Selkirks and the Rockies in the latitude of Vancouver. In the Rockies everything is on a smaller scale, and yet the scenery is far more imposing because you can see it all.

A gorge of the Rimac, showing ancient terrace cultivation.

It is only when, after considerable pondering, some faint conception of the colossal scale on which the Andes is built, begins to dawn upon you—when you see grass green and flowers blooming at an elevation from which you could look down on the highest summit of the Rockies, and when from there you see great, red-brown, rugged rock-walls rising thousands of feet above you, and above them again, the dazzling fields and pinnacles of eternal snow and ice soaring up into the sky and over-topping the highest clouds—that the overwhelming impression of your own infinite littleness and the immeasurable grandeur of these Titans of the Tropics bursts upon you with a force that leaves you, not at first appreciative, but only half stunned and dumbly wondering whether or not you have been translated into some other world whose glories your poor human faculties are unable to do more than guess and marvel at.

It was just about sunrise that we pulled out of the Desemparados Station at Lima, and ran at a very respectable speed up through the wide, gently sloping plain between two great spurs of the foot hills which a few miles farther on gradually approach each other to form the Valley of the Rimac. On the one hand was the broad rugged stony bed over which the Rimac pursues a course which is somewhat noisy at its quietest. In the rainy season, when the snows are melting and the deluges falling on the mountains beyond the rainless zone of the coast, it thunders and foams in a succession of cataracts, like the daughter of the mountains that it is.

On the other were wide expanses of emerald-green cane-fields, and beyond these the rounded, red-brown mountains rising group beyond group and range beyond range away into the dim distance to right and left and in front of us, to be crowned at last by the still invisible diadems of the Nevados of the Cordillera.

To-day the vegetation of the Rimac Valley is entirely confined to the level, but a few miles out of Lima the train brings you within sight of evidences that once upon a time it must have worn a very different aspect. As the mountains come closer together you see that they are terraced almost to their summits, and moreover, as you open up the lateral valleys on either hand, you find that nearly every one of them contains the grey ruins of a city, or town, or village, standing silent and forlorn in the midst of a brown, waterless plain upon which no drop of rain falls or ever has fallen within the memory of man. Yet once upon a time, in the days when these towns and cities were filled by a lost people, and were the homes of a vanished civilisation, the plains on which they stand were green and well watered, and verdure and flowers rose in terrace after terrace up the now leafless and sunbaked sides of the mountains, watered by some system of irrigation whose secret is as utterly-lost as are those who devised it.

A run of thirty-three miles up the valley of the Rimac, on an ever-increasing grade, brought us to Cosica, 2800 feet above the station we had started from, and here the actual climbing began. Fourteen miles further on, at San Bartolomé, we had climbed 2000 feet higher, and then we came to the first tunnel. The tunnels on the Central Railway form a distinctive feature, second only to the enormous elevation over which it passes. There are sixty-five of them in a distance of 136 miles, and fifty-seven of these are between San Bartolomé and Casapalca, a run of under fifty miles. Of course, they are not long tunnels, but they are quite long enough when you go through them on an oil engine. In fact, each of them struck me as a miniature, but thoroughly characteristic entrance to the Infernal Regions.

Out of the clear, crisp, sunlit mountain air we plunged suddenly into darkness, made visible by the fierce yellow glare of the furnace. A thunderous roar filled our ears, and a perfectly awful atmosphere, compounded of oil fumes, dense brown oil smoke, and some half-dozen strange and quite indescribable smells, penetrated to the inmost recesses of our lungs. For my own part, I never before knew what a nuisance it is to be obliged to breathe, however little you want to do so, for, to draw a single breath even through several thicknesses of silk handkerchief, felt like breathing a blast from Tophet.

In the shorter tunnels it was possible to hold our breath from end to end, and come out gasping and blear-eyed, and half blinded by the smoke and grit; but in the longer ones we simply had to breathe, and, however sparingly and gingerly we did it, the effect was enough to make us pray fiercely for the other end.

As an additional excitement, the passage of the train often shook chunks of rock out of the top of the tunnel, and, while we were holding our breath to bursting point, with heads bent down and buried in handkerchiefs, one of these would take us between the shoulder-blades, and knock out the wind that we were trying so hard to keep in. I found fifty-seven of these experiences in one afternoon about as much as I thought I should want for the rest of my life.

Another experience, which at first was a little disquieting to unaccustomed nerves, was the enormous height of some of the winding gradients on the mountain sides. For mile after mile the train runs along mere ledges of rock with nothing but a foot or so of level ground between the wheels, and a precipice which sometimes drops from 1500ft. to 2000ft. almost sheer into the valley, while on the other side another rock-wall towers to an equal or greater height, and to sit on the tender of an engine, swinging round curves, and jumping into and out of tunnels on a little ledge that seems to hang between heaven and earth, is just at first more calculated to give one the creeps than to fill the soul with unadulterated delight. But this soon wears off, and then, saving only the intermittent suffocation, one's sensations are all of wonder and exhilaration.

A "V".

It will be readily understood that a train does not climb over nearly 16,000ft. of mountains in less than 140 miles without a considerable amount of winding about and not a few devices for overcoming the difficulties of the route and the force of gravity. The most useful of these is a system of what are called "V's," and a glance at the illustration will show what these are better than a page of description. The engine has pulled the train up the grade to the right, out of the valley below. Round the corner it has been detached and run back on to the turn-table. It is just being swung round. When that is done it will come back on the down grade, back the train on to the V-piece round the corner, and then pull it along the up grade to the left. This contrivance is used in places where there is no room for a curve of the necessary radius. In this place, for instance, which, as will be seen, is not very far below the snow-line of the Andes, say some 15,000ft. above sea-level, the mountain side has been chopped away to make room for the "V." A curve would be impossible, for the mountains here form a complete cul de sac, and without the device of the " V," the railway must have stopped there.

In other parts of the line, the ascent is made by long, winding curves.

It may be worth while to mention here that the thin, zig-zag lines on the mountain sides are mule tracks, that is to say, the nearest approach to a road that the mountain districts of Peru can boast.

The railway passes through three distinct zones before it reaches its highest point at the mouth of the Galera tunnel. First there is the arid rainless region of the coast, with its valleys of brown-grey sand and its gaunt, sun-scorched mountains of red earth and black rock. Then at about 12,000 feet comes the zone of seasonal cloud and rain, with fertile tree-clad valleys and enormous mountain masses green with grass to their summits. Here there is, of course, an abundance of water, and unmistakable evidences of very extensive cultivation, which utilised every foot of ground in the valleys, and turned the mountains into a sort of hanging gardens with terraces on which the golden maize once waved and rustled, but which are now broken down and barren, and, like almost everything else in Peru, neglected and going to ruin.

Beyond this zone is another where, albeit under the Tropics, the limit of vegetation is passed. This is a region of wild, glaring wastes of sand and rubble, of huge ragged rock masses, foaming cataracts, and deep, dark mountain tarns, and around and above all is the white majesty and awful grandeur of the mighty Nevados themselves—range after range of shining snowfields and glaciers and glittering peaks, dazzling in their unearthly purity and fearful beauty, untrodden and unapproachable, the virgin abodes of a silence that never has been, and never will be, broken by the sound of a human voice, and of a winter that will never end as long as the eternal Andes stand.

A Ride to the City of the Sun.

ONE of the shortest journeys that you can take as regards time, if not distance, is from the Pacific coast at Mollendo, which is the southern sea-port of Peru, to Sicuani, which is the north-eastern terminus of the southern railway of Peru. A word or two of explanation is necessary just here. Mollendo is probably that "sea-port" of Arequipa which, in the historic pages of Prescott, you will find mentioned as the place at which Gonzalo, younger brother of the great Francisco Pizarro, "caused galleys to be built to secure the command of the sea."

Now, Arequipa, whose name in the old Quichua tongue of the Incas meant "the Place of Rest," is, unfortunately for the execution of this laudable project, a hundred and seventeen miles by rail from the seacoast and seven thousand five hundred feet above it, and there is no water near it on which you could sail anything like the largest toy yacht that is accustomed to race across the Round Pond at Kensington.

The journey from Mollendo via Arequipa to Sicuani takes three days, and the travelling is not at what we should call express speed even on a line running, say, from London to the South Coast, but if one takes into consideration the fact that the train starts from the sea-shore—the sleepers are literally laid down in the sands at Mollendo—and that before the journey is ended it has climbed up zig-zags, and round hill-spurs, over bare, brown mountains which in Europe would be more than half covered with snow; that it deposits you for your first night's rest in a large and populous city which is only a thousand feet lower than the pass of the great St. Bernard, and about a thousand feet higher than the Mont Cenis tunnel; that it will put you down for your second night's rest at a forlorn little junction named Juliaca which stands on a plain between four and five times as high as Snowdon; and that one of the stations, at which you will stop for refreshment, is the highest regularly inhabited place in the world, or at any rate the highest railway station, standing as it does 14,666 feet above the surface of the Pacific, and that your journey will end in a smiling valley in the midst of which nestles an old, picturesque, and by no means over-clean Spanish town at an altitude which in Europe would be beyond the limits of conventional or at any rate convenient life—then it will be understood by the reader who is possessed of sufficient intelligence to get safely through this somewhat involved sentence that the journey after all isn't a very long one.

More than that, the journey not only carries you over the second highest point in the world at which a steam-engine works, and past a little, undistinguished-looking tarn in the gorge of the Vilcanota, which is the true source of the longest river in the world, but by the time that the train finally pulls up on the evening of the third day at Sicuani you will find in a very few hours' experience that you have travelled from the Pacific sea-board to the end of the Nineteenth Century—and that is not a bad journey for three days.

But when you are bound for the City of the Sun, as I was, and get up the next morning early, as everyone in Spanish America does whose evening's indulgence in any way bears the test of the morning's reflection, and go out to make the final arrangements for your further journeying, you will find that this three days' railway travel has done more than take you to the, end of the

—The sea coast —

— from —

The start —

Nineteenth Century. As a matter of fact it has taken you back through a couple of centuries into the Seventeenth.

At Sicuani the traveller exchanges a really comfortable seat in a very respectable first-class carriage for the hurricane deck of a mule, astride of which he has to ride for three days more into a land which in all its outward aspects is hardly changed, save perhaps for the worse, during three hundred years of Spanish tyranny and misrule. Here too, you will also find that every pound of freight which has been brought up in the baggagewaggons has now to become part of a cargomule's load.

It is in this sense that Sicuani is the connecting link between two Ages, and so far as transit is concerned this is the same thing as saying that it is the touching point between the steam engine and the mule—that is to say between the most tractable and the most intractable means of conveyance that human genius has so far discovered.

There is only one road from Sicuani to the City of the Sun, and it lies through a succession of valleys separated from each other by passes, through which the muletrack winds up the sides of gorges between whose rock-walled slopes the River Vilcanota —soon to be known as the Urubamba, then the Ucayali, and then the Amazon—gathers up its now broad waters

— the summit —

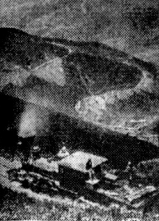

— to —

—and the steps —

into roaring, tumbling torrents, only to spread out again a mile or so further on amidst the pleasant meadows which form the floors of these oases in the wilderness. On either side of this string of valleys there is nothing but a vast chaos of mountains, tangled into ranges, and knots, and cross-ranges, bleak, barren, and lifeless—a mighty maze to which only the Indians of the Sierras hold the key.

Probably the first thing that you will do the next morning, after drinking your cup of early coffee and copy of fire-water—the Castilian tongue doesn't call Peruvian brandy aguardiente without reason—will be to enter on the preliminaries of a swindling-match with reference to the hire of the mule that is to take you to Cuzco.

Crucero Alto—the highest railway station and regularly inhabited house in the world, 14,036 ft. above sea level.

As you come out of the Hotel FerroCarril—which in English we should call Railway Hotel—and turn to the right, the first thing that will strike you after you have traversed a very unkempt piece of ground will be a mixed and more or less struggling mass of mules and humanity. Close along the goods-depot of the station is a sort of compound, a stone-paved quadrangle with a floor of entirely indescribable mud and filth, in which the arrieros or mule-train men are transferring the baggage from the waggons to the backs of their long-suffering and muchenduring animals.

The South American mule, like his NorthAmerican brother, has anything but a good character. Those who know him best like him least—and that isn't a good thing to say of anything. It is a common saying there that you may make a friend of an individual mule for ten years and do your best by him, and all that time he will be waiting for a chance to kick the life out of you, and if that chance comes on the last day of the twelfth month of the tenth year he will do it, and from what I have seen I should say that there is no libel in the statement.

But for all this there is something, to be said in extenuation for him, and of this quite a casual glance over the loading-up square at Sicuani will furnish sufficient evidence for there you will see a brute even more callous and cruel than the Peruvian mule-and that is the Peruvian arriero. You will see him roping a heavy load on to a wretched animal whose back is a mass of sores, and putting his foot against its side and hauling on the knotted, raw-hide lashing like a sailor on a rope, until you wonder how .the wretched beasts can breathe, let alone carry such a burden over the fearful tracks which lie for a hundred and twelve miles before them.

Mute as his sufferings by the way are, they must still atone for many of his sins. Moreover, the mule is here an absolute essential to commerce, and as such surely deserves a little consideration. Everything that goes from Sicuani to Cuzco, from a reel of cotton to a case of champagne, has to cross that hundred and twelve miles on the back of a mule, and all the products of the interior going down to the coast for export have to do the same.

There are no wheeled vehicles, for the simple and sufficient reason that there are no roads for them to travel upon. In short. without the mule, vicious, ill-conditioned, unfriendly beast as he is, the trade between the eastern slopes of the Andes and the Pacific coast would be impossible.

Ruins of the great Temple of Viracocha, on the Plain of Cacha. Its original dimensions were 337 ft. by 90 ft. Several villages, churches, and bridges have been built out of its ruins.

As with trade, so with travel, and therefore the first thing that I had to do the morning after my arrival at Sicuani was to find an animal. It was not very long after the Revolution, and thousands of mules and horses had been stolen by both sides and had either been killed in battle or kept by the soldiers in default of pay; hence they were scarce. Happily I was armed with a "recommendation" from the Manager of the Transport Company, and with this I secured one of the only two animals which Sicuani could just then produce. The proprietor's name was Mendoza, and should have been Barabbas. The mule was a tall, gaunt beast, with a more than usually projecting underlip, which gave him a quite indescribable expression of cynicism and world-weariness.

Our first day's journey tools us to a township called Checacupe. The tracks followed the banks of the Urubamba almost constantly, and we passed from valley to valley, each one greener and more pleasant to the eye than the last, and more and more plentifully dotted with haciendas and villages. On either hand the great brown mountains towered up bare and barren, but still marked with the terraces which, in the days of the Incas, were green and golden with crops of maize and bright with variegated flowers.

It is while riding through this series of valleys that one becomes sensible of that peculiar charm of Peruvian scenery which overcomes all the difficulties and discomforts of Peruvian travel, and exercises a sort of spell which years afterwards makes you want to go back. It is the ever-present contrast between the oasis and the desert—the mountain, brown, bare, and barren, and the valley, green and fertile, and laughing in the same sun light which makes the hills look so lifeless and forlorn.

A few miles on mule-back from Sicuani is, as I have said, the equivalent of a time excursion through two centuries. When you take the turn in the winding road which hides the railway station from you, you are back in the seventeenth century. In the white-walled haciendas which stand on the lower slopes of the hills, embowered in a prodigal wealth of foliage, the remnant of the old proprietors, of the descendants of those of the old Conquerors who settled upon the soil, are still living in exactly the same style as their ancestors of two hundred years ago, saving only for the difference between prodigal wealth and a very great difficulty in making both ends meet.

"There they live in their great rambling, white-walled houses, most of which date from the times either of the Conquerors or the Spanish Viceroys, the days when the land teemed with gold and silver, and the now forgotten system of Inca irrigation still clothed the hillsides with verdure. In those days the chain of valleys which stretches from Sicuani to Cuzco must have looked very different to what they do now, although the houses and churches are so solidly fashioned —many of them are founded on the old Inca temples and palaces, and even built out of their ruins—that they are practically the same today as they ever were.

When you get into the towns, or close to some of the great haciendas, you see unmistakable signs not only of ruin and neglect,

but also of hopeless poverty, which, to some extent, makes that neglect inevitable. French and German bounty-fed beet-sugar has done for these valleys what it has done for our own West Indies, and the dwindling canepatches are now grown chiefly, for the purpose of making chacta, or cane-brandy, which is decimating the unfortunate Indians even faster than the Peruvian method of conducting a general election with Maxim guns and Mannlicher rifles.

The population of these valleys must at one time have been very considerable even under Spanish rule, for, as you follow the mule-track as it climbs up the mountain sides and round the hill-spurs, and ever and anon dips down into the next valley, to rejoin the broad, shallow river, you see hacienda succeeding hacienda, and village and town following each other every two or three leagues or so; but many of the old quadrangular mansions have been turned into granaries and brandy-mills, and half the houses of the towns are empty, or only occupied by a few wretched Indian families.

The fighting face —

It is no uncommon sight when riding through these pueblos to see a white, massive archway surmounted by the arms of some proud family of Castile, leading into a courtyard ankle-deep in rubbish and filth, and surrounded by the spacious chambers of what was once a mansion and is now only a rookery in which a score of families herd together in listless idleness and hopeless poverty.

Sometimes you will see one of the hillspurs crowned by the ruins of an Inca palace or fortress, and on the slope below it the remains of a stately pleasure-house of one of the lordly old Conquerors—ruin looking down upon ruin, emblems of the fate which has befallen both conquerors and conquered. The roads are perhaps the most villainous in the whole world, but here and there you come upon fragments of that wonderful paved causeway which once ran for hundreds of miles, north and south, from Cuzco through the Sierra region, and along which the gorgeous monarchs of the Land of the Four Regions were borne in their golden litters, escorted by long trains of warriors and princes, through the silent throngs of their adoring people. But this, like everything else in the interior of Peru, has fallen to ruin. The Spaniards and their Peruvian descendants, being too lazy to work quarries themselves pulled up the stones to make the foundations of their adobe houses and churches.

The Spaniards, it is true, did build some splendid bridges for military purposes, as the suspension bridges of the Incas were too frail for cavalry. But a ford is quite good enough for the modern Peruvian, so these, too, have gone to wreck and ruin, and, as a rule, all that is left of them are two piers and two or three huge fragments of concreted masonry lying in the river bed. The Peruvian never repairs anything unless it is absolutely unavoidable, and in the whole 112 miles I can only remember crossing one stone bridge that was in a decent state of preservation.

As we rode on from bolson to bolson the mournful evidences of the vanished Inca. civilisation became more and more frequent,, and towards the afternoon of the second day we rode out into the broad green plain of Cacha, on which stand the grey ruins of the great temple of Viracocha, which was one of the most splendid and famous buildings in the land.

Its walls of polished stone once inclosed a space 337ft. long and 90ft. broad, but, as usual, Spanish laziness and vandalism dragged the splendid structure to pieces for the sake of its stones. Several churches and two or three bridges, as well as nearly the whole pueblo of Cacha have been built out of them, but there still remains a huge broken wall some forty feet in height. It might perhaps be better described as a series of pillars or piers about twenty feet wide and eight feet apart.

— of the great Inca fortress.

There are twelve of these still standing, but the whole of the triangular plain or terrace, about a mile wide, from which the pillars rise, is thickly covered with foundations and remains of buildings, which were no doubt the houses of the priests, the convents of the sacred vestals, and other splendid adjuncts to the shrine of the fair-haired, blueeyed god. Even to this day his memory lives among the degraded descendants of his worshippers, and it is no uncommon thing for a traveller from the far-off north with fair hair and skin and blue eyes to be greeted with the words, "Tai-tai, Viracocha !" A few leagues on from Cacha the mountains come together again, and the river gathers up its broad waters and rushes in a torrent through the narrow gorge; the rising path winds through a wilderness of ancient ruins, and in the next valley it runs round the hill-spur on which once stood the fortresstown of Quijijana. All round this little valley are cliffs pierced with rock-tombs in which thousands of the old inhabitants must have found their last resting-places. The painting on them is still visible in places, and the colours look as bright as though they had only been laid on a few months ago.

Out of this valley the road rises sharply up the mountain sides on the left hand and at the very top of the ridge skirts a strange lonely lake whose dark smooth waters must be something like 13,000ft. above sea level. It has no apparent out-let, but it has a story which makes the traveller look over it with more than common interest, for this is the Lake of Urcos, in which, as the old tradition tells us, the fugitives from Cuzco sank the great Golden Chain of the Incas. If we may believe the tradition, the chain was as thick as a man's arm and no less than a mile long.

After passing through the forlorn, disreputable village of Urcos the road dips sharply down again into the broad and pleasant valley which well deserves its musical name of Andahuaylillas, where we spent the night at the Hacienda Pocuto—an old-world mansion which I would fain stop to describe in some detail did space permit.

After Andahuaylillas, which we left soon after daybreak, the ruins of towns and fortresses became more and more numerous, for now we were fast approaching the heart of the ancient empire of the Incas, and at length, about midday, an upward turn in the road brought us to the still huge remains of the great fortress-gate of Piquillacta.

Here, as is believed, the actual domains of the first Inca began. The valley narrows to a width of about fifteen hundred feet, and is fenced in on either side by high cliffs, and from side to side runs a huge wall, nearly a thousand feet long. It is pierced by two broad gateways, faced with massive and beautifully dressed stones, cut with such precision that, although no mortar was used, they are still perfectly in position, after standing for, perhaps, eight hundred or a thousand years.

The wall was once crowned by two lofty pyramids, or watch towers, which have been destroyed for the sake of their stones; but the mighty fortification is still some thirty feet high, and more than twenty thick. One of the gateways is choked up with brushwood and fallen stones, and the path through the other is very different to the smooth, level causeway of former days.

As you ride through it you come upon some fragments of this, and as you look about you, you see proofs on every hand that you are now in the very heart of Inca-land. The beautiful valley which stretches out green and sunlit before you is the bolson of Oropesa, the next to that of Cuzco itself. To the left is the Lake of Muyna, once inclosed by flower-strewn terraces faced with stone. On the hill-slope above it are the thickly scattered ruins of one of the pleasurecities of the Incas, and, now as you ride along, you scarcely see a hill-spur that is not crowned by the hoary remains of a fortress, a palace, or town.

All about you, too, are evidences of the most laborious and skilful cultivation of terraces and water-courses, now broken down, choked, and dry—pitiful remnants of the civilisation which flourished here before the blight of Spanish cruelty and Spanish sloth fell upon the land.

Inca burial tower, built of dressed stone so perfectly fitted that no mortar is needed.

The bolson of Oropesa ends in the narrow pass of Angostura, which, in the old days, must have been very strongly defended, for all the heights about it are covered with the ruins of massive walls and broken towers. This is the last of the passes, and the downward pathway from it leads through the villages—or rather towns—of San Sebastian and San Jeromino, inhabited by the Ayllos, or descendants of the old Inca nobility, tall of stature and still proud of carriage, with the red flush of the Sacred Blood showing through the olive-brown of their cheeks.

Here, too, is the last ford of the river, which we cross once more for about the fortieth time, and when we have climbed the steep bank on the far side we find ourselves on a broad, level. grassy plain, once the Plain of the Oracle, on which the picked regiments of the Incas were wont to perform their war-like exercises, and where the festivals of the Sun and the Moon were once so splendidly celebrated, and across this, some couple of leagues away, we see, nestling at the foot of its guardian hills, and still looking white and stately, and beautiful in the enchantment of distance—soon to be miserably dispelled as we enter its mean and filthy streets—the capital of El Dorado that was, Cuzco, the once golden and glorious City of the Sun.

A Paradise of Tomorrow

From the Arctic Regions to the Tropics in a journey of five days, on what an American fellow-traveller of mine described, with as much accuracy as picturesqueness, as the hurricane deck of a mule, is a succinct and correct description of the trip from Cascapalca to the Perené District, which immediately followed the ride on an oil-engine from sea-level to a considerable distance beyond the clouds, which I attempted to describe in a former number of this magazine.

The Galera Pass

As readers of that number will probably remember, the railway was closed then beyond Cascapalca (ninety-five miles from Lima, and fourteen thousand feet above sea-level) on account of the revolution which had ended a few days before I left the Peruvian capital. In consequence of this, the muleback journey had to be begun on the Western instead of the Eastern side of the Cordilleras, and this meant climbing along a track, which, I think I am justified in describing as one of the most villainous in Peru, which is the same as saying one of the worst in the Solar system.

It runs out of the valley in which the town of Cascapalca and the silver works of Messrs Bakus and Johnson lie over the Galera Pass some thousand odd feet higher than the famous railway tunnel, which is equivalent to saying nearly seventeen thousand feet above the now far off waters of the Pacific.

It would scarcely be in order to describe a trip beginning at such an elevation as this without saying something on a subject which for his or her own sake, will, I trust, be absolutely strange to every reader of this article. This subject is sorroché.

Sorroché, so far as a fairly comprehensive acquaintance with the ills that flesh is heir to enables me to speak with anything like authority, is the one malady that is worse than sea-sickness. Its other name is mountain-sickness. But neither in Spanish nor in English does its name convey any idea whatever of its multiplied abominations.

Physiologically speaking, it is the result of changing your elevation too quickly. That does not sound much, but it means a great deal. At sea-level or thereabouts, every square inch of body-surface bears, as most people are supposed to know, an atmospheric pressure of, say, fifteen pounds. This pressure balances exactly the expansive force of the fluids and gases of which the human organism is very largely composed.

We don't know anything about it save in the theoretical sense because the balance is so exact. The full grown man walks about unconcernedly with a pressure of something like seventy-five tons enfolding him in its imperceptible clasp: but when it begins to be taken off to any extent, the matter is far otherwise.

At seventeen thousand feet, the fifteen pounds per square inch is diminished to about eight, and the proportion of oxygen in the air has come down to about thirty or thirty-five per cent. The combined effects of the reduction are anything but pleasant. The skin puffs up as though air had been blown in underneath it : the eyes bulge out as though they would start from their sockets the roots of one's hair seem loosened and the scalp rising from one's skull.

The most trifling cut or the smallest puncture is not only distressing but dangerous, for the blood, relieved of so much of the controlling pressure, spurts out like water from a prick in a hose-pipe, and if you are what is called of a full habit of body blood will flow of its own accord from eyes and nose and ears. Respiration is carried on by means of a series of quick, choking gasps, and the heart pounds away wildly in its efforts to pump the expanding and half-oxygenated blood through the veins. The slightest exertion brings you up in a moment, gasping for breath and trembling in every

The divide of the Cordilleras.

joint, and your brain, under the spur of the swift-flowing blood, plays tricks that make reason reel upon her throne.

That is sorroché, or as near to its diagnosis as I can get; and when a wanderer has got it riding through the fearful solitudes of the Upper Andes, be only needs one thing more to complete his misery of mind and body, and that is the sight of the bleaching bones which lie scattered by the wayside, all that the condors have left of men and animals that have dropped down to bleed or starve to death, or to be frozen, as they may be in an hour or so by the terrible winds which sweep through the passes and over the bleak and lifeless plateaus from the glaciers and snowfields of the mighty mountain chains which tower to the skies on every hand.

From Cascapalca to Oroya by the muletrack, is a ride of about forty miles, beginning at fourteen thousand feet, crossing the head of the pass at nearly seventeen thousand, and ending in a desolate nook twelve thousand feet high, buried amidst bleak masses of rock separated by valleys and slopes, covered fairly well with grass, but utterly treeless, and with no other signs of life than here and there, a wretched hut of rough stone and clay, a herd of llamas, or a still rarer mule-train.

The Galera pass, is, I believe, the highest in the world that is practicable for animals, and yet it does not reach the line of perpetual snow. In fact, when I crossed it, the scanty herbage was green beside the road, and the lake of Corachura, a little of which can be seen in the illustration, was free from ice. As the surface of this lake is over sixteen thousand feet above sea level, I should think it safe to say, that it is about the highest unfrozen lake known, or unknown, to the geographer.

I am loth to attempt even the most sketchy description of the scenery of this portion of the inland ride, since there are literally no words that could convey any fairly adequate idea of the colossal scale on which Nature has worked in these regions, lying, as it were, between earth and sky; of the unearthly loveliness of the sky-piercing snow-peaks and ice-fields, of the sombre grandeur of the tremendous masses of rock upon which they are poised; of the illimitable distances of vision that are made possible by the incomparable purity of the atmosphere, and, perhaps above all, of the awful loneliness and desolation, in the midst of which man feels himself a stranger and an intruder in a region which Nature seems to have chosen for herself as the home and the throne of her sternest and most solitary majesty.

This, at least; was the impression forced in upon my mind during that long and weary, and yet most marvellous, day's ride, and, as though no element was to be wanting in the scene of unspeakable grandeur, a furious thunderstorm broke out just before nightfall, and the darkness came down upon such a vision of fearful splendour as could only be realised by one whose good fortune it had been to see it.

But the next day, though the first few hours of the morning were spent in crawling over a howling wilderness of bare rock and loose stone, took us literally from the desert to the gates of Eden. Gradually the grass began to grow greener and thicker in the lower parts of the valleys, and soon we were riding past patches of golden, rustling maize.

Then shrubs and trees began to cluster round the more sheltered pools that opened out in the course of the noisy brook, which, beginning far away up under the snow-line of the Western Cordilleras, wanders through pleasant valleys, gloomy gorges, broad grass-lands, and almost illimitable forests, until it loses itself in the mighty flood of the Amazon, to form part of its tremendous tribute to the Atlantic.

Farther on the road, ever descending, sometimes more steeply than is pleasant, the climate and the vegetation, first of Scotland and then of England, are reached, and the familiar trees and shrubs and flowers begin to show themselves on the unfamiliar hillsides. Then the road takes a sudden turn, and it passes at a somewhat sharp incline between two steep, rocky hills, each crowned with the remnants of an Inca fortress, for this is one of the outposts of the now vanished empire of the Children of the Sun.

As the road winds on through the valleys, the air becomes warmer and softer, the sky bluer, and the earth greener. The snowy giants of the Cordilleras have vanished into their remote solitudes; but still on either hand, rise great rounded mountain masses, five and six thousand feet above the roadway, and along their steep, smooth sides, the eye ranges for miles and miles without interruption; and every here and there, far away up in the sky, apparently beyond the reach of human hands or feet, a tiny bright green patch shines out amidst the grey brown of the mountain sides, marking the maize-fields which the toilful Indian, dispossessed of the valleys that were once his own, climbs up to plant beyond the reach of Spanish sloth.

A turning point on the way.

The day's ride of some five-and-thirty miles ends in the delicious Vale of Tarma, which lies 9,800 feet above sea-level, surrounded by lofty mountains, green from base to summit, save where they are crowned by cliffs and soaring pinnacles of rock.

Embosomed in

trees of exquisite foliage the town of Tarma lies in the midst of its level valley, surrounded by fields that are always green or golden, and gardens in which the flowers bloom for ever and the fruit is ripening on the trees all the year round. For in this much-favoured spot there are no seasons save one, and that is eternal spring, warming in July and August into a brief summer, distinguished only by two or three degrees of temperature from the spring, into which it imperceptibly fades again. The crops can be sown at any time in the light, rich, volcanic soil, and sowing, and ripening, and reaping, and harvesting, all go on together, governed only by the pleasure of the husbandman.

The rainfall is only about fourteen to fifteen inches a year, but the streams from the mountains are perennial, and so the rivers never run low and the irrigation canals are always full. But, bright and beautiful as this Eden is, it is not all a paradise, for the curse of Spanish sloth and misrule has fallen heavily upon it.

The Indians, hopelessly degraded by their three centuries of servitude, herd together in mud huts of unspeakable filthiness, and you cannot ride half a mile along the Vale of Tarma, or for fifty yards through its streets, without meeting some poor wretch, ragclothed and filthy, and hideous beyond description with leprosy and elephantiasis. From Tarma, the road to the Montana lies through the gorge Of the Chanchamayo, a long narrow valley hemmed in by almost unscalable moumains along the sides of which the narrow, stone muletrack alternately dives through long, dark tunnels hewn through impassable cliffs and zig-zags in and out of the side gorges, often climbing so high that from such a turning-point as is shown here you may look down more than a thousand feet over precipices of rock and a dense tangle of vegetation to the narrow white band that lies along the bottom of the gorge, whence a distant murmur rises to remind you that it is a torrent and not the brook that it seems.

By the end of this day's ride, you have passed through the temperate zone, and at night you will sleep on the borders of the Tropics. The afternoon of the next day brings you to what might well be called the Gate of Paradise.

Here the great gorge of the Chanchamayo narrows to a few yards. A huge dome-shaped hill rises abruptly before you, clothed with dense and gorgeous vegetation, from the torrent at its base to the clouds which often hang about its summit. This is the Pan de Azucar, or Sugar Loaf, and round its base the track winds along a rocky ledge with the mountain wall on one side, and on the other a boiling flood, roaring and raging over huge boulders.

This passed, you are in the tropics. The warm, moist air is heavy with the scent of flowers, tree-ferns droop over the water's edge, and great, slender-trunked palms tower high above the dense undergrowth. The red rock-walls of the valley are covered with flowering creepers thickly interlaced and festooned with orchids, and every now and then you have to lean down level with your animal's neck, as the road passes under a canopy of verdure, whose thickness for the moment shuts the sunlight out. As the swift dusk falls, myriads of fireflies flash their golden lights out of the green glooms of the forest, and the humming and singing of insects mingle with the roar of the torrent.

By the time you unsaddle you have cleared the gorge, and the next morning you will see the sun rise over one of the loveliest lands of earth—a land of broad, swift-flowing rivers, of wide fertile plains, and great, forestclad mountains rising to the clouds, and beyond them, green with abundant rains, and yet bright with eternal summer; an Eden in which there is neither disease nor poverty, where the generous earth repays the lightest labour with increase many hundredfold; for this is the paradise of the Chanchamayo and Perene regions, and for hundreds of leagues north and south and east its valleys and plains and mountains, so far scarcely touched by the hand of industry, and in great part even untrodden by the foot of discovery, lie in their almost virgin beauty, waiting to be made the homes of the millions who will one day delight in them, when the hand of a just strong rule shall have put an end to the sloth and savagery of the Peruvian and the Indians, who are either his slaves or his untameable enemies.

But for the curse of Spanish-American corruption and mis-rule, this paradise of tomorrow might well have been a paradise of today. The railway would have been brought from its eyrie among the mountains of Oroya, over the wilderness into the Vale of Tarma, and thence through the Gorge, out on to the broad valleys and plains of the Chanchamayo and the Perene, past the point where the Cascades of the Perene river make navigation impossible, and there the iron-way would join with the water-way, as some day no doubt they will do.

Then, on the wharves of some city of the future that will stand on the banks of the broad Ucayalé, the train from the Pacific will run alongside the steamer from the Atlantic, and the products of the East and West will be exchanged in the markets of the metropolis of one of the richest and fairest lands of earth, a land which now, for the most part, is lovely only in its magnificent wildness, and rich only in its splendid possibilities.

The Gate of Paradise

THE MOST MAJESTIC OF MOUNTAINS.

THERE is nothing like the close contemplation of a big mountain—a really big one, not a trifling excrescence of four or five thousand feet—to bring a man to a proper sense of the perspective relationship between himself and the world he lives in. There is nothing, in a word, that will bring the thermometer of his self-conceit down with such a sudden run, especially when he sees a veritable giant for the first time from a near and advantageous point of view.

A dweller in cities, who has never stood face to face with the unrobed majesty of Nature, is prone to think himself, even in a physical sense, a very considerable item in the economy of mundane things, but bring him suddenly within fair view of such a mountain as El Misti, seen from the verandah of the Observatory at Arequipa, and straightway into his soul, if, peradventure, he has one, there will rush such a sense of his utter littleness, that he will begin to wonder why the same Creator, who could make a thing so mighty and so marvellous, should have taken the trouble to create such an insignificant atom as himself.

Nothing hides or takes from the austere majesty of El Misti's splendid nakedness. Before you is a deep, wide valley; beyond that a rugged, slightly sloping plain, and from this his mighty bulk rears itself, bounded by two long, straight lines which meet in a gleaming point of snow, dazzling white against the blue beyond, more than twelve thousand feet aloft. Between the lines, there is nothing but great, gaunt precipices of bare rock, and vast, smooth fields of black, volcanic sand. No forests cluster round his base, and neither ridge nor valley breaks the contour of his sombre symmetry. Sheer up from the earth to the sky he towers in naked, unflawed majesty, perhaps the most perfect example of the pure volcanic cone in the world.

It takes two days to make the ascent from Arequipa, which itself stands nearly 8000 feet above sea level. I had the privilege of the conduct and company of one of the assistant astronomers of the observatory, whose duty it was to take the readings of the instruments at the different stations that have been established between the observatory and the summit.

As this gentleman was that day making his forty-sixth ascent, he naturally didn't think so much of it as I did. As for me, there was something in the vast black bulk of the mountain so near to me, as my mule crawled mile after mile and hour after hour round his base, which seemed to stupefy me with an utterly overwhelming sense of the sheer majesty of Size and Shape in concrete form. I could not think, I could not even admire save in a dim, dazed sort of fashion. My eyes mechanically followed the long straight lines, and wandered over the vast black, smooth slopes, but that was all. My mule could have done as much, and I, just then; could do no more. I was mentally paralysed. I learnt the reason of this later on. It was all in the point of view. While you are climbing a mountain it is your master. When you have got to the top you have conquered it.

The first day's work consisted of a slow and weary ride of thirty miles over villainously rough tracks and wildernesses of black burning sand under a sun which from year's end to year's end is seldom or never dimmed by a cloud. At twelve thousand feet, on the old Puno Road, my companion took his first readings; our beasts were taken to water, and we made a late and light lunch of sandwiches and the red wine of Moquegua—it is well to be modest in eating and drinking when you are going nearer than usual to the stars, lest the terrible mountain-sickness takes you and you find reason to wish that you had died somewhere lower down.

From here the real climb began, and there was four thousand feet of it to do before supper and sleep. It was here, too, that the journey ceased to be merely wearisome, and became toilsome—between which there is, perhaps, even more difference than there is distinction. Every few hundred yards of the winding way it was necessary to climb down and lead the mule over ticklish places or round the corners of rock-spurs which even a South-American mule could not be safely expected to negotiate with a load on her back.

A very little of this sort of work goes a very long way with the average man, and, the higher we got the more often I sat down to get my breath, and ask the mule what she thought of it. This is not a confession of weakness. It is only a way of stating the fact that, when you are between fifteen and sixteen thousand feet above the sea, there is a good deal more hard labour in scrambling twenty yards over rocks and loose stones and sand, than there is in running a couple of hundred yards at full speed at a normal elevation.

I have bound corn-sheaves after a reaping machine from dawn to dusk of a blazing Australian day, but I don't think I ever put as much hard labour into six hours as I did in climbing that four thousand feet—with the assistance of the mule. Without it, I might have taken the rest of the mountain for granted, and, like some other mountaineers, just gone back and talked about it.

The mountain mule

Thanks to the mule, whose portrait I think it only proper to introduce here, I was not more than three hundred yards behind the astronomer when he and José reached the door of the roughly built but just then most homelylooking hut —half stable, half living and sleeping room —which stands on the eastern slope of the mountain, just sixteen thousand feet above the Pacific coast, which lies over a hundred miles to the westward. Our thirty-mile ride had thus brought us half-way round the bulk of El Misti, and eight thousand five hundred feet nearer to the stars.

So far, I freely admit, I had been too busy attending to my breathing and other pressing physical concerns to pay much heed to the marvels which had all the time been multiplying about, or, rather, beneath me. But when I was able to sit down on a big stone by the door of the hut, and accumulate a sufficient reserve of wind to keep a pipe going, I looked about, and—no, I have honestly tried to translate the unearthly beauty of that nightfall into something like adequate verbal description, and I have failed. There are times when Nature reveals herself, but does not permit herself to be described, and this was one of them.

The halfway hut.

I am not in the least ashamed to say this. Byron tried to describe Mont Blanc, and failed. Who am I, that—sitting a few hundred feet higher than the utmost peak of the Alps, with that black cone towering four thousand feet above me, and with the unscaled heights of Charchani and Pichu-Pichu rearing their snowy crests five thousand feet higher on either side of me, and with range upon range before me rolling away into the dim twilight distance, and breaking here and there into foamcrests of snow and ice—I should try to precipitate all those visual miracles in the poor little testtube of printed speech?

That night I ate and slept higher than I had ever done before, and I did both well. No other machine has such a marvellous faculty of adaptation as the human system. A couple of months before I had slept in a bed whose four legs stood fourteen thousand feet above sea level, and my sleep was like a vivid dream of Purgatory. This night, after a good supper of tinned beef, bread, and cocoa as hot as the diminished atmospheric pressure would let us get it, I lit a pipe and went outside to look at the stars, hanging so low down in the firmament that it seemed as though I could see behind them, and then I crept into my sleeping-bag and slept. That is to say, I shut my eyes, drew one long, satisfying sort of breath, and woke, hearing the astronomer telling me that it was morning. I wriggled reluctantly out of the bag, pulled on my long, Norwegian, reindeer-skin boots, and wrapped a thick poncho round me—one puts off the early morning wash at sixteen thousand feet, and 4.30 a.m. and went out. To me it looked like such a morning as Adam might have seen from the top of a hill in Paradise. In the mingling of the growing light and the waning darkness the world below loomed up, not quite without form and void, but like an infant Cosmos new-born from the womb of chaos. Above, the low-hanging stars were fading from gold to silver, and far away to the east the horizon was brightening from silver into gold.

Twenty-five miles away towards the sunrise Urbinas, the satellite and safetyvalve of El Misti stood, seeming to support a vast aerial island of level-hanging smoke whose upper surface I could just see across, and over this the coming sunbeams streamed, changing it from black and brown to gold and rosy red, and then-it doesn't take long for the sun to rise in seventeen south of the Line—the sunbeams leapt from peak to peak and range to range of the snow and ice-crowned Cordilleras, the nether world rose in a moment out of darkness into day, and then the astronomer called me in to breakfast.

It took, if I remember rightly, five hours for the laborious, all-enduring mules to make their winding way up the other three thousand three hundred feet—to be quite accurate—to the top of the crater wall.

Here in the midst of the broad snow-field which had looked such a tiny little white patch from the city, we dismounted. The astronomer took the readings of the most elevated set of meteorological instruments in the world*—all I gathered from the process was the fact that the barometer marked somewhere about fourteen inches, and that, therefore, about half the earth's atmosphere, measured by weight, lay below us—and then we had lunch, and after that I joined El Misti, who was also smoking, in a pipe. If I ever eat a more elevated meal, or blow a more supra-mundane cloud than that, it will be in another world, which, in more senses than one, is, I fear, a trifle problematical.

The crater of El Misti

* The whole of these instruments were stolen a few years ago. The priests taught the Indians that they were used for unholy purposes, and would make El Misti erupt, and cause another earthquake. The Indians took the hint, and the apparatus vanished.

The view? No! Once more I must confess that I am not equal to the task. Imagine yourself perched on the top of a craterwall nineteen thousand three hundred feet above the level of the sea, in an absolutely cloudless and transparent atmosphere, through which the eye wanders until, like a traveller along an endless road, it is wearied out and daunted by an infinitude of distance; and, if you can do this, you will see more than I can make you see through the medium of many pages of necessarily inadequate description. If it be true that words were given to man to conceal his thoughts, it is also true that there are times when he can find no words to express them without doing them violence.

It was now that I found that the sense of the paralytic mental depression that had afflicted me on the way up was merely due to relative position. Comparatively speaking, I was something very much less than a fly, but I was on the top of the wheel now, and that was everything. Dejection gave place to exhilaration as my eyes ranged hither and thither over the boundless expanse of earth and ocean which lay round and beneath me. There seemed to be nothing else in the world quite as high as I was, though, as a matter of fact, both Charchani and PichuPichu are some hundreds of feet higher than El Misti. The mountains over which the train had toiled on its way from the coast, looked like little ridges and furrows scored on the surface of a vast plain. Arequipa, the Pompeii of South America, looked through the crystal atmosphere exactly like a town marked in white in the middle of a green patch on a brown map. I could see every street and square and bridge distinctly, but it was nearly twenty-five miles away, and so they looked small, as, indeed, everything else in the world did, seen from that tremendous elevation.

On the way up, I had seen what looked like a white, almost diaphanous, cloud overhanging the cone. From the top of the wall I could see the cause of it. El Misti has two craters, an old and a new, and the new is within the old. Every now and then from his mighty throat, down which you could look between the sulphur-streaked rocks into a fearful chasm eight hundred feet deep, there came a puff of yellow-brown vapour which, as it rose into the sunlight, changed to snowy whiteness. The Titan's pipe is still alight, and for over thirty years now he has puffed away peacefully, only giving himself a little shake two or three times a year to show that he is alive.

Meanwhile Urbinas, the safety-valve of that region of the Continent, is fulfilling his functions admirably. But if ever anything goes wrong with his satellite, El Misti will awake in his wrath and Arequipa will be numbered among the cities that were and are not. The inhabitants are apparently looking forward to this,

The Observatory at Arequipa

for they keep the place pretty much as the last earthquake left it. They cleared away the stones which fell down, but they left the rest as they were, even on the splendid arches of the cathedral front. Their genius is a waiting one, and they take no trouble save in politics and revolutions.

There is the usual legend as to a vast Inca treasure buried in the old crater of El Misti. I have used the idea in fiction already and so those to whom the suggestion may seem promising are hereby requested to apply elsewhere. But whether this be romance or not, there certainly are remains of human habitations under the snow on the floor of the old crater. It was a strange place for anyone to make his home in. It may have been the abode of the guardians of the treasure or a place of banishment, in which case it was well chosen; or, again, it may be that the Harvard University is not the first learned body that has used El Misti for scientific purposes, and that in the days that are forgotten men read the stars from that lonely erie as they did from the mountains made with hands in the Land between the Waters.

"Los Medanos"

The Strange Sandhills of the Peruvian Desert

IN a former number of PEARSON'S MAGAZINE I gave some description of the railway journey from Mollendo, the coast-town and terminus of the Southern Railway of Peru, up to Arequipa, the Southern Capital of the Republic, and thence over the wild uplands that lie between the two great ranges of the Andes to Sicuani, which locality I described as being at once the end of the railway and of the nineteenth century.

A view of the sandhills of the Peruvian desert, with railway in the foreground

In this article I mentioned incidentally a very curious natural feature of which, thanks to the kindness of the Superintendent of the Southern Railway, I am now able to reproduce some photographs that will give my readers a clear idea of one of the most singular freaks of nature that could be found in many a long day's travel.

After the train has climbed from the seacoast over the foot-hills for a distance of about eighty-four miles the traveller, looking out of the windows of the car to his righthand side, sees one of the most extraordinary mirages to be found in the world. The train has descended slightly from the last curve out of the hills on to the broad desert plain of Quishuarani. Thirty or forty miles away on the other side you catch your first glimpse of the Cordillera proper, a vast, black mountain-wall stretching north and south as far as the eye can reach, and crowned with twinkling points of snow, which gleam out so dazzlingly white that the whitest cloud looks grey beside them. When the train first wound out of the foothills, after many miles of sinuous and toilsome climbing, it seemed exactly as though it was running straight into the midst of a sea crowned by innumerable, foaming breakers. I looked and looked, and the longer I looked the more perfect the illusion was. I knew that the train was carrying me across an absolutely waterless desert more than six thousand feet above the level of the sea, a desert which in the old days, before the advent of the railway, had been the last resting-place of many a man and beast that had struggled up through the arid wilderness of the coast region, only to go mad, and die of thirst, in sight of the mountains, amidst which are to be found many green valleys watered by perennial streams.

I got out my field-glasses to obtain a closer look at the foam-crowned sea which I knew was not a sea; but they only brought it nearer, and did nothing to destroy the illusion. Overhead the sun was blazing down from a cloudless sky. The burning, rarefied air was shimmering like a curtain of impalpable gauze all round, forming, the enchanted medium through which I saw the ghostly sea.

But presently, as the train was apparently running into the midst of it, I saw, a hundred yards or so away from the line, one of the billows of the sea, and then, although the illusion was still present to the eye, faith had been destroyed by sight. The billow in its concrete form was a mass of silver-white sand, rising from the grey-brown soil of the desert, It was, in short, a sandhill, but of a shape which I had never seen before. It was almost exactly in the form of a crescent moon, highest where it was thickest, and tapering off

One of the sandhills at close quarters, the photograph shows clearly its crescent shaping and its enormous size comparison with a man.

thinner and lower towards the horns until the points of them lay level with the plain.

As the train ran on, more and more of these came into sight, and I was not long in noticing that the horns all pointed the same way. I asked a fellow-traveller what they were, and he told me that these were the Medanos, or moving semi-lunar sandhills which, as far as he knew, were only to be found here and on the great desert of the Sechura, far away to the North of Peru, which Pizarro and his companions had crossed with such terrible suffering some three hundred and sixty years before.

Later on I made a few more inquiries into the nature of these Medanos. I found that though no one seemed to know where the silver sand came from, because it is absolutely different from the soil of the desert—which is good brown mould needing only water to make it bear three or four harvests a year—the wind, blowing constantly from the mountains, brought it from somewhere, and from these premises I deduced the genesis of the Medano as follows :

The fine sand falling from the air and being swept along the level ground would naturally collect on the weather side of any little obstruction. It would begin, of course, as a tiny heap of sand. In fact, I saw many baby Medanos as we crossed the desert. The constant wind, sweeping over the smooth surface, would bring new contributions of sand, and all these would be deposited where the Medanos were growing. It is, indeed, to the constancy of the wind

A near view of a sandhill, the ridges of sand on its surface being clearly discernible at the left of the photograph.

and the unfailing supply of sand that the symmetrical shape of these strange sandhills is due, and this is also the reason why the bend of the half moon is always to windward. The wind sweeps the sand from the level plain up the outer slope of the bow, over the ridge, and down the inner side. But on the lee side of the ridge there is, of course, a calm, and so the drifting grains fall to the earth, down the inner slope, and along the two horns, both sides of which are wind-swept, the outer naturally more so than the inner.

But if the sand grains composing the mass are thus constantly in motion under the impulse of the wind, it stands to reason that the mass itself must also be in motion, and this is actually the case. Nearly all the Medanos, from the baby ones, only three or four feet high, to the giants of sixty and seventy feet, are moving slowly but constantly to leeward. Their average rate of motion is about twenty feet a year, but there are some, both here and on the Sechura desert, which have formed about a core of rock projecting from the soil, and these, of course, are stationary.

The Medanos move slowly, but there is no resisting or opposing their progress. Some of the big ones must contain thousands of tons of sand, and when the two horns begin to approach the railway, or one of the few buildings scattered across the desert along the track, it is time to begin thinking about leaving the building to its fate or moving the track. The horns, of course, can be swept or dug away, but that makes no difference to the movement of the main mass, and, sooner or later, the slowly moving avalanche of silvery sand makes a hopeless block.

The height of some of these Medanos, and the wide sweep of the horns, will be seen from the photographs by comparison with the height of a man standing below and on top of them, while their formation and motion will be gathered from the general view of the desert shown at the head of this article. This view has been taken from leeward; that is to say, the Medanos are advancing towards the observer.

The thin double line in the foreground is the railway. The right hand horn of the big Medano has already touched it. Some day it will have completely covered it, and it will then probably be both cheaper and easier to lay the track round the Medano than to keep the line clear of the constantly encroaching mass. This is perhaps one of the most peculiar difficulties ever encountered by the makers of railways in the wild places of the earth.

The Snake-Dancers of Arizona

Illustrated with Photographs by W. H. MAUDE.

Snake-dancers ranged in parallel lines

THE most wonderful portion of that Land of Wonders, which the Yankee curtly and comprehensively describes as "Out West," is, by general consent, admitted to be the region geographically known as Arizona and New Mexico.

It is a land on which Nature appears to have taken pleasure in lavishing her wonders a land of wide waterless deserts, exquisitely fertile valleys, strange flat-topped hills called mesas, whose summits are often green prairielands crowned, some with towns and villages, and others, from which the water supply has vanished, with the sun-baked, crumbling ruins of them; of huge ranges of mountains towering, snow and ice-clad, to the ever cloudless sky, and of canyons, at the bottom of which hundreds, and sometimes thousands, of feet below the general level of the country, boil and thunder the waters of the rivers, which, by boring out these deep channels for themselves, have left the regions above waterless.

It is a land, too, where Nature has been by no means niggardly of her treasures. In the chronicles of the old Spanish conquerors, the followers and successors of Cortez, there is an account of a lawsuit over a block of solid virgin silver, which weighed twenty-eight hundred pounds; and twenty years ago when their lead ran short, the Apaches and Navajos thought nothing of shooting down the hated Paleface with golden bullets.

In those days, too, it was by no means an uncommon thing for Indians to go into the then frontier towns with pieces of gold weighing anywhere between a few pennyweights and half a pound, and trade them away for any trifle that happened to take their fancy. But, little value and all as they seemed to put on their gold, so jealously did they guard the secret of its source, that no white man has ever found it, or, if he has done so, lived to tell anyone else.

In the human sense, the most extraordinary characteristic of this strange land is the fact that it is inhabited by two absolutely different kinds of people—people who differ from each other in character and modes of life as widely as the Hindoo villager differs from the Tartar nomad of the Asiatic steppes. As far as I know, the human family affords no other example of people so widely different from each other inhabiting the same tract of land side by side for centuries. True, they are all called Indians, but with the name all r e s e m b l a n c e between them begins and ends.

Entrance to the "estufa," or underground chamber where the secret rites are performed.

The Apache, the Comanche, and the Navajo are, and have been for centuries, hunters, wanderers, and warriors. The Zunis, Moquis, and the Queres are town dwellers, artisans, and agriculturists. They are, or have been, warriors, too, and have waged many a fierce fight with their hereditary enemies in defence of their fortress towns.

It would be interesting to speculate upon the origin of these two widely different and irreconcilably hostile races, but it must suffice here to say that the town dwellers, or Pueblo Indians, with whom only we are here concerned, claim descent from the ancient Aztecs and Toltecs, and carefully preserve in their vague and fantastic traditions the sacred memory of the great Montezuma and many legends of the glory of the empire which Cortez and his companions destroyed.

Every Pueblo has one or more underground chambers or "estufas," in which the most secret rites are practised, and it is probable that no white man has ever witnessed these rites any more than he has penetrated the secrets of the priests and medicine men who perform them. Some of the ceremonies are, however, performed in the open air, and anyone, white, or brown, or red, may watch them. They only take place at rare intervals, and they are probably the public finale which proclaims that the inner mysteries have been duly performed. The underlying idea of all of them seems to be that of seeking protection from the Power of Evil through the aid of certain creatures or "totems," of which the justly dreaded rattlesnake is by far the most important of the creatures of earth, while the eagle is supreme among the inhabitants of the air. The Pueblos are, perhaps, the only people who have tamed the monarch of the air, and made him at once a deity and a street scavenger.

The Moquis, too, would appear to have tamed the other more formidable deity just as effectually. They keep huge rattlesnakes in certain secret and sacred places, and one of their most venerated offices is that of the Keeper of the Snakes.

In the illustrations accompanying this article, which are the first ever successfully taken of the snakedances, practised by the Moquis every two years, it will be seen that the snakemen are actually handling the deadliest reptiles found on the American continent with as little fear or apparent danger as if they were eels. It does not appear to be snakecharming, nor is anything done to make the reptiles harmless.

Professor Bandalier, who was recently commissioned by the

Archeological Institute to study the customs and institutions of the Pueblo-Indians of the Southwest, records in his report that among the Tehuas, another branch of the Pueblos, there is a priestess whose title is Sa-jiu, or the Mother, and one of her duties is the custody of a liquid called frog-water. This is a greenish fluid, and, according to the learned professor, it is an infallible cure for snake-bites, no matter how powerful the venom may be.

Unhappily, however, no white man has ever been able to obtain any of it, or to learn how it is made. It seems a pity that a few obscure and almost unknown semi-savages should be the sole possessors of what might be made a priceless blessing to thousands, and, in fact, millions, in such a country as India, to say nothing of explorers in tropical countries. The snake-dance as practised among the Moquis lasts nine days, but the first eight of these are devoted to preparations and the secret rites which take place in the estufas. There are two sets of dancers, as will be seen in the photographs. One set are the Antelope-priests, and the other are the Snake-priests.

The meaning of their various weird ceremonials is shrouded in mystery. It may be that the antelope is the symbol or token of good, and the deadly rattlesnake that of evil and destruction. This seems the more likely, because the flesh of the deer would have been the commonest meat food and nourisher of the people in the past, while, next, perhaps, to the Navajos and Apaches, the deadly

Antelope-men marching around the snake-dancers.

snakes of the wilderness would have been their most formidable enemies. It will be seen from the last illustration that, when the dance is over, the snakes are thrown down, apparently inert and harmless, and this typifies the final overcoming of the evil spirits by the powers of the priests.

The accompanying photograph is the first revelation of the secrets of a Pueblo estufa ever made. It represents an altar in the secret chamber of the Antelope-priests. On the first day of the dance the Antelope-priests collect various coloured sands, and make a sort of mosaic on the floor of the estufa The markings on the mosaic are supposed to represent thunder-clouds and lightning, but this is only guesswork, for no explanation can be got from the priests. The various articles placed round the altar represent offerings to the different powers that are to be propitiated.

The second day is devoted to the making of prayer-sticks or plumes, which play an important part in the dance. They are to the Pueblo what the prayer-wheel is to the Buddhist and the rosary to the Catholic. To the top of the stick are tied light feathers and down, chiefly taken from the sacred eagle. These wave and float in the air, and are, as Professor Bandaleur explains, emblems of thought. "A prayer is a thought, and often a suppressed sigh only; consequently, the plume is above all the emblem of prayer. Were it

The altar in the secret chamber

Snake-dancers carrying handfuls of snakes.

left to float at will, it might wander astray; therefore, it is tied to the spot where it is uttered by being attached to a stick."

His prayer-plume is also the greatest and most acceptable votive offering that the PuebloIndian can make at the shrine or altar of the totem which on any particular occasion he desires to propitiate, as, for instance, when he is going a long journey or is threatened by some specific danger.

On the third day the Snake-priests go out into the wilderness to hunt for snakes, preferably the rattle-snake. Before setting out they anoint their bodies with the mysterious frog-water, and when the dances are over this operation is carefully repeated. The water would therefore appear to be used both as a preventive and a cure. Meanwhile the Antelope-priests build the kisi, or conical structure of boughs, in which the snakes are kept till the final dance of the ninth day. Then they descend into the estufas to perform the secret rites, while the uninitiated pray that the results may be propitious. The first public dance begins about five o'clock on the evening of the eighth day. This is the antelope-dance, which appears to be a sort of preparation for the snake-dance. No snakes appear in it.

At the same hour on the following day the two sets of priests come out from their estufas and range themselves in two parallel lines, bowing and swaying and making a sort of humming chant.

Oraibi, the Moki Indian village where the snake-dance is held

Each has a snake-whip in his hand, which he waves rapidly in the air. Then one of the Antelope-priests walks between the lines carrying a bowl of charmed liquid, with which he sprinkles the dancers, and also throws out with his fingers towards the four points of the compass. After this he walks round the dancing-ground sprinkling consecrated corn-meal. On his way he comes to a plank covering an underground chamber. This is Shi-pa-pu, the entrance to the nether world, and on this he dances and stamps to make sure that it is securely closed.

After this the real snake-dance begins. The Snake-priests divide themselves into three groups—the carriers, the huggers, and the gatherers. The carriers bring the snakes out of a big earthen jar in the kisi, and take them by the back of the neck in their mouths. Then the huggers put their left hands on the carriers' shoulders and brush the snakes' heads with their whips, so as to keep them from striking their faces. In this way they make about three-fourths of the circuit of the dance - ground. Then they stop. The carriers throw the snakes to the ground; the gatherers pick them up, and pass them to the Antelope-priests.

These evolutions are repeated for about twenty minutes or half-an-hour. Then all the snakes are flung down in a hideous, writhing, slimy heap at the base of a wall, and the priestesses and their assistants come and sprinkle them all over with consecrated meal. After this the priests gather them up in their arms, each taking as many as he can carry, and rush off with them from the top of the mesa, or hill on which the pueblo is built, down on to the plain below. Here the snakes being released are allowed to escape unharmed and discuss their strange experiences among themselves.

The priests then race back to the top of the hill, and drink considerable quantities of a liquid placed in a big earthen jar near the

Snake-kisi. This acts as a violent emetic, and as they invariably get severely bitten during the last part of the dance this probably has some connection with the action of the frog-water. They then retire for a short time to their secret chambers for the concluding mysteries, and by a little after sundown the whole of the strange ceremonial is over.

Rattle-snakes thrown down in a corner after the ceremony.

To France by Air.

Being some Account of the First Intentional Crossing of the Channel from London by Balloon.

THE aerial navigator of to-day is practically in the same position as the first primitive mariner who stood up in his dug-out, or on his raft, and held up a palm-leaf or roughly-woven grass-mat for the wind to catch and blow him along.

He can only go with the wind. He cannot move an inch to right or left. He is as helpless as a man on a raft without oars or poles, or the power of using his hands, drifting down the current of a huge river, only it is not a river but an ocean that he is floating in. It is above him and below him, and on all sides of him, and where its currents flow there he must go. He can only control his motions in two directions, up and down, and for many reasons he has to be very chary of using this power, especially in coming down, for every escape of the precious gas is a loss that cannot be made good.

There is just as much difference between the balloon of to-day, and the air-ship of tomorrow, as there is between the primitive mariner's raft and an Atlantic greyhound. But, given only the fair wind, and all is well. Who would travel in a rattling, jolting train, or in a grinding, shuddering, reeling and rolling fabric of steel when he could enjoy the pure luxury of motionless locomotion in companionship with the clouds?

The sensations of earth-travelling are in air-travelling absolutely reversed. In the train or the steamer you are constantly aware that it is the vehicle which is carrying you over earth or water, but in balloon-voyaging your vehicle stands still in the midst of a profound silence—through which some few of the voices of the world now and then filter up just to remind you how utterly alone you are—and land and sea, like a vast, flat, painted panorama, slip swiftly away behind you.

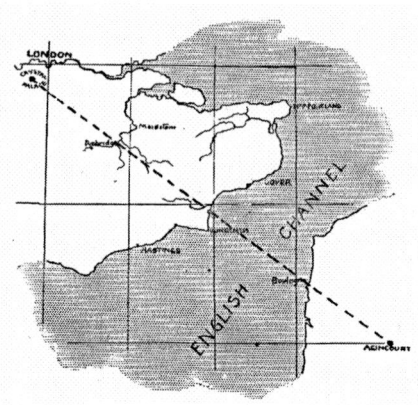

The route taken

To the novice, such as I was when I started in the good craft "Queen of the West" with Mr. Percival Spencer at 11.20 on a fine February morning from the balloon ground at the Crystal Palace, the first sensation is one of separation, merging swiftly into one of absolute isolation. You do not leave the earth; the earth leaves you—at least that is how it impressed me when the Skipper gave his last order: "Are you all clear? Has she enough lifting power? Then let her go!"

There was just a little rocking as the men took their hands off the edge of the car. The next moment everything was absolutely still; the wind had suddenly stopped blowing; the Crystal Palace with its grounds slipped away downwards and backwards with rapidly shrinking outlines; and a score of townships came out with map-like distinctness, fringing the vast smoke-and-mist-shrouded gulf in which London lay.

Away to the north-east gleams of sunshine fell through openings in the clouds on the distant Thames, sweeping in long, shining curves, broken here and there by a patch of mist or a mass of drifting smoke. It seemed to us as though the sun shone over the clouds, and as though I was looking down along the sun-beams,

Waiting for the gas. The white object is the unfilled balloon covered by the net. The two figures on the left are Mr. Spencer and Mr. Griffith.

for in those first few minutes we had silently and imperceptibly, without a jar or a swing of the car, mounted some three thousand feet into the air, and so some of the clouds were below us. Presently the clouds to the north-west broke, and through them we caught a magnificent bird's-eye view of the southern suburbs of London, projecting like a huge triangular wedge of bricks and mortar, interspersed with trees and gardens, into the open country beneath us. I had never before seen so clearly how the monster London is eating its way out into the fields and woods about it as I did just then. In twenty minutes from the start we recognised Sevenoaks, with its long, white High Street showing up very clearly from a depth, according to our point of view, of 4600ft., with its lordly parks clustering dark about it. The air was clearer now, and we could see away over Maidstone to the east, and Redhill to the west; south of us the long, straight stretch of the South-Eastern Railway, from Redhill to Ashford, lay like a black line drawn with a Titan's ruler across the fields and forests of the Weald of Kent.

Half-full

During the next half-hour we dropped nearly a thousand feet in consequence of heavy clouds coming between us and the sun A balloon is never quite stationary as regards elevation. In fact, it may be described as an exceedingly sensitive balance poised between Heaven and earth. Quite contrary to my expectation, the throat of the gas envelope was left wide open over our heads. Indeed, we could see up to the valve at the top of the balloon quite

Ready to hitch on. The balloon is held down by sandbags until the car in the foreground is hitched on.

plainly. And when, to relieve the silence, we shouted up into it, our voices were echoed back very distinctly, but strangely changed in the thin gas.

Now when the sun shone directly upon our 36,000 cubic feet of gas they immediately became rarified and expanded, and all this time the balloon rose steadily, but the moment a cloud-bank cut off the direct rays, there came an instant shrinking, and down we went through a distance which, if there had been any sudden stop at the end, would have constituted a very respectable fall.

Happily for one's nerves there is no sense whatever of falling. Only the barometer gives you any hint of it. In fact, while we were in mid-Channel, a sudden contraction of the gas, due to this cause, brought us down 2400ft. in five minutes. Now the idea of a drop from 7000ft. to 4600ft. between 1.25 and 1.30 on a February afternoon, with nothing under you but the empty air and the broad sea, would be just a little terrifying if you could stand somewhere else and watch the balloon do it. And yet in the car the only indication

Off!

1000 ft. up. The last photograph taken from the ground.

that we had fallen a distance nearly equal to that from the top of Snowdon to the sea was a movement of the indicator of the barometer through a few degrees-so perfect is the adjustment of the aerial balance.

We passed over the straight stretch of line in the neighbourhood of Tunbridge. By this time the air had become so clear that my hopes of getting some good photographs of the Channel began to rise with the expanding balloon. Presently, far away to the westward, a sharp headland jutted up through a dim, grey layer of misty looking clouds into the sunlight above. It was Beachy Head some forty miles away, and high above it again floated layer upon layer of clouds, with the southern sun streaming in between. Looked at from the car of the balloon at a good elevation, the world appears built in several storeys, each more gorgeously fantastic than the one below it, the prosaic earth itself being the ground-floor, or, perhaps, it might be better called the basement.

But presently, far down and away to the southward, there shone out a broad flash of intensely silver white light that was neither sky nor cloud nor earth. It was the Silver Streak, living well up to its name, but looking just then more like a sea in Fairyland than the turbulent piece of water of which so few people have any but unpleasant recollections. We were looking down at it from a height of nearly five thousand feet, through a rift in the lower clouds, and all

1000 ft. down.
The first photograph taken from the air.

round the edges of this the silver melted away into the grey, so that the sea had no shore, or, for the matter of that, any visible connection whatever with the solid earth.

Then came another of the magical transformation scenes which were constantly taking place about us. We passed into a warmer stratum of air, the balloon rose nearly a thousand feet in a few minutes, the clouds melted into mist, and the mist into air, and there, nearly six thousand feet below us, was the unbroken coastline from the South Foreland to Beachy Head, with the broad, shining waters of the Channel joined to it by a tiny, winding fringe of surf. Of course, the cameras went to work at once; but, alas! the developing bath showed that the sensitive plates could see mists that were invisible to our eyes, and the results were exasperatingly disappointing.

The last glimpse of London

We could now see our cross-Channel course distinctly. Right ahead of us the point of Dungeness jutted out, looking for all the world like a triangle of fresh brown mud, which had been thrown up from the sea during the night. At the one angle of the base Rye Harbour, with its little network of streams and outworks of groynes, nestled under a brown s'ope; and at the eastward corner

Bits —

was Romney, looking somewhat forlorn and insignificant, as though conscious that its occupation had gone.

It was now a quarter to one, and our elevation was 5500ft. directly over the coast. There was the wreck of a steamer lying just off Dungeness Point, and a few other craft under steam and sail were sprinkled about. Of course, they looked absurdly diminutive, and yet strangely real; but what was stranger still, was the appearance of the Channel itself.

— of Kent —

Where the sun fell on the water one could see the waves with their crests distinctly, but the distance was too great to detect any movement; and so it looked as though we were floating over a sunlit sea which had been instantaneously frozen, foam and all, into green ice frosted with snow. Of course, the tiny ships were fast frozen in it, and the steamers appeared to be turning a lot of coal into smoke to no purpose whatever. Every now and then a low growl of the surf drifted up out of the silence, and more rarely the hoarse hoot of a steamer's whistle, possibly bidding us good-afternoon.

— and Sussex

Just as we crossed the English coast the haze to the southward dissolved, and the bold outlines of blacktopped Cape Gris Nez came into view, thirtyfive miles away. The sun took us again now, and we reached our greatest height so far since the start. It was, I confess, a somewhat eerie sensation to look sheer down at the water through a distance of

Dungeness from 6000 ft.

over 6000ft. It was a sensation that one could only have in a balloon, because not the least piquant portion of it was the utter absence of any visible means of support.

From the top of a mountain you cannot, of course, look straight down for any distance, and from the top of a column or very high building you see a solid material connection between yourself and the earth. But from that little basket, hung up to nothing, twenty times higher than the cross of St. Paul's, looking down into that vast emptiness, was a proceeding which made you catch your breath, and instinctively take hold of something, no matter whether it was fastened to anything or not. The idea of falling out was naturally too utterly paralysing to be entertained for more than a second or so.

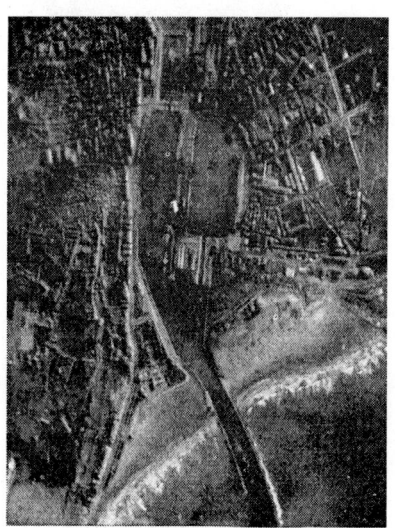

Boulogne from 8000 ft.

I just happened to be thinking about this when another transformation took place. Land and sea and sky vanished like the geography of a dreamworld. The bright sun had gone, and there we were in a dim, white world all to ourselves. The sudden sense of solitude was almost crushing. There was neither sight nor sound beyond the confines of the little basket, which, by the way, was hardly bigger than those which some ladies seem to consider necessary for the accommodation of their dresses on a journey. I don't think I ever realised what absolute solitude is like so clearly as I did then.

But presently we had a companion. The sun broke through the upper part of the cloud, the moisture on the gas-envelope began to evaporate, and there, on the white curtain which lay spread between the world and ourselves, appeared, perfectly distinct, the ghostly counterpart of our aerial craft encircled by a complete rainbow halo. It accompanied us for two or three minutes, during which I took a couple of shots at it and then, as we soared up into the sunlit blue above us, it vanished. So did the cloud a few seconds later, and from a height of 6700ft. we saw the splendid expanse of the English Channel with its French and English shores, looking like some gigantic river debouching through the Straits of Dover, and broadening away to the ocean until land and sea lost themselves in the sunny haze which shrouded the western horizon.

It was now twenty minutes past one, and we could see the day boat from Folkestone lying motionless on the blue-green water with a long trail of black smoke behind it. She looked absurdly small and futile, and the idea of anyone suffering the colossal woes of seasickness on board her seemed entirely incomprehensible.

The matter looked rather different a few hours later when our stately and symmetrical "Queen of the West" had collapsed into a bundle of yellow stuff wrapped up in a dirty sheet like a big weekly wash, and lay beside the car on the deck of the steamer Empress between Calais and Dover. So much difference is there in points of view.

We could see her destination now quite clearly, and I was glad to find that we, too, were going directly towards it. It was just here that we made our big drop. A bank of clouds rolled up, hiding the English coast from view and shutting off the sun. Then down we went with a run, and when we found ourselves again we were only 4600ft. above the sea, with Boulogne town and harbour dead ahead, and coming clearly into view, with little black dots sprinkled about outside the breakwater which soon resolved themselves into fishing luggers.

Now we rose another 1200ft. with the help of the sun, and got our first good view of France and its coast-line from Dunkirk to the mouth of the Somme. Then came another drop to 4200ft., and we heard loud and prolonged hootings rising from Boulogne, which was now slipping fast towards us. They may possibly have been signals from the Customs officials summoning us to come down and have our baggage examined, but from our serene altitude we smiled at such puny, mundane bars and barriers, and, as if to show her royal con tempt for them, the "Queen of the West" leapt upwards again, and at two o'clock we were looking straight down at Boulogne from a height of 7700ft.

The air of France was sunnier than that which we had left behind us in England, and so we kept on mounting up into the clear blue. Eight thousand feet was passed, then 9000ft., and then 10,000 feet was just touched. Away to the northward we could see the long white line of the English cliffs like a thread running through the dim distance. But the French coast was sharply defined, and Napoleon's white column stood out on its heights above the town with marvellous distinctness. France itself, of which we could see about 2000 square miles, was a flat, brown land dotted with red-roofed villages, and patches of forest threaded with white roads and long, winding, silver streams.

just after we had drifted over Boulogne, and had the open country beneath us, I had an opportunity of visually demonstrating the truth of a mathematical precept which hitherto, I confess, I had taken rather as a matter of academic faith than of conviction. We had now accomplished the principal object of our trip, we had done what had not been done since the great Nassau balloon started sixty years ago from Cremorne, and, after losing itself in the upper regions for a night, came down in Nassau. We had started from London and we had crossed the sea to Europe.
Under the circumstances we felt justified in indulging in a mutual whisky-andsoda. Our altitude was nearly 10,000ft., and I thought I would try if a soda-water bottle would make the difference, so I leant over the edge of the car and dropped it. There were several villages sprinkled about under us, but they only looked like the collections of houses and trees which you buy in the Lowther Arcade, set out in order, and quite too small to hit from such a distance.

Now, Science says that if you drop an object from a moving vehicle that object retains precisely the motion of the vehicle till it comes to rest on the earth, and that is just what my soda-water bottle did. The air was brilliantly clear just then, and I could follow the course of the bottle quite easily, for it looked like a green spot of light against the brown earth towards which it was flashing down.

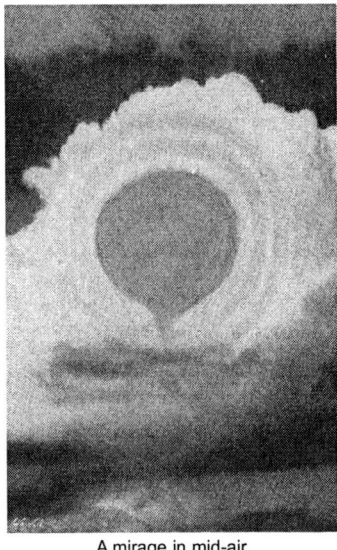

A mirage in mid-air.
(A cloud effect caused by bright sun above and a bank of mist below.)

In spite of my academic conviction, I expected to see it left behind, but it was not. We were travelling about thirty miles an hour at the time, and at just that speed it flitted over field, road, and wood. Then we drifted over a village, and I began to feel sorry that I had let it go, for it would have gone through the roof of a house like a thunderbolt. But no; there was a yellow field beyond, and I saw its final twinkle over this. It vanished exactly under the car, and my academic belief was triumphantly transformed into a demonstrated certainty.

But it was now getting on towards three o'clock, and the February sun was working down towards a vast Alpine region of Cloudland. Another hour or so and the air would cool. Our gas, of which, judging by the smell in the car, we had already lost a considerable quantity, would contract and down we should come. True, we had nearly four bags of sand left, and the judicious emptying of these would have kept us afloat for a long time.

If the wind had gone round a point or so to the northward we should have had a try for Paris, but the map showed that our course so far had been almost a bee-line, and that it would take us a good hundred miles north of Paris. So we decided to cast about for a nice place—not too rough or hard or spiky with trees or chimneys—to come down on.

The country ahead was very promising, sprinkled with villages and hamlets, and fairly well wooded, with wide stretches of arable land between, and, as we might have gone further and fared worse, Captain Spencer decided to say good-bye to Cloudland. Now it will not need any, explanation on my part to show that in ballooning coming down is a very much more tick- lish operation than going up, or stopping up. Our little system, to use an astronomical term, consisted of a gas envelope of some 36,000 cubic feet capacity and a car, which, with its contents, weighed some six hundredweight, while the earth contains more than 260,000 million cubic miles of solid matter, and weighs, I believe, some 163 billion tons. Hence, anything like a forcible collision between these two systems was, on our part, emphatically to be avoided.

I had had a little experience of this part of balloon-voyaging at the end of our unsuccessful trip on the previous Thursday. We were then approaching the eastern coast of Kent at a speed of forty miles an hour, and had to come down somewhere before we were blown into the North Sea. Our 300ft. drag-rope began by mixing itself up with hop-poles, and the effect in the car was that of an earthquake about every second or so. Then we hit a ploughed field very hard in several places and at all angles, hopped across another one in giant strides of 400ft. or 500ft. each, scraped over a little wood, jumped another field, and brought up with our drag in a wire fence, and a final thump on a moderately soft portion of the broad bosom or Mother Earth.

It was one of the busiest experiences that I had ever had, considering the time it took, and so the recent memory of it caused me to look with lively interest, not to say apprehension, upon the now rapidlyapproaching earth. The sublime peace and stillness of the journey was now over. The world below ceased to move only in one direction, and began to spin round as it swept ever faster and faster beneath and towards us. A balloon rarely spins save when it is caught between two crosscurrents, or when it is descending very rapidly, and the latter reason is why the world seemed turning about us.

We drifted rapidly downward over a pleasant little red-tiled village, out of which the inhabitants had already come into the streets and fields, and were welcoming us, and the English and French flags which we hung out from the car with shouts and cheers in many keys. Dead ahead was a church with a twisted spire, and just beyond it a fine chateau standing in broad, wooded grounds. It seemed curious that, after a hundred and thirty mile flight directed by the will of the wind, we should very nearly have hit just that one tiny little point in all the wide land of France. And yet, as a matter of fact, we only missed the church spire by a few feet.

The drag-rope began to get in its necessary but unpleasant work now, catching in trees, and jerking the car about like the pendulum of an insane clock as it ripped the branches off. But this didn't last as long this time. On the other side of the trees behind the chateau there was a broad, smoothlysloping stretch of ploughed land, and, when the dragrope had drawn clear of the trees, it fell upon this, checking our speed, and breaking our fall beautifully. In the intervals of keeping myself in the car I had been hanging on to the valve-rope while the Skipper had been regulating the descent with ballast, and so exactly did he balance matters that the final bump and roll would scarcely have hurt a baby.

Of course, we had hardly touched the ground before a small crowd of labourers, men, women, and children, all bare-headed, came running up from every direction, and soon half-a-dozen stalwart sons and daughters of France had gripped the edge of the car, the huge envelope was lying prone on the muddy furrows, billowing itself into shapelessness as the gas roared out of the valve, and our aerial voyage was over.

As soon as it was safe to do so I took out my watch. It was 3.25 English time, so that we had been exactly four hours and five minutes on our flight of a hundred and thirty miles. The son

The end of the journey.
(The drag-rope catching the trees behind the Chateau de Verchin.)

of the owner of the chateau came up with the rest, and told us that we had made our descent in the village of Verchin in the Department of Pas de Calais. Then out came our map and the next moment we made the agreeable discovery that we two were the last Englishmen to fall on the ever-glorious field of Agincourt. International courtesy, of course, forbade any allusion to the subject; but I could not help wondering what gallant King Harry and his iron-clad warriors would have thought or done if such strange visitors from his good city of London had dropped as from the clouds in their midst. M. de Wailly de Wandonne, the lord of the chateau, welcomed his unexpected visitors with true French hospitality, and we held quite a levee while we were satisfying our aerial appetites in the big salle-a-manger.

The journey home via Anvin, Etaples, Boulogne, and Calais was both dilatory and disagreeable in comparison with the serene directness of our aerial voyage, but nevertheless I got back to my house in Kensington with the milk exactly twenty-two hours after I had started to join the "Queen of the West" at the Crystal Palace.

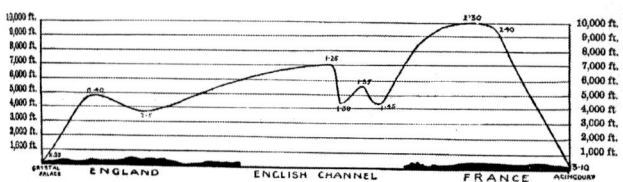

The trip in vertical elevation.

When Will the 20th Century Commence?

The human intellect has played many queer pranks, even since it has been educated up to the standard of the nineteenth century. Certainly the queerest of them has manifested itself in the discussion as to when that century ends and the twentieth begins. Everybody knows that the Act of Union, which made the United Kingdom one, took effect on the first day of the present century— that is to say, on the 1st of January, 1801. Everybody knows, too, that a child is one year old on the first anniversary of its birth, and that exactly the same is true of the Christian Era. Hence the nineteenth century cannot end until Christendom has counted nineteen hundred complete years. These facts are so exquisitely elemental that any serious controversy about them appears quite incredible.

But there is another sense in which the question: "When does the twentieth century begin"? may be asked without laying the speaker open to the suspicion of stupidity. Further, the asking of this question implies another, and that is: "Where does the twentieth century begin"? These questions each admit of two answers, and in each case one answer is conventionally, and the other mathematically or astronomically, true.

By way of making this as plain as possible, let us imagine the Equator to be a double line of railway stretching round the world. Let two trains, travelling in opposite directions at exactly equal speeds, start from a portion of the necessary Equatorial ocean-bridge, which would be situate in the Atlantic Ocean exactly on the meridian of Greenwich. Where would those two trains meet?

Each would have travelled over one-half the circumference of the earth, and, since there are 360 degrees in this circumference, they would meet on the 180th meridian of longitude. There is no land just here. The nearest would be Byron Island, about ninety geographical miles away to the south-west, so we will imagine an oceanic station here at which the passengers could exchange greetings, and other things. One of the first facts that they would learn from each other would be that they had arrived on different days. For instance, suppose that the eastbound train arrived on Monday, the 31st of December, 1900, the west-bound would arrive on

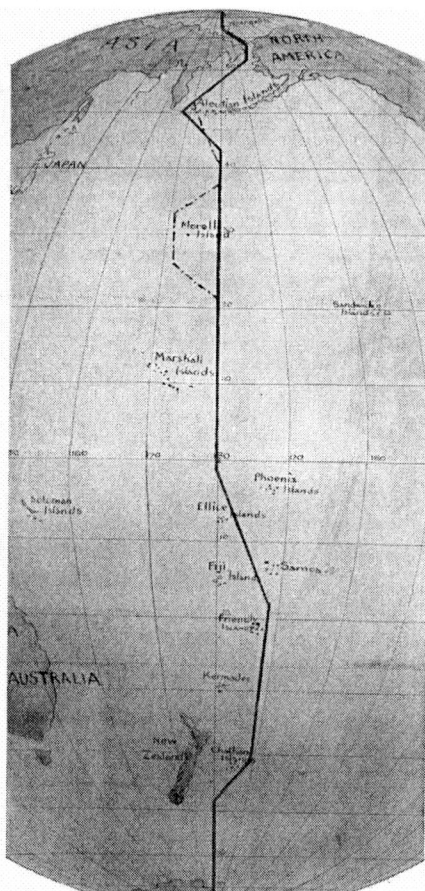

To the right of the black line, eastern time is kept, to the left western. Some authorities differ as to whether eastern or western time is kept on Morell Island. There is no need for anxiety. Morell Island was never inhabited, and for the last twenty years it has not even been sighted.

Tuesday, the 1st of January, 1901. Granted, further, that they pulled up alongside each other exactly at midnight on the 31st of December—Greenwich time—the engine of the east-bound train might be whistling its first salute to the twentieth century, while the engine of the west-bound would be blowing off steam in the nineteenth. In short, the former would have lost and the latter would have gained exactly twelve hours.

For this reason the hundred and eightieth. meridian of longitude, the line where east becomes west and west becomes east, has been adopted by the civilised nations of the world as the date-line-that is to say, the line along which, conventionally speaking, the day changes at the sixth stroke of midnight, and as east becomes west, so p.m. becomes a.m. In the sense of this argument, therefore, it may be taken that the twentieth century will actually begin when the clocks along this line have struck the sixth stroke of twelve on the night of the 31st of December, 1900.

There are, however, certain other conventionalities which interfere with the actual correctness of this conclusion. For political reasons time is counted in the regions adjacent to this line according to the systems of those nations within whose "sphere of influence" they lie. The result is that the line on which the date conventionally changes does not coincide with the 180th meridian, but is deflected every now and then to the westward and the eastward. Moreover, there are no fewer than four of these date-lines laid down by different authorities.

The one shown on the accompanying diagram is the most recent and most generally accepted, and may therefore be taken as serving my present purpose best. To the left of the line Asiatic time is counted; to the right, American. Thus, on that momentous midnight, the conventional date will change first for the inhabitants of the Eastern Friendly Islands, and twenty-five minutes later for the dwellers on the eastern coast of Vanua Levu, the largest island in the Fiji group.

Hence, curiously enough (still according to conventional time), the Friendly Islanders will be in the twentieth century twenty-five minutes before the Fijians, while a Samoyede standing on the extreme point of East Cape, overlooking the icebound Strait of Bering, would get there twenty-five minutes earlier still. Wherefore, according to the arbitrary date-line, the answer to the question: "When and where will the twentieth century begin"? will be "At midnight at East Cape, Siberia."

But now arises another very important question, a question which, as far as I am aware, no one has yet tried to answer with appropriate correctness: "When and where will the first day of the twentieth century actually dawn? Who will first see its first sunrise, and at what hours will they see it?" At first sight the answer would appear to be very simple. We have all learnt from our geographies that it is noon at the same time at all places situated on the same meridian, and if this were also true of sunrise and sunset, then, of course, the dwellers along the 180th 80th meridian and those who happen to be crossing to the eastward at sea at dawn on January 1st, 1901, would be the first to see it. But, as a matter of fact, the spot at which our two imaginary trains are supposed to

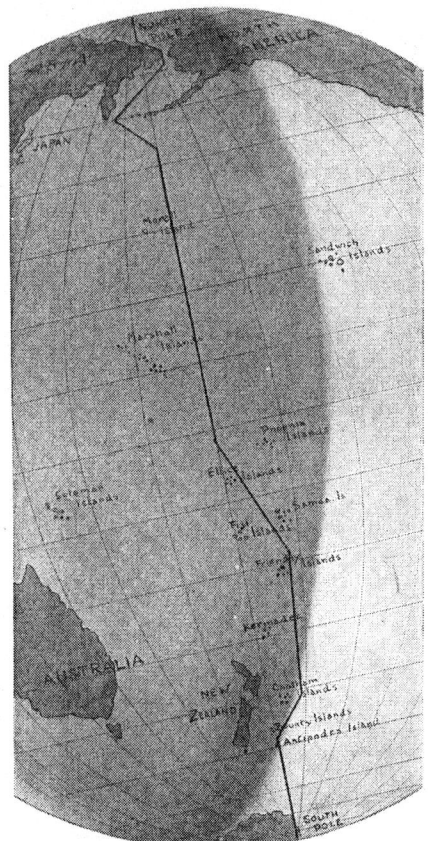

The inhabitants of Antipodes Island will be the first persons to see the first sun of the 20th century.

draw up for exchange of greetings is the only spot on earth or sea where, if the passengers chose to wait for the first sun of the new century, they would see it rise at six o'clock-that is to say, exactly between midnight and noonday.

The reason for this is that the dawn-line—the line which represents the flow of the dawn-flood round the world—never, except on two special dates in the year, coincides with the date-line. If the axis of the earth—the line which runs through it from pole to pole—stood at right angles to the plane of its path round the sun this would be so. And the sun would rise and set at the same moment on every place situated on the same line from pole to pole. There would be eternal summer in the tropics, eternal spring in the temperate zones, and eternal winter at the poles. In other words, there would be no change either of days or seasons.

But the axis is tilted at an angle of twentythree and a half degrees to the plane of the orbit, and therefore we have to draw our dawn-line for the twentieth century not along the 180th meridian, but across it at this angle, or, to be more exact, twenty-one degrees from north-east to south-west. The difference is due to the phenomenon known as the precession of the equinoxes, the explanation of which may be found in any work of astronomy.

This brings us to a somewhat different view of the facts as they actually are. Some of these facts, indeed, appear a good deal more curious than they did before, for not only will the twentieth century actually dawn at different times for everybody living along the mathematical date-line, or 180th meridian earlier as you go southward, and later as you go northward—but, according to our reckoning, conventional and astronomical, the twentieth century will never dawn at either of the Poles, since the North Pole went into darkness and the South Pole came into light each for a six months' spell on the 22nd of last September. Hence, the North Pole will not see its first twentieth century sun till the 22nd of next March, while the South Pole saw its last nineteenth century dawn three months ago, and will not have a sunset for three months more.

If the change of the centuries took place at either of the equinoxes—March 22nd or September 22nd—then, since on those days the earth's axis is at right angles to the plane of the orbit, and there is equal day and night all over the world, the matter would be very easily decided. The dawnline would coincide with the date-line, and from Pole to Pole the first sun of the new century would rise at the same moment.

But, unfortunately, this is not so, and the consequence is that the line of dawn, as it sweeps round the earth, first touches the date-line to the south of the Equator, and then gradually creeps up this line till it leaves it far to the north. So the first sun of the twentieth century will rise on the places along or near the date-line in the order of their position from the south upwards.

Now there is no land along this line from the Antarctic Circle to Antipodes Island, hence this tiny spot of earth will first see the twentieth century dawn. A few minutes later Bounty Island will see it. Then it will sweep along the north-east coast of North Island, New Zealand; then over Vanua Levu in the Fiji Islands. Next it will shine on the scattered coral islets of the Ellice group, and after travelling about nine degrees more to the north, the light-tide will touch the crossing of the dawn-line and date-line at six o'clock. Two hours and five minutes will have to pass before it reaches the banks of the Yarra. In six hours and twenty-five minutes it will gild the temples and palaces of Calcutta. In nine hours and fifty minutes it will be flowing over Lion's Head, and down the rugged sides of Table Mountain. In twelve hours and twenty-five minutes it will have crossed Montmartre and touched the base of the Eiffel Tower in Paris. Five minutes later it will have passed the cross of St. Paul's and be flowing up Fleet Street. In seventeen hours and twenty minutes from the time it crossed the dawn-line it will be flowing round the feet of the Statue of Liberty, and in three hours more it will have reached the Golden Gate. Thence it will cross a stretch of ocean unbroken by rock or islet back to the dawn-line, and so will be accomplished the evening and morning of the first day of the twentieth century.

There are two stories told among globetrotters which have a rather quaint connection with the subject of this article. It is well known that a ship going eastward meets the sun, and, therefore, on a voyage round the world loses a day; hence, in order to keep the calendar right, a day, has to be added when the vessel crosses the date-line or 180th meridian. Conversely, a ship going round the world to the westward gets a day behind the sun, and so has to take one off. In one instance a party of missionaries going from China and Japan to America were disquieted to find that there were two Sundays in the week, and the question arose which of these was to be kept as Sunday; and, further, would it be right to indulge in secular amusements on the other Sunday? The question was referred to the Captain, who decided that the first Sunday was the real one.

The other case, which came under my own observation, was still more serious. I was coming westward from Australia on a French mail boat, and we had a bishop and several curés and sisters on board. The dear old bishop knew more about theology than astronomy and navigation, and he had made all preparations for the celebration of mass on a certain Sunday, when to his horror he found that there wasn't one, since that was the day on which we crossed the 90th meridian, and it became, astronomically speaking, a dies non. The service was held on what should have been Sunday, but for all that it was Monday.

George Griffith Bibliography

Poems General Secular and Satirical (1883) *
The Dying Faith (1884) *
The Angel of the Revolution: A Tale of the Coming Terror (1893)
Olga Romanoff or, The Syren of the Skies (1894)
A Heroine of the Slums (1894)
The Outlaws of the Air (1895)
Valdar the Oft-Born: A Saga of Seven Ages (1895)
The Romance of Golden Star (1897)
Britain or Boer? A Tale of the Fight for Africa (1897)
Men Who Have Made the Empire (1897) *
The Gold Finder (1898)
The Knights of the White Rose (1898)
The Destined Maid (1898)
The Virgin of the Sun: A Tale of the Conquest of Peru (1898)
The Great Pirate Syndicate (1899)
Gambles with Destiny (1899)
Knave of Diamonds (1899)
The Rose of Judah: A Tale of the Captivity (1899)
Brothers of the Chain (1900)
Thou Shalt Not (1900)
Denver's Double: A Story of Inverted Identity (1901)
A Honeymoon in Space (1901)
Captain Ishmael: A Saga of the South Seas (1901)
In an Unknown Prison Land: An Account of Convicts and Colonists in New Caledonia With Jottings Out and Home (1901) *
The Justice of Revenge (1901)
The White Witch of Mayfair (1902)
The Missionary (1902)
The Lake of Gold: A Narrative of the Anglo-American Conquest of Europe (1903)
A Woman Against the World (1903)
The World Masters (1903)
Sidelights on Convict Life (1903) *
With Chamberlain Through South Africa (1903) *
A Criminal Croesus (1904)
The Stolen Submarine: A Tale of the Japanese War (1904)
His Better Half (1905)
An Island Love Story (1905)
A Mayfair Magician: A Romance of Criminal Science (1905)
The Great Weather Syndicate (1906)
A Conquest of Fortune (1906)
The Mummy and Miss Nitocris: A Phantasy of the Fourth Dimension (1906)
His Beautiful Client (1906)
The World Peril of 1910 (1907)
The Destined Maid (1908)
John Brown Buccaneer (1908)
The Sacred Skull (1908)
The Lord of Labour (1911)
The Diamond Dog (1913)

* Non-Fiction

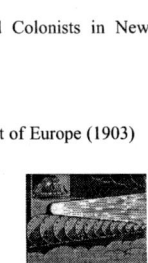

ROUND THE WORLD IN SIXTY-SIX DAYS.

(FROM OUR CORRESPONDENT.)

Dover, Monday Night.

At Dover to-day Mr George Griffith, an enterprising globe-trotter, who left Charing Cross at eleven o'clock this morning on an attempt to perform a task which at first sight seems impossible, was interviewed. He says he is going to lower the round the world record from 74 to 66 days. If he does this he will leave Miss Nellie Bly, of the *New York World*, eight days behind. He has been working up connections for some months past, and he claims that he has hit upon a series that will not occur again in combination for years to come. The achievement is just possible, given all trains and steamers on time. The longest wait by schedule is 12 hours, and the shortest 10 minutes. The former is at Yokohama, and the latter at Montreal, where he changes from the Canadian Pacific to the Delaware and Hudson Railway. His route is via Paris, Rome, Naples, Suez, Colombo, Singapore, Hong Kong, Yokohama, Vancouver, Montreal, New York, Southampton, London. If he succeeds he will land at Southampton from the American liner New York on the morning of May 16th. This is Mr Griffith's fourth trip round the world, but it is his first attempt at record breaking. His last trip was from Melbourne via Raratonga, Cape Horn, and Cape of Good Hope. His time was 245 days, but he went in a sailing ship and was not trying to make any record. He claims to make his present journey by availing himself solely of the ordinary means of travel, without special trains or steamers, relying wholly for success on punctuality and promptness. This makes his enterprise essentially different from that of Miss Nellie Bly, who made use of special means of transit.